current
problems

progress

A. STADNICHENKO

Monetary Crisis of Capitalism

Origin, Development

PROGRESS PUBLISHERS
MOSCOW

Translated from the Russian by Leo Lempert

Редактор русского текста Л. Чернова

АЛЕКСЕЙ ИВАНОВИЧ СТАДНИЧЕНКО
ВАЛЮТНЫЙ КРИЗИС КАПИТАЛИЗМА

На английском языке

First printing 1975

C $\frac{11105\text{-}035}{014(01)\text{-}75}$ 106-74

CONTENTS

PREFACE

The world monetary crisis is a striking display of capitalism's general crisis at its present state-monopoly stage. This crisis assumes diverse forms: so-called "gold rushes", abrupt speculative flows of capital from one country to another, extreme instability in the balances of payments, inflation, sharp and frequent fluctuations of discount and interest rates, instability of the exchange rates of national currencies, with the latter resulting in changes of currency parities—devaluations, revaluations, and the like.

All this tends to exacerbate the hidden and open competitive struggle between the gigantic monopolies and between the principal capitalist states and intensifies the socio-economic instability of capitalist society.

The monetary crisis adversely affects the living conditions of the masses in capitalist countries and intensifies the class struggle. It has become a chronic malady of capitalism, alarming the monopoly bourgeoisie, which utilises the state machine in its own interests. With the help of the state and international financial and economic organisations, these circles have been vainly seeking to mitigate the monetary upheavals of capitalism and to find a way out of the crisis.

This monograph deals with the major aspects of the world monetary crisis of capitalism.

The main guideline in this study was Lenin's methodological proposition "...not to forget the underlying historical connection, to examine every question from the standpoint of how the given phenomenon arose in history and what were the principal stages in its development, and, from the

8 PREFACE

standpoint of its development, to examine what it has
become today".[1]

In examining the development of the world monetary
crisis we have drawn on Western literature and relevant
works published in the USSR. Particularly useful were:
Imperialism and the Crisis of World Capitalism, edited
by P. Y. Bregel, (1968); S. M. Borisov, *Gold in the Economy
of Contemporary Capitalism* (1968); F. P. Bystrov, *Terms
of Payments in International Trade Transactions* (1963);
Currency Handbook (1967); I. D. Zlobin, *Monetary-Financial
Contradictions of Imperialism* (1959); I. I. Konnik, *Laws
and Interconnections of Commodity and Money Circulation
under Socialism* (1968); F. I. Mikhalevsky, *Gold in the
Capitalist System After the Second World War* (1952);
K. Y. Chizhov, *International Monetary and Financial
Organisations of Capitalism* (1968); L. I. Frei, *The Credit
and Monetary Policy of Capitalist Countries* (1962).

The need for an historical approach is also dictated by
the fact that attempts are made in Western literature to
sever present-day monetary relations from their historical
roots, to prove that earlier objective laws of currency circulation have either completely or largely lost their validity,
claiming, for example, that gold as world money has become
a "relic of barbarism". This is done to make the reader believe
that the Marxist doctrine of money and money circulation
is obsolete. Various bourgeois concepts of monetary circulation are put forward, mostly of Keynesian origin.

Roy Harrod, the well-known British economist, and
some other Western researchers claim that a "Keynesian
revolution" occurred in the interwar period in financial-
economic theories and capitalist practices. In this way they
are trying to sever the unity of the process of decay in capitalism's monetary system and the emergence of its chronic
crisis.

In contrast, the purpose of this work is to demonstrate,
from the standpoint of the Marxist doctrine of money and
money circulation and in the historical perspective, how
the entire development of currency relations in the capitalist world made the present crisis inevitable.

---

[1] V. I. Lenin, *Collected Works*, Vol. 29, p. 473.

MONEY CIRCULATION AND ITS ROLE
IN DIFFERENT SOCIO-ECONOMIC SYSTEMS

The present international monetary system is a result of the prolonged development of money and money circulation, with objective laws predetermining the similarity of stages in money circulation in different countries during the succession of various socio-economic systems.

Let us recall that money or the money form of value, for all its simplicity and use over the centuries, was for a long time elevated into a fetish and remained an incomprehensible riddle. Marx pointed out that "the value-form, whose fully developed shape is the money-form, is very elementary and simple. Nevertheless, the human mind has for more than 2,000 years sought in vain to get to the bottom of it, whilst on the other hand, to the successful analysis of much more composite and complex forms, there has been at least an approximation. Why? Because the body, as an organic form, is more easy of study than are the cells of that body. In the analysis of economic forms, moreover, neither microscopes nor chemical reagents are of use. The force of abstraction must replace both." [1]

The approach to the contemporary international monetary system and its protracted crisis largely depends on a proper understanding of the essence of money and its role in different socio-economic systems. This is the more important because gold, which long ago became world money, plays a major role in the development of the present-day monetary crisis in the capitalist world.

---

[1] Karl Marx, *Capital*, Vol. I, Moscow, pp. 7-8.

So what is money? Studying the nature of the value form in acts of exchange, Marx established that in all cases two different commodities stand opposed to each other so that the value of the first commodity is in the relative form of value, while in the other it is in the equivalent form. Subsequently, when a wide range of commodities is drawn into exchange, one of the commodities assumes the form of the universal equivalent and as such is "ousted" by all other commodities from their midst. This is the objective process whereby the equivalent value form is developed. Lastly, the "particular commodity, with whose bodily form the equivalent form is thus socially identified, now becomes the money-commodity, or serves as money".[1]

There is no need to relate in detail how in different countries at the early stages of mankind's development various commodities, e.g., livestock among nomads, were used as money.

In the history of mankind the process of exchange is the process of the formation of money. Marx pointed out that "as they develop, the interrelations of commodities crystallise into distinct aspects of the universal equivalent, and thus the exchange process becomes at the same time the process of formation of money."[2] It should be noted that as early as several centuries B.C. precious metals, gold and silver, began to function as money. In some countries either gold or silver served as money and in others both were used. The first instance is called monometallism and the second bimetallism. There were cases when copper and its alloys (bronze) were used as a money metal for a long time but ultimately gold became the principal monetary material, the measure of value and the main means of international payments—world money, in fact.

As a universal money material capable, as it were, of preserving its value when hoarded, gold passed through the centuries from the money-boxes and chests of satraps and slave-traders into the safes and armoured vaults of the tycoons of contemporary state-monopoly capital.

---

[1] Karl Marx, *Capital*, Vol. I, p. 69.
[2] Karl Marx, *A Contribution to the Critique of Political Economy*, London, 1971, p. 52.

Gold is a measure of value because it itself has value. The relative magnitude of the value of gold is established at the site of its production and in direct trade. When gold goes into circulation as money, its value is already given as labour value, but to serve as a standard of prices a definite weight of gold must be fixed as the unit of measurement.

In actual circulation, however, the weight unit of gold cannot be established during every exchange or every purchase of a commodity. In ancient times coins were introduced, originally as pieces of metal of a fixed weight, converted by minting into a definite shape. The British pound sterling was the money name of a pound of silver. But when silver yielded its place as the money commodity to gold, the name "pound sterling" was applied to a smaller quantity of gold. The pound as a monetary unit and as a unit for measuring of gold did not coincide. The weight of precious metal in coins 'is usually fixed by law and thus becomes mandatory.

This was particularly important at the early stages in the development of commodity exchange, when precious metals, gold and silver, directly participated as money in acts of exchange, in the purchase and sale of commodities.

Coins, as a legislatively established money standard for prices, began to be used long before our era. This is confirmed by historical and archaeological evidence, in particular by the unearthing of coins themselves. Some authorities hold that metallic money appeared some 900 years B.C.[1] and possibly even earlier because the role of coins could be performed not only by money in our understanding of the term (minted pieces of circular metal) but also by various rings, metal pins, and so on. Serving as ornaments, these objects were constantly carried on one's person, and participated in exchange, which at times assumed the form of a rite, an exchange of gifts concealing trade in commodities, and so on.

Metallic money is known to have existed in Libya in 600 B.C.

---

[1] See W. Stanley Jevons, *Money and the Mechanism of Exchange*, London, 1899, p. 55.

In the seventh and sixth centuries B.C. money circulation became widespread in Greece, thanks largely to the Greek colonies in the Mediterranean. This is demonstrated, alongside other remains of ancient Hellenic culture, by the coins of Greek cities with splendidly preserved minted portraits or scenes.

Trade contacts between ancient peoples undoubtedly led to the gradual spread of minting know-how but at that time there could be no international monetary system, although exchange and mutual settlements were apparently made at a certain parity. More often, however, coins circulated only locally and, after conquest, the currency system of one people was imposed on another.

Be that as it may, the circulation of metallic money developed further. In Rome silver and copper coins depicting the two-faced god Janus and other deities and battle scenes were used in the third and second centuries B.C.

In the ancient world metallic money circulation in the form of coins serviced chiefly the commodity exchange of the surplus product created either on slave-owning estates or in the subsistence farms of peasants grouped into communities. Such trade was necessarily limited and irregular. During more or less prolonged interruptions of the circulation process money had to assume the form of hoards, and for this purpose money made of precious metals was the most suitable. Such money and precious articles were used for the payment of tribute in Asian countries several centuries before our era. In some countries, e.g., in Lydia under Croesus (560-546 B.C.), money circulation made great advances. Lydia is considered the first ancient country in which gold became the principal money metal.

Substantial quantities of coins had to be minted even in ancient times. That is why both oriental rulers and the authorities of ancient Greek city-states attached great importance to the minting of money. They introduced strict regulations governing the issue and circulation of coins. Persons who violated these regulations, especially counterfeiters, were punished severely. The most widespread method of counterfeiting coins in antiquity was to make coins out of base metals and then cover them with a thin layer of precious metal.

The choice of a metal for minting money depended on its availability in the country. This explains why, in contrast to the prevalence of gold coins in the countries of Western Asia, copper coins were dominant in ancient Rome.

The money systems of individual countries appear to have been closed. Such concepts as stable parity or exchange rate did not exist as yet. In view of the prevalence of direct commodity exchange merchants who engaged in trade between countries did not need them, though a certain part of the commodities was probably paid for in local or foreign money. For local coins to gain the status of a means of payment beyond the bounds of their own country only one thing was needed—the establishment of their full value, i.e., the content of the precious metal. This was done by weighing, listening to their ring and even by testing their hardness with one's teeth or making an incision in the coin.

It was only in the Middle Ages that the exchange of metallic coins minted in different cities began in the trade centres of Italy. A definite correlation of currencies was gradually introduced in exchange practice according to their intrinsic value or precious-metal content (parity) and, possibly, also according to a rate based on the demand and supply. Shops of exchangers also began to discharge functions which remotely resembled the operations of contemporary banks, namely, transfer operations. This was done in a very simple way.

If a merchant had to buy goods in another city but did not want to take the risk of carrying on his person a considerable sum in coins, exchangers in different cities who maintained regular contact came to his aid for a set fee. The merchant turned over to the local exchanger the money in coin and received a receipt and on his arrival at the other city he was paid the sum indicated on the receipt in another exchange shop. At times payment for the goods purchased was made directly by these receipts, especially if the seller himself wanted to travel and buy goods in the city where the exchanger who had issued the original receipt had his office. Thus, the receipts to some extent performed the function of credit money, which became widespread under capitalism. But just as the exchange shops themselves only remotely resembled banks unde. capitalism, the receipts issued by these offices can only vaguely be considered as the prototypes of modern bank notes.

The progress of money circulation observed in the Middle Ages in Italian trading centres was the exception under the conditions of feudal stagnation in terms of money circulation prevailing in the rest of feudal Europe. Under feudalism the fragmented economy engendered a corresponding proliferation in money circulation.

Many feudal lords issued their own money, which often had only a limited circulation within the bounds of a particular fief. The feudal rulers were not bound by any rigid rules in coinage, and if such rules were established for a certain time they were often violated, which greatly hindered trade.

The situation changed for the better only where centralised feudal monarchies arose through the forcible elimination of feudal fragmentation. Since they had an interest in the development of trade, such monarchies not only protected merchant trade, but also sought to normalise money circulation, organised minting offices, and so on. In this they were supported by the merchants and the artisans of the feudal towns.

The feudal towns were the mainstay of a stable money circulation. Indeed, in the Middle Ages the development of towns, inhabited primarily by artisans and merchants, reached a high level and the circulation of commodities on the basis of metallic money took on a large scale and improved forms.

The need to exchange the coins of one country for those of another, on the one hand, introduced into international trade the practice of settlements in precious metal bullion and, on the other, developed the money exchange business and improved its forms. The individual exchangers were replaced by exchange offices whose connections extended beyond the bounds of their own country. More frequent use was made of bills or receipts from exchange offices. The exchange of different coins according to a parity and rate was improved.

The exchange business was gradually combined with cash operations which the exchange offices performed on the instructions of their regular clients, the merchants. Lastly, more powerful institutions appeared which operated on the basis of definite statutes, e.g., the Amsterdam Exchange Bank (1609) and similar banks in Venice, Genoa, Stockholm and Hamburg. But the operations of these banks were still based on metallic money circulation, which depended on the financial policy of the state authority. This authority, particularly as feudal monarchies gained in strength, could either normalise or derange the money system. The latter happened during wars and financial difficulties resulting from other causes. This was done, as before, by deliberately debasing money, reducing its weight and decreasing the content of the precious metal in coins. Although in this way resources were temporarily obtained for waging wars and covering the expenses of the court, eventually the debasement of coins threw the money circulation into disarray and, after a certain time, order had to be restored. Most frequently this was done with the help of onerous taxes and levies.

When a state allowed the payment of taxes with non-full-value coins*, it could imperceptibly reduce the amount of them in circulation. An equilibrium was achieved even when non-full-value coins remained in circulation if this was required by the needs of commodity turnover. Thus, the conclusion was gradually drawn that a certain quantity of coins as tokens of value, although they were not of full value, was necessary for the exchange of full-value money of higher denominations. Such exchange (billon) money of small denomination has been preserved in the local trade of all countries up to the present. The circulation of non-full-value metallic money led to the idea of using money made of another material, paper money. Nevertheless, metallic money circulation in the form of coins was the main type in Europe up to the epoch of the disintegration of feudalism and the emergence of capitalism, the epoch of the spread of colonial conquests and the expansion of world trade.

---

* There is no exact English equivalent of the Russian *полноценные деньги* and *неполноценные деньги*. We use the term *full-value money* to designate specie which contains the full specified quantity of precious metal and *non-full-value money* for worn, abrated or deliberately debased coins which do not contain the full specified quantity of precious metal. —(*Translator*).

In the 16th and 17th centuries, which Marx named the period of the infancy of contemporary bourgeois society, worship of the money system based on precious metals gave rise to mercantilism as a system of views which proclaimed money with intrinsic value, gold and silver, as the only wealth.

The idea of using paper money tokens was applied in Asia much earlier than in Europe. In Asia the early Middle Ages witnessed the formation of colossal authoritarian empires which encompassed many nationalities. It was apparently the need for trade in such vast empires with a shortage of full-value metallic money and the difficulties of circulating it as the volume of trade expanded that acted as a stimulating factor in the introduction of paper money.

Paper money was known in the 13th century in China during the empire of the Mongol Kublai Khan. It is believed that it was used even earlier in China under the Sung dynasty defeated by the Mongols, but it is difficult to form a definite idea of the nature of the pre-Mongol paper money circulation owing to the lack of data. As for money circulation under Kublai, there is very definite information about it in the descriptions given by the Venetian merchant Marco Polo, who lived for a long time in China during the rule of Kublai in the second half of the 13th century.

Marco Polo gave such a detailed description of the issue of paper money and its circulation in Kublai's Mongol empire (the Yüan dynasty) in China that there can be no doubt about the sophistication of the money system which existed at that time.

From Marco Polo's descriptions we know that a special paper was made for the printing of money and that it was "cut into pieces of money of different sizes, nearly square, but somewhat longer than they are wide".[1] These pieces were used for paper money of different denominations. The preparation of this paper money "is authenticated with as much form and ceremony as if it were actually of pure gold or silver", Marco Polo continues. We are also told that to each note a number of officers, specially appointed, not only subscribed their names but affixed their signets as well.

[1] *The Travels of Marco Polo*, London, 1928, p. 174.

In conclusion "the principal officer, appointed by His Majesty, having dipped into vermilion the royal seal committed to his custody, stamps with it the piece of paper, so that the form of the seal tinged with the vermilion remains impressed upon it, by which it receives full authenticity as current money."[1] This established procedure for the issue of paper money with the participation of several officials maintained a strict system and mutual control during this process.

Unfortunately, Marco Polo does not reveal the principles by which the officials were guided in determining the volume of paper money to be issued. He only remarks that "in large quantities, this paper currency is circulated in every part of the Great Khan's dominions". The inquisitiveness of the Venetian did not go to such lengths as to be interested in this side, which is important for understanding the economic essence of paper money circulation during the rule of Kublai in China. But we learn that paper money not only had mandatory circulation ("nor dares any person, at the peril of his life, refuse to accept it in payment"), but, most important, it also had stable purchasing power, for it was possible to buy any commodity with it and it was freely exchanged for precious metals. "Should anyone be desirous of procuring gold or silver for the purposes of manufacture, such as of drinking-cups, girdles, or other articles wrought of these metals, they in the like manner ... apply to the mint, and for their paper obtain the bullion they require."[2] Should a person happen to possess paper money which from long use became damaged he could take it to the mint where, by paying only three per cent of the value, he could receive new notes in exchange.

Pointing out that the troops of Kublai Khan received their pay in paper money which for them had the same value as gold and silver, Marco Polo makes a quite profound observation: "Upon these grounds, it may certainly be affirmed that the Grand Khan has a more extensive command of treasure than any other sovereign in the universe."[3] This

---

[1] Ibid.
[2] Ibid., p. 175.
[3] Ibid.

remark shows that not only the power of the sword but also the financial basis supported the might of the Mongol Yüan dynasty in China.

Judging by the fact that the paper money of Kublai Khan could be freely exchanged for precious metals, it replaced the latter in circulation and saved precious metal from debasement and wear in the process of money circulation.

The appearance of paper money in Europe belongs to the period of the disintegration of feudalism, the strengthening of trading capital and the expansion of the European countries' colonial possessions in America.

Of the two types of paper media of circulation (paper money of mandatory circulation and credit money) credit money appeared first in European countries, in Britain in particular, while in the colonial possessions in America paper money of mandatory circulation came first.

The introduction of paper credit money was associated with the efforts of private bankers, who in Britain, for example, originated among the goldsmiths.

As for paper money of mandatory circulation, its appearance everywhere was linked with the activities of governments, although their power could not in the least be compared with that of Kublai Khan.

But whatever the differences between the two types of paper money and the chronological order in which they originated in various countries, there were common reasons which determined the emergence of paper media of circulation, alongside the circulation of full-value metallic money. These were the development of commodity circulation, the expansion of the market to an inter-continental scale in view of the settlement of the colonies of European countries in America by people from the metropolitan states and also the natural increase of the population in the colonies.

Moreover, both the geographical and the economic expansion of the world market (increase of purchasing power owing to the curtailment of the subsistence forms of the economy and their replacement by commodity forms) proceeded in an epoch when the means of transport remained unchanged— sail boats on sea and horse-drawn carts on land. This meant that the increased mass of commodities in circulation with the exceedingly slow transportation facilities required a much larger volume of money. This applied particularly to overseas trade in view of the long time required for the shipment of goods.

The shortage of full-value metallic money in Europe apparently provided the main stimulus for mercantilism, a system of views which regarded money—gold and silver— as the only wealth. Essentially, it concealed the highly complex process of the development of commodity relations, on the one hand, and the disintegration of feudalism, on the other. This intricate process, growing in breadth and depth, demanded an ever greater stock of money. The quest for money was the determining motive in the activity not only of the trading strata of the population but also of the feudal elements who were cramped within the bounds of the subsistence economy.

Account should also be taken of the fact that the stratum of craftsmen, including wage workers, servants, apprentices, and so on, increased in the cities, and for them money earnings were the source of livelihood. Expansion of paid services had to be met by a corresponding increase in money to pay for the services and for the purchase of means of subsistence by those, who performed the services.

Last, but not least, money was also needed in the overseas possessions themselves, especially in the American continent, where European settlers in the colonies of Spain, Britain, France and Portugal reproduced commodity-money relations even faster than in the metropolitan states. All this created a new need for money, which corresponded to the extending process of commodity-money relations in the European metropolitan countries and in their overseas possessions.

Although at that time new silver mines and goldfields were discovered in the colonies, the production of precious metals was vastly insufficient to satisfy the need for full-value money. It is this that should be regarded as the main cause of the origin and development of various substitutes for full-value money, namely, paper media of circulation. To put it differently, the historical socio-economic process led mankind to the need to supplement the existing system of full-value metallic money with a system of paper money of mandatory circulation and credit money.

We have already touched on paper money of mandatory circulation in the description of Kublai Khan's 13th-century empire. In contrast to paper money, credit money is a category of circulation media which received adequate development together with the broader spread of commodity-money relations and it merits a special analysis. Moreover, although the development of paper money and credit money often proceeded in parallel, the logical path of full-value metallic money can be traced primarily through non-full-value coins as tokens of value to paper money of mandatory circulation. This was the case in the early Middle Ages in Asia and the same happened later in Europe and the European overseas colonies; moreover, priority should evidently be given not to the metropolitan countries but to their colonies in North America.

Though precious metals, silver and gold, began to be mined in the European colonies in America soon after their formation, the acute need for full-value metallic money was the reason for the appearance of paper money in North America. The main cause was that precious metals from the colonies were exported mainly to the metropolitan countries. The royal governments in the metropolitan countries regarded the minting of coins as their own profitable prerogative. While paying lip-service to mercantilism, the ruling élite in some of the royal courts of Europe deliberately prevented the outflow of full-value metallic money to the overseas possessions, disregarding the economic interests of commodity circulation, which was growing in scale there.

It is not surprising that in Massachusetts, one of the oldest English colonies in North America, a mint producing silver coins was organised as early as 1652. But in 1684 it was closed by King Charles II "on the ground that it violated the royal prerogative of coinage".[1]

In the meantime the colonies began to trade not only with their metropolitan countries but also among themselves. Particularly important was the trade between the colonies of England and Spain and also of other states.

Foreign, some of them Spanish, vessels anchored at the coast of Massachusetts and other English possessions as

---

[1] Arthur Nussbaum, *A History of the Dollar*, New York, 1957, p. 7.

early as the 1630s. It is not surprising that money of Spanish coinage penetrated local circulation which suffered from a shortage of money. The abundance of silver in the Spanish possessions in America, mined in newly discovered deposits, apparently enabled the Spaniards to coin money for circulation in the overseas possessions on a wider scale. It became more profitable to sell silver in coins than to market silver as a commodity.

In any case, during the 17th century the Spanish silver peso, weighing 423.7 grains, was quite widespread throughout the American continent. Gold coins from "Portuguese" Brazil, where the production of gold was extended were also imported into English possessions in North America. French and Venetian coins also turned up there. Quite frequently foreign coins were put into circulation by the pirates, who came ashore at the colonies to buy provisions.

It goes without saying that the wide circulation of foreign coins in England's North American possessions could take place only owing to the shortage of legal English currency. This applied equally to French possessions in present-day Canada.

The need for money rose during war periods, even deliveries from the treasuries of the metropolitan countries to pay officials and military men were delayed for various reasons. This, incidentally, further spurred on the introduction of paper money.

It is a fact that in 1685 paper money of different denominations was issued in the French colonies to pay the soldiers and it was to be exchanged for silver money immediately upon the arrival of a vessel from France.

But most definitely the initiative in the issue of paper money was displayed in the selfsame English colony of Massachusetts. In this colony, the lively trading centres of Boston were already functioning in the 17th century.

The direct reason for the issue of paper money was the need to participate in financing the protracted war (1688-1697) which King William was waging against the French colonies. Owing to the shortage of metallic money credit notes of various denominations were issued in Massachusetts in 1690. They had to be accepted in all official payments on a par with full-value coins. In 1692 these notes, issued for a sum of not more than £7,000 in small denominations, were recognised as legal tender. As such they can be regarded as the first paper money of mandatory circulation introduced in North America on a more or less considerable scale.

In Europe paper money was introduced by the Bank of Stockholm in the 1660s. But nowhere did paper money become so widespread as in North America, especially during the War of Independence. It was also during this period that the economy was hit ¯by inflation for the first time.

Without going into a detailed history of the spread of paper money, it may be said that at least a quarter of a century before John Law organised the notorious General Bank in France (1716) and its failure, the colonies in North America were subjected to the trials and tribulations of paper money circulation. It was in the 17th century that paper money really came into its own owing to the disintegration of feudalism, the emergence of capitalism and the formation of a truly world market.

The possibility of the circulation of paper money as tokens of value replacing metallic money was predetermined by the fact that non-full-value coins were already in circulation as substitutes for full-value money. "The fact that the currency of coins itself," Marx wrote, "effects a separation between their nominal and their real weight, creating a distinction between them as mere pieces of metal on the one hand, and as coins with a definite function on the other— this fact implies the latent possibility of replacing metallic coins by tokens of some other material, by symbols serving the same purposes as coins."[1]

This is in fact achieved with the help of paper money. How paper money is introduced into circulation depends on the existing conditions. Since paper money is by its nature intended to replace metallic money with intrinsic value (gold and silver), in the classical cases of its use it must be freely exchangeable for full-value money. In this case its rate can be preserved theoretically and practically at the same level as metallic money. In the absence of free

---

[1] Karl Marx, *Capital*, Vol. I, p. 126,

exchange the exchange rate of paper money usually declines. Metallic money of full value is preferred. This difference in favour of metallic money becomes greater as more paper money is put into circulation compared with the stock of full-value money really necessary for the current volume of commodity circulation.

If there is an excessive issue of paper money, e.g., during the financial difficulties of a state at war, it becomes so depreciated that its parallel circulation with full-value money becomes impossible. The latter is not put back into circulation by those in whose hands it finally lands, and full-value metallic money disappears. Paper money which cannot be exchanged, in turn, loses its purchasing power.

But let us recall that besides being a medium of circulation money also acts as a means of payment. In this function any liabilities can act as substitutes for full-value metallic money. Duly endorsed, they can circulate as a kind of paper money but of a different economic essence. This is money with the help of which liabilities "circulate" or are transferred from one person to another. In contrast to paper money of mandatory circulation, it is credit money, which circulates in the credit sphere. Marx pointed out that "credit-money springs directly out of the function of money as a means of payment. Certificates of the debts owing for the purchased commodities circulate for the purpose of transferring these debts to others."[1]

Such credit money at the higher stage, e.g., present-day bank notes, do not differ outwardly from paper money as tokens of value which replace full-value metallic money. But at its initial stage such credit money was an undisguised liability, a receipt or bill, drawn up in a proper form, often on special blanks. They appeared in all countries at a comparatively high development level of commodity circulation. At first such bills circulated only with the endorsement of the holder.

Originally credit money was, as it were, the forerunner of oncoming capitalism; now it is the main medium of circulation of capital. It is not by chance that credit money

---

[1] Ibid., p. 139.

was introduced and most developed in England, where capitalism gained its full stature sooner than in other countries.

Credit money in the form of commodity bills originated in private trade. The issue of a bill by one merchant to another presupposed that the buyer of the commodity would repay the bill as soon as the commodity was resold. But if the bill holder who had sold the commodity himself needed money to pay for another commodity or to redeem his debts, he could settle his accounts with the bill by endorsing it and transferring it to his creditor. The repeated transfer of bills represented their circulation as primary credit money.

The receipts of London goldsmiths to whom rich urban dwellers gave their money or jewellery for safekeeping acted as credit money even before the 17th century. But their circulation was limited.

The circulation of bills that goldsmiths issued to their creditors represented a big step forward in the development of credit money. The great trust enjoyed by the persons who issued these bills ensured them wider circulation, at first, apparently also with the endorsement of the creditors.

Only the last step remained, to issue a bill payable to the holder (and not to a definite person as in a bill of exchange) and in certain amounts convenient for settlements, for these bills to turn into bank notes. This actually happened in the first decades of the 18th century.

As for the goldsmiths themselves, they even long before this, in fact, performed the functions of bankers, because they accepted money for safekeeping and furnished credits to private persons, especially to kings and the feudal nobility at quite high, usurious interest rates.

When paper money appeared, royal governments began to utilise it as an additional source of replenishing their treasury instead of the old method of debasing coins. That is why the policy of the English kings, from the 17th century onwards, amounted to manipulating paper money circulation. At the same time, for example, the first Romanovs in Russia were still compelled to resolve their financial difficulties with the help of the old methods, like reducing the weight of coins (Tsar Mikhail Fedorovich) or the issue of non-full-value copper coins (Tsar Alexei Mikhailovich).

The financing by goldsmiths of the English royal court which repaid them with tax revenue was profitable for the creditors and demanded an ever greater mobilisation of resources. To attract them, goldsmiths introduced the payment of interest for the money deposited with them for safekeeping. "Around 1645 they devised a method of placing this custom on a quite solid basis. They began to pay four per cent for the sums placed in their safekeeping."[1] This comparatively high interest for deposits was easily compensated at that time because the goldsmiths themselves furnished credits at 10, 20 and even 30-per cent interest. The burden of such usurious credit accelerated the disintegration of feudalism, while money capital, personified originally by ordinary goldsmiths, turned into bank capital.

The power and influence of private English banks in the second half of the 17th century rose to such an extent that the royal government could not but reckon with it. Forced to resort to their help, it was prepared, if the occasion presented itself, to wage a struggle against them. Thus, in January 1672, Charles II declared that his treasury was unable to pay the debts to the goldsmiths and temporarily closed it. This formal declaration of the treasury's bankruptcy triggered off a chain reaction. Some of the King's creditors went bankrupt but the majority of the bankers suffered only a partial loss of their capital. Apparently their accumulations were sufficient to withstand such a financial blow.

The high credit interest rates which depended on the discretion of the private London bankers were not only oppressive for the royal government, but also restrained the development of trade within the country and with the overseas possessions. The incipient world market demanded the organisation of banking and credit along wider public lines. Economic thinking in the 17th century persistently worked on these problems both in England and other European countries. Many schemes for organising banking

---

[1] I. I. Kaufman, *Istoriya bankovskogo dela* v *Velikobritanii i Irlandii* (History of Banking in Great Britain and Ireland), St. Petersburg, 1877, p. 165.

and credit appeared, including some for setting up a central bank with the functions of a state bank (the chief credit institution of a country), the establishment of mortgage banks for supporting the feudal landowners who were being ruined, banks for financing trade, and so on.

For us it is important to trace the development of the principles for centralising credit and issuing credit money which subsequently received their consummate form in the activities of the central national banks which play the decisive part in the contemporary world monetary and financial system of capitalism.

CENTRALISATION OF THE ISSUE OF MONEY AND BANKING AND THEIR INTERCONNECTION WITH PUBLIC FINANCE

One of the results of expanding the specific circulation of credit money was the conversion of agents of pre-capitalist money circulation — money-lenders, exchangers and goldsmiths—into money capitalists, bankers. The latter added to the functions of the former agents the concentration of money resources in the form of accounts and deposits entrusted to them by various sections of society against bank receipts or loan liabilities. In their simplest form: these liabilities were notes or bills of exchange given to definite persons. Such bills had a limited circulation with their endorsement. But as soon as the issue of bills payable to the holder was started, the possibilities for their circulation increased. Such bills, in fact, turned into bank notes.

In addition to bills of exchange and bank notes, other forms of credit money were introduced at the dawn of capitalism. Cheques drawn on bank deposits came to be particularly important. Every cheque personifies the payment or the receipt of a credit: payment when the bank redeems the cheque of the client, using partly or fully his deposit in the bank; it is a receipt of credit if the bank itself, on agreement with the client, makes available to him credit up to a certain sum, within whose limits he can draw cheques on the bank.

But whatever form credit money assumes it must not be identified or confused with paper money of mandatory circulation. Credit money is a means of payment, debt liabilities in circulation. "Just as true paper money takes its rise in the function of money as the circulating medium," Marx wrote, "so money based upon credit takes root spontaneously in the function of money as the means of payment."[1]

With the appearance of two kinds of paper media of circulation they began to perform important functions formerly discharged usually by metallic money. This to some extent eased the acute need for specie felt in Europe and North America because of growing internal trade.

On the other hand, foreign trade, increasingly becoming intercontinental, presented a bigger demand for circulation media. This demand was satisfied not only by expanding the production of precious metals in the colonies for the minting of coins in the metropolitan countries. It was also met by the further development of credit money. The issue of credit and paper money was easier than accelerating the production of precious metals. The opening up of new deposits in many cases depended on accidental circumstances and required the investment of capital and time for their development. It is for this reason that the replacement of full-value metallic money by credit money in internal commodity circulation in some countries, especially England, acquired great economic significance. This was mainly exploited by emerging bank capital, which grew out of the pre-capitalist agents of money circulation.

At that time the young private English banks made the issue and circulation of credit money a profitable means of augmenting their wealth. They not only mediated the circulation of bills of exchange by discounting them, but in place of the discounted commercial bills began widely to introduce their own bills payable to the holder which actually were private bank notes. The degree of reliability of the notes of private banks in the process of mutual settlements depended on the financial stability of the bank which issued them.

Circulation of the notes of private banks signified a substantial saving in specie as a means of payment. This saving accrued fully to the private banks. Moreover, they utilised this opportunity to finance commodity circulation

---

[1] Karl Marx, *Capital*, Vol. I, p. 127.

for obtaining an additional profit by raising the interest on bank loans. The development of banks and credit money extended the possibilities for trade, with the lion's share of the benefits being appropriated by the new stratum of money capitalists. At the same time, at this initial stage of accumulation banks did not yet possess financial possibilities corresponding to the growing volume of commodity circulation.

In the mid-17th century the need for credit in England was already clearly not being satisfied by the operations of private banks and goldsmiths. It is this that explains why trading capital itself began persistently to look for a way out. Hence the idea of organising a powerful joint-stock bank and thus increasing credit along joint-stock lines, gained ever more supporters.

In the first half of the 17th century, during the reign of Charles I, Samuel Lamb, a big businessman, energetically advocated the idea of organising public banks. During the Cromwell dictatorship in the mid-17th century he even submitted a plan to Cromwell, arguing that in this way it would be possible to expand trade with the colonies, to bring back gold and silver to England, and so on. The bill for opening a public bank was discussed in a special parliamentary committee.

From the 1670s and up to the end of the 17th century such bills were successively put forward by Lewis, Chamberlain, Patterson, the ill-famed John Law and others. In 1694 such a bank was organised on the basis of Patterson's idea. Notwithstanding the strong resistance offered by private banks of goldsmiths and a considerable section of the House of Lords and other public circles, in April 1694 the bill providing for the establishment of a public bank was passed and approved by the king.

Without going into details about the organisation of the first Bank of England on public lines, let us note that these were the selfsame joint-stock principles of organisation which subsequently ensured the unprecedented concentration and centralisation of capital. Of course, the principles for organising the joint-stock bank were not entirely new and incorporated only in the given bill. Companies organised along joint-stock lines already existed in commerce. But in this particular case the form of joint-stock capital was applied to banking, which affected both trade and the financial interests of the royal government, i.e., the political sphere (let us recall the great dependence of the royal government on usurious capital, goldsmiths and so on).

Subscription for the shares of the bank amounting to £ 1,200,000, announced at the beginning of June 1694, contrary to pessimistic forecasts, was very successfully completed in a few days. In January 1695 the Bank of England commenced operations, of which the issue of bank notes was basic.

One characteristic detail is worthy of note. Apparently not expecting that banking operations of this financial institution organised along joint-stock lines would bring a profit, the legislators incorporated in the act a clause that the king would receive £ 100,000 from new tax revenue for annual payments to the subscribers of the bank shares. In other words, the government guaranteed profits to the bank shareholders. It is not surprising that from the first days of its operations the bank began to help the king's government in settling financial matters, particularly in reminting old coins. It exchanged the coins for its notes.

At first the private banks of goldsmiths tried to boycott the bills or the bank notes, but failed. Then they resorted to another tactic. Taking advantage of the fact that the bank indiscriminately accepted all coins both of full weight and also abraded and worn out, they presented them in large quantities to the bank demanding that they be exchanged for bank notes. Thus, private banks accumulated a large quantity of the notes of the Bank of England and then presented them to the bank, demanding their exchange for full-value coins. But since the bank was supported by royal authority, its notes increasingly acquired the force of legal tender to the detriment of the notes of private banks. That is why the issue of notes by private banks was curtailed and came to an end in the mid-18th century. At the same time the role of private banks as holders of deposits for different sections of society steadily increased. What was particularly important was that the banks began to concentrate merchants' deposits and make mutual settlements by crediting respective sums of money from one current   account to another. In this way the banks turned into public cashiers and gained the opportunity to credit and control the sphere of circulation

In contrast to private banks, the issue of notes by the Bank of England, which was connected with the government, raised its financial and economic role in the state. How this happened was conclusively shown by Marx. Having started its activity with loans of money to the government at an annual interest rate of 8 per cent, the Bank extended its operations. It was authorised to coin metallic money; it used its notes, granting loans at high interest rates, discounting commercial bills and buying up precious metals. Bank notes began to function like coins. The role of the bank in the state increased: "Credit-money, made by the bank itself, became the coin in which the Bank of England made its loans to the State, and paid, on account of the State, the interest on the public debt."[1]

It may be said that from the moment this role of the bank was established in public finance, a new era arrived in the development of money circulation in general: metallic money circulation was gradually replaced by the circulation of paper and credit money. And this, like any other novelty, began swiftly to spread in other European countries. But here, too, the development of banking initially did not always proceed smoothly. In France the history of banking was associated with John Law's venture, which to this day is an instructive example of how not to abuse the issue functions of a state bank.

John Law, a Scotsman, advanced his plan for organising a joint-stock bank at the end of the 17th century, first in England, but unsuccessfully. On moving to France, he gripped the minds of the more temperamental Frenchmen. Moreover, he was looked upon as a living embodiment of English experience. What happened in the first quarter of the 18th century in France is, as it were, a prototype of contemporary paper money inflation.

The bank founded by John Law in 1716 at first operated as a joint-stock venture. Its bank notes could be regarded

---

[1] Karl Marx, *Capital*, Vol. I, p. 755.

as ordinary notes of private banks. After the bank was reorganised into a state institution in 1719, the issuance of its notes without any limit whatsoever turned into the worst kind of issue of paper money. Eventually, it all ended in a tremendous crash and the flight of the initiator of the whole swindling operation. An astronomical figure of the bank notes issued by John Law's bank is named— 3,071 million *livres*.

Whether this figure is true or not, it is beyond doubt that in this case the French public in the early 18th century faced a fantastic anomaly in the issue of bank notes, which became paper money and which fully disregarded the laws of money circulation. Like any other experiment, John Law's experience was useful at least in demonstrating how not to act in issuing paper money. That is why both the Bank of England which already existed at that time and also state and joint-stock banks set up with the right of state banks in other countries avoided a recurrence of this bitter experience in their issue of bank notes.

It should be emphasised that, while the sphere of the issue of paper money by one central bank under the auspices of the government was extended in every capitalist country, private banks also utilised the joint-stock form for mutual penetration through shareholding. This enabled them to compete with government banks or to co-operate with them, depending on the circumstances.

Such united and, consequently, enlarged banks succeeded especially in concentrating all kinds of deposits, which even further increased their role as public cashiers. The use of deposits in the form of current accounts resulted in a situation in which the owners of deposits utilised their accounts in banks for repeated day-to-day settlements, issuing corresponding written instructions to banks. A cheque, representing a blank with such instructions, became one of the widespread forms of credit money. Two essential features should be differentiated in the nature of cheque circulation both at the early and the subsequent stages, depending on who acts as creditor and who is the borrower. If a person deposits in advance a definite sum in the bank he becomes a creditor of the bank. Every cheque of his paid by the bank, in essence, is a repayment of the credit by the bank to the amount corresponding to the sum of the cheque. This as it were, is a deferred repayment of the credit by the bank

The situation is the opposite when the bank itself opens an account for a definite sum to some person and authorises him to draw cheques within the limits of that sum. In this case every payment of a cheque by the bank is a credit to the person issuing the cheque who is a receiver of the loan. In both cases, however, the cheque is a form of credit money.

Cheque circulation, an invention of private English banks at an early stage, became widespread, alongside bank notes and paper money. Formerly it stood, to a certain extent, opposed to the circulation of bank notes; now it supplements it.

The rise of such an original institution as the clearing house is linked with the development of cheque and bill circulation. The organisation of this institution was prompted by daily practice. The point is that as early as the 17th century the clerks of various London banks had to deliver daily many cheques and bills and to receive or pay money on them. As time went on, they noticed that the cheques and bills of different banks largely cancelled each other out and at the end of the day money had to be used only to settle the difference. Then bank employees began to meet at designated street corners to exchange cheques and bills. But, since it was not very convenient to wait for each other in the street, especially in bad weather, they hit on the idea of combining business with pleasure and began to meet in a definite tavern. Lastly, when the bankers became aware of this arrangement, they rented a building for this purpose in 1775 for the convenience of their employees, thus opening the first page in the history of clearing houses. A clearing house, after the exchange of cheques and bills, uses money only for settling the difference.

Circulation with the help of cheques replacing money reduces the need for the latter, but it has a number of specific features: first, cheque circulation is primarily of a local nature; in international settlements cheque circulation involves settlements only with a definite bank, which is of benefit to this particular bank but is not always convenient for the clients. Cheque circulation also carries a certain risk. Banks are able to increase, without control, the quan-

tity of circulation media by granting unjustified credits
for speculations fraught with bankruptcy.

As compared with cheques, bank notes have a more universal and greater speed of circulation. This feature clearly
emerged after the issue of bank notes in every country had
become the privilege of only one central institution known
as the state bank of issue. In contrast to cheques which
carry a definite date for payment, bank notes are not limited
in time. But, as demonstrated earlier, in the case of John
Law's bank in France, the excessive issue of bank notes
can completely upset their circulation, turn them into
fiat money and lead to inflation. That is why with the
establishment of banks of issue the question of the laws of
the issue of paper money in general became very acute.
Differing points of view on this question were voiced already
in the 17th century. Ever since then much attention has
been paid to paper money circulation both by theoretical
economists and statesmen.

As time went by, paper money circulation and the issue
of money turned into an instrument of the class policy of
bourgeois states, and hence it is not accidental that in his
works Marx gave much attention to a theoretical analysis
of these questions. They are of great political poignancy at
present in view of the monetary crisis of capitalism and
require special examination.

The first theoretical and practical question relates to the
interdependence between full-value metallic money, gold,
and paper media of circulation and payment—paper and
credit money. The latter became so widespread that at
present precious metal coins have been completely ousted
by paper money in all capitalist countries. The small change
preserved in retail trade has become mere money tokens.

Metallic money was not ousted from internal circulation
at once; it was a drawn-out process, accompanied in all
countries by painful financial and economic upheavals.
The replacement of metallic by paper money is linked with
the expansion of credit, the development of banks and the
many various forms and functions of credit money.

The first sphere from which metallic money was ousted
by credit money was large-scale wholesale trade. Marx
pointed out that "to the same extent as the system of cred-

it is extended, so is the function of money as a means
of payment. In that character it takes various forms peculiar
to itself under which it makes itself at home in the sphere
of great commercial transactions. Gold and silver coin,
on the other hand, are mostly relegated to the sphere of
retail trade."[1] This, by the way, explains why bank notes,
the most developed form of credit money, are usually issued
in more or less bigger denominations which do not suit
small-scale trade. The first notes issued by the Bank of
England were for £ 20. But in trade on a smaller scale, too,
full-value metallic money, gold and silver, could be preserved only up to a certain time. With the growing scale
of circulation in small trade, full-value coins could be
replaced by smaller coins made of alloys of non-precious
metals or paper money. In both cases the non-full-value
coins or paper money became legal tender only by state
authority. We should not think, however, that state com-
pulsion is capable of imparting purchasing power to any
quantity of paper money.

"The issue of paper money," Marx emphasised, "must not
exceed in amount the gold (or silver as the case may be)
which would actually circulate if not replaced by symbols."[2]

This, however, is not the actual situation. But whether
the replacement of full-value money by their paper symbols
proceeded according to the principle formulated by Marx
or with deviations from it, full-value metallic money was
ousted by paper and credit money from internal trade. The
service rendered by Marx lay in the fact that he was the
first to formulate theoretically the law governing this process.
The history of money circulation in different countries has
fully corroborated his conclusions.

Indeed, full-value metallic money was fully ousted by
credit money from large-scale wholesale trade. In retail
trade it was replaced by paper money, but prior to the
First World War it was exchanged for coins. But even when
preserving the conversion of paper money for coins it had
a mandatory circulation for the reason that the state determined the nominal value of paper money and the procedure

---

[1] Karl Marx, *Capital*, Vol. I, pp. 139-40.
[2] Ibid., pp. 127-28.

for its exchange for full-value gold or silver coins. Since gold became the main monetary metal from the end of last century and up to the First World War, the exchange of paper money for gold coins was an indispensable condition of the gold monetary standard.

But such a harmonious combination of metallic money (implying everywhere full-value and not token) and paper money was preserved only during brief historical periods. Usually paper money was issued in quantities larger than required for replacing metallic coins. In this case their parallel use in circulation was rendered difficult. Metallic money was ousted from circulation by paper money. An agio and a mark up to the price of gold coins in paper money was allowed during settlements. This meant a decrease in the rate of exchange of paper money as compared with metallic money.

Nevertheless, during all kinds of financial difficulties, e.g., in wartime, all states resorted to the issue of paper money as a supplementary source of finance. And although this upset the money circulation, it often made it possible to avoid a more dangerous economic catastrophe. It is this that constitutes paper money inflation. In this case under difficult conditions the state creates means of payment by force of law and imposes them on commodity circulation. John Maynard Keynes, one of the chief proponents of the new bourgeois political economy, wrote that "the creation of legal-tender has been and is a Government's ultimate reserve; and no State or Government is likely to decree its own bankruptcy or its own downfall, so long as this instrument still lies at hand unused".[1]

And so with the appearance of paper money the state even in the period of the preservation of metallic money in circulation, instead of the archaic method of deliberate debasement and depreciation of coins, gained a new financial source—the unlimited issue of paper money. In that case what happened to full-value money, gold?

Experience has shown that, after brief simultaneous circulation with paper money, gold and silver coins ultimately disappear entirely. This applies in particular to gold coins

[1] J. M. Keynes, *A Tract on Monetary Reform*, London, 1924, p. 9.

and gold, which are turned into a hoard. But a hoard of precious metals, with the undivided domination of metallic money and after the extensive spread of paper money of mandatory circulation and of credit money, acquires a different nature.

With purely metallic money circulation hoards, as Marx points out, "serve as conduits for the supply or withdrawal of money to or from the circulation, which in this way never overflows its banks".[1] With the help of the conduit of hoards, metallic money circulation is, as it were, automatically regulated. But with the development of paper money circulation and the employment of all types of paper money media of circulation and payments the role of precious metal hoards changes, which is particularly noticeable under capitalism. "While hoarding, as a distinct mode of acquiring riches, vanished with the progress of civil society, the formation of reserves of the means of payment grows with that progress".[2] This was written by Marx 100 years ago during the period of pre-monopoly capitalism. In our days hoarding and the "formation of reserves of the means of payment" is most strikingly confirmed in the formation of state gold reserves as full-value means of payment in international settlements.

It is in this form that gold now acts as universal world money. But this does not mean that there is no private hoarding of gold and that hoards in their former sense have completely disappeared. They exist but they no longer play their former role.

At present gold in the form of coins is no longer used as world money. At the present scale of foreign trade direct settlements with the help of metallic money is impossible from the economic point of view. Credit money (drafts, cheques, promissory notes, the transfer of money by a bank from one account to another without the use of cash) have become regular media of circulation in foreign trade. Liabilities are to a considerable extent mutually cancelled out on the respective bank accounts. But during every span of time, say, a year, a certain difference in mutual payments is formed.

---

[1] Karl Marx, *Capital*, Vol. I, p. 134.
[2] Ibid., p. 142.

It is in such a case that either hard currency or gold, usually bullion, is used. It is this gold that constitutes full-value world money. "Money of the world," Marx writes, "serves as the universal medium of payment, as the universal means of purchasing, and as the universally recognised embodiment of all wealth. Its function as a means of payment in the settling of international balances is its chief one."[1]

In the past, when gold coins circulated, the statement that the path upon which gold enters on leaving the mint eventually brings it to the melting pot which turns national coins into bullion necessary in international settlements, corresponded to the actual situation. Now the stocks of monetary gold are mostly kept in the form of bullion. Final settlements on international balances with gold signify that, together with the act of settlement, value is transferred from one country to another in the form of universal wealth, world money. No other form of wealth possesses such universality.

As for credit money, its stability depends, above all, on the presence in a bank's portfolio of short-term commercial bills with even consecutive maturity. In that case the bank notes, as the bills are settled, can more or less evenly return to their initial point, to the cashier's office of the bank. But this does not happen in reality. The point is that besides the bill holdings for which, as they are redeemed, the bank constantly receives its own notes, it has also liabilities on current account deposits. An excessive demand for the return of deposits and also the presentation of its bank notes to be exchanged for full-value metallic money can always place a bank in a difficult position. This happens most often in periods of socio-economic upheavals, during a war, and the like. Then, as was the case in the past, the exchange of bank notes for gold is stopped.

By stopping the exchange of bank notes for gold a government usually vests the bank notes with the force of legal-tender. The bank in such cases can satisfy the demand of the depositors by its bank notes. The latter acquire mandatory circulation, as was the case with the notes of the Bank

---

[1] Marx, *Capital*, Vol. I, p. 143.

of England in 1797, which turned into paper money of mandatory circulation. Such a method of converting credit money or bank notes into paper money has become possible because the state treasuries of capitalist countries by their intervention in the affairs of central banks converted the latter into the chief weapon of government financial policy. This is also facilitated by the widespread practice of the issue of bank notes not only secured by the bank's portfolio of short-term commercial bills but also by treasury bills and state bonds. The latter are by their nature long-term securities and cannot serve as a basis for ensuring the stability of bank note circulation.

But paper money can also be introduced into circulation directly by the authorities, irrespective of the nature and prestige of the authorities themselves. Thus, as early as the period of colonial dependence paper money began to be issued in the English possessions in North America. In the colony of Massachusetts, as we mentioned earlier, the notes in circulation in 1692 amounted to over £ 7,000. In 1723 credit bills were issued in Pennsylvania. In 1730 in Virginia, owing to the shortage of media of circulation, there appeared so-called tobacco notes which were legal-tender in all settlements for tobacco within the bounds of a given county. The Mortgage Bank in Boston, organised in 1740, began to issue its own paper money. This activity, however, was stopped under the pressure of the English Government. In 1751, obviously sensing a political and economic threat in the issue of paper money in the North American colonial possessions, the English Parliament passed an act prohibiting the issue of any paper money in the New England colonies, in North America. A similar prohibition extending to all the colonies was adopted in 1763.

The issue of paper money, like a mirror, reflected the political and economic interests of the independent capitalist development of the colonies across the Atlantic, on the one hand, and the interests of English ruling circles, on the other. Here the scales obviously tipped in favour of the colonies. Without the issue of paper money the development of capitalist relations would have been hampered. That is why the issue of paper media of circulation in the colonies was continued under various guises. Thus, short-term

treasury bills for six months or a year and bearing interest
were issued and they actually circulated as money. Lastly,
in 1771 the Municipal Assembly of New York, which by
that time had advanced to a leading place in trade, was
allowed by the English Parliament to issue paper credit
notes. This was done to mitigate the shortage of media of
circulation and to some extent resist the counterfeiting
of money, which was generally rife in the American colonies.

It is no exaggeration to say that the shortcomings of
money circulation in England's North American colonies
was one of the important reasons which accelerated the
outbreak of the struggle of English colonial possessions in
North America for independence.

The revolutionary war for independence which broke out
in 1775 at once faced the Continental Congress in Philadel-
phia with the question of sources for financing the war. The
introduction of a tax in the absence of a central tax machinery and centralised statehood was out of the question.
Continental credit bills or paper money of mandatory circulation were issued as the only real means for financing
the War of Independence. Economically, this played an
important part in the struggle for independence.

The original amount of issue (two million dollars equated
to silver dollars of Spanish coinage) authorised by the
Continental Congress in 1775 had already in 1776 begun
to rise so swiftly that the various silver and gold coins circulating in the colonies started to disappear.

In 1779 the amount of credit bills in circulation reached
a total of more than $ 241 million. Inflation became un-
curbed. The depreciation of paper money assumed disastrous
proportions, further exacerbated by the unusual spread of
counterfeit paper money. New York, occupied by English
troops, was one of the main centres for the spread of counterfeit money. Huge sums of counterfeit continental bills
were circulated by agents of William Howe, Commander-
in-Chief of the English Army in America, for the purpose of "crushing the rebels" by undermining their financial
basis.

The history of paper money circulation in the United
States during the War of Independence stimulated the

development of banking in America. For the first time it demonstrated the role of paper money circulation in socio-economic upheavals.

Russia was by no means the runner-up behind European states in the issue of paper money as a financial resource. After six years of the reign of Catherine the Great at the beginning of the first Turkish war, in 1768, the State Assignation Bank was founded which issued paper money, called assignations, for 1,000,000 rubles. True, in order to secure the issue of this paper money, the Government deposited in the bank an equal sum of coins, which ensured its exchange. For this reason bank notes during the first years of their issue circulated on a par with silver coins and even with a certain agio as compared with copper coins. Notwithstanding the increase in the issue of paper money (up to 20 million rubles in 1774), their circulation on a par with silver, was preserved.

Thus, the Russian autocracy received a new fully modern source of revenue, the issue of paper money. It is not surprising that as the issue of paper money was extended, in Russia just as in other countries, its rate, as compared with metallic money, declined.

The revolutionary events in France and the war situation in Europe in the 1790s stimulated the issue of paper money in all European countries, Russia included.

A study of money circulation during the years of the French Revolution by I. I. Kaufman led him to the conclusion that the period of the issue of paper money during the revolution was divided into two unequal parts: between August 1789 and up to April 1, 1795 paper money for more than 8,300 million francs was issued; these issues even with the drop of the exchange rate yielded a financial effect amounting to 39.5 per cent of the nominal value. After April 1, 1795, when more than 37,000 million francs were put into circulation, the financial benefit of paper money issue was reduced to naught. Such is the logical end of any inflation.

The issue of paper money in Austria which began, just as in Russia, long before the revolution in France, (in Russia 21 years and in Austria 17 years earlier) also reached large dimensions.

The long period of the Napoleonic wars in Europe led to the discontinuation of the exchange of bank notes in England and the derangement of money circulation in Austria and other countries.

As for Russia, in the initial period of the reign of Alexander I, when it seemed as though the military aspirations of Napoleon would bypass Russia, the rate of Russian paper money stabilised at a level of 70-80 per cent of their nominal value. The situation sharply deteriorated as soon as the threat of an attack on Russia by Napoleon arose.

As a result of the war against Napoleon, during the six years from 1811 to 1816, when more than 256 million rubles of paper money was issued, its rate dropped to 23.5 per cent of its face value. But paper money depreciated and money circulation was upset at that time to varying degrees in a number of other European countries. This confirmed the general rule: the upsetting of paper money circulation in the past was linked with socio-economic upheavals. Only several years after the abolition of the Napoleonic military dictatorship was money circulation in European countries stabilised.

The period of upset money circulation from the beginning of the great French bourgeois revolution and up to the end of the Napoleonic wars in Europe compelled economists to take the theoretical problems of money circulation seriously.

One of the results of the Napoleonic wars was the clearing of the way for capitalist development in Europe by uprooting feudal survivals. Developing capitalism needed normal money circulation, and this became the aim of government policies.

In the second quarter of the 19th century, the concentration and centralisation of capital was accelerated by the joint-stock companies, which spread widely. But simultaneously capitalism's intrinsic flaws became pronounced, particularly during trade crises, including the crises of 1825 and 1836.

The cyclical nature of the development of capitalist economy was felt increasingly. Approximately every ten years economic advances gave way to crises in which money circulation played a special part. Crises were followed by periods of an upturn in trade, which again led to stabilisation of money circulation.

Machine-based factory production has developed widely since the mid-19th century. A technological revolution occurred in the merchant marine, the transition from sailboats to steam ships. An unusual boom in railway construction spread on the basis of the joint-stock form of capital.

All this demanded mobilisation of public capital and the maintenance of stable money circulation. The governments of European states strove for it in order to facilitate capitalist development, basing themselves on the theoretical conclusions which by that time had been drawn following a long period of theoretical studies. The results of these studies were analysed in detail in the works of Marx. No serious student of the contemporary world monetary crisis can ignore them. It is particularly important to discuss, even if only in general outline, the theoretical problem of money circulation, because at the present time, too, all kinds of theories, like the quantity theory of money and others, are utilised to justify the need for limited inflation and other measures in money circulation. All these steps are taken in the interests of finance capital to the detriment of the working people, and can be exposed only on the basis of the Marxist theory of money circulation.

EVOLUTION OF SOME THEORETICAL VIEWS
OF MONEY CIRCULATION

The present world monetary crisis has given rise to quite
a few theories of money circulation used by bourgeois economists and financial tycoons for explaining its cause and
exploring acceptable ways of coping with it. On closer
scrutiny, however, some of the "original" theories often
turn out to be a mere rehash of paper money "theories"
known long ago. This applies particularly to the so-called
quantity theory of money.

Its basic principles were formulated in the 1670s in the
works of David Hume, an English philosopher and economist and the most outstanding exponent of this theory.
In Hume's interpretation, the quantity theory of money
proceeds from the premise that commodities enter the
process of circulation without a price, while gold and silver,
full-value money, are without value. The price of commodities and the purchasing power of money, as it were, arise
in the process of circulation from the quantitative proportion of the mass of commodities and the quantity of money.
Thus, gold and silver receive value to the extent to which
they function as money. Their value is a result of their
function as money.

This functional viewpoint of the nature of the value of
money, gold and silver, with the development of paper
money circulation, often helped to identify paper money
with metallic money circulation and give preference to the
former over the latter. If gold and silver receive their value
from their function as money and the level of this value

is determined by the proportion of their quantity to the mass of commodities, why not also carry this over to paper media of circulation? Hence the views of bourgeois economists who denied the objective laws of the value of money and began to replace them by subjective factors—legislative acts of the state which determine the nominal value of a money unit.

This nominalist theory of money blossomed to the full before the First World War in the works of G. F. Knapp, a German economist, and some other bourgeois academics.

After the First World War this theory, in one way or another, was developed by the Keynesians, and after the Second World War by the apologists for American finance capital and the proponents of giving preference to the American dollar over gold.

All these theories are cognate with Hume's theory of money circulation because it underestimated precious metals and their role as money. Once labour value is not inherent in precious metals and their value stems from their money function and quantitative relations to the mass of commodities, this opens the way for further justifying a similar function for paper media of circulation.

When, however, credit and paper money began to play an essential part as substitutes for full-value metallic money, the functional quantitative theory of money circulation first led to an identification of all circulation media and then also to giving preference to artificial symbols of money. The wrong premises logically led to wrong conclusions.

In opposition to the functional quantitative theory of money other views of the nature of exchange value and money emerged in the 18th century. Views which contained rudiments of labour value were developed in classical bourgeois political economy and received their consummation in the works of Marx.

Recognition of the intrinsic labour value of commodities presupposes that the mass of commodities, entering into the process of circulation, has a definite sum of prices. These prices are merely specified by the supply and demand in the conditions of market competition. Thus, prices do not depend on the quantity of money in circulation. Money itself as the money metal enters into circulation having an immanent labour value. That is why, if it is a question of purely metallic money circulation, a definite quantity of money (gold and silver) is needed for the circulation of a given quantity of commodities available in the country. Just as the weight of a commodity is determined by weights because they themselves have weight, similarly the prices of commodities in the process of circulation are determined by full-value metallic money because this money has immanent value.

If there is more of monetary metal than is needed for circulation of the given mass of exchange values of commodities the surplus precious metals will assume the form of hoards, will be utilised for production needs, jewellery, and so on.

During a shortage of metallic money hoards, conversely, are turned into functioning money, as deferred payment arises and commodity credit and credit money are generated. The latter, discharging its function under normal conditions, returns to its starting point. If it was an ordinary bill, which circulated thanks to the endorsements, it ultimately returns to the person who issued it because upon maturity it will be presented to him for payment by the last holder of the bill. If it takes the form of bank notes, they will return to the bank by way of repaying the bill discounted by the bank.

The shortage of metallic money can also be alleviated by symbolic money tokens, paper money, if its quantity does not exceed the quantity of full-value money it replaces.

It is necessary to differentiate the circulation of credit money as a medium of payment. It is determined by the sum of prices of commodities alienated or already transferred into other hands on which payments have been deferred. In that case the quantity of money as a medium of payment depends on variable factors, the terms of the commercial credits.

As for the direct circulation of commodities in the form of acts of purchase and sale, in this case the necessary quantity of money depends on the objectively existing sum of the prices of commodities divided by the number of turnovers of the same money units. During the existence of only metallic money circulation or during the free exchange of paper circulation media for full-value metallic money at their nominal value, say, under the gold monetary standard, money circulation has a tendency to regulate itself automatically.

The problem of the quantity of money begins to arise because the media of circulation, including metallic and paper money, are available in a quantity larger than necessary for commodity circulation. Then paper money, as was the case for a long time in Russia (from the 1770s and up to the mid-19th century) circulates at a rate considerably lower than its nominal value. This disagio from the nominal value of paper money in general corresponds to the surplus of substitutes for full-value money as compared with the quantity of metallic money needed with the given sum of prices of commodities in circulation. It should be emphasised that the comparatively high rate of paper money in Russia was maintained by artificial measures, like the fact that fiscal agencies were strictly ordered by the Manifesto of April 9, 1817 to collect taxes only in paper money. Consequently, for the payment of taxes it was necessary to obtain paper money, exchanging for this purpose silver coins or selling goods for paper money.

A case was recorded when the Penza treasury office was strictly reprimanded by the Finance Ministry on May 18, 1817 for the fact that the Penza and Insar *uyezds* of the Penza *Gubernia* made payments of taxes not in paper money but in silver coins at a definite rate. The order of the Finance Ministry on this score stated: "Henceforward only state paper money or copper coins shall be demanded and received in payment of all taxes, and as for silver and gold they shall not be accepted from anyone on the penalty of the severest punishment under the law."[1] Copper coins in this case were mentioned alongside paper money because their rate was also maintained by artificial measures to avoid a considerable disagio. In this case the Russian financial authorities displayed a certain far-sightedness and understanding of the nature of the mandatory circulation of paper and non-full-value metallic money.

---

[1] Quoted from I. G. Tainoy, *Zolotoye obrashcheniye i tsentralniye banki* (Gold Circulation and Central Banks), St. Petersburg, 1910, p. 38.

For the circulation of paper money it is highly important to what extent the treasury itself accepts it in payment of taxes and state levies and also for other state services, e.g., the post and telegraph.

In the 18th century and in the pre-Marxian period in the 19th century most West European economists had an insufficient understanding of the nature of paper money as tokens of value of mandatory circulation. They confused their circulation with bank note circulation or the circulation of credit money. This was displayed both in the theoretical inability to find rational criteria for the issue of both and in the practice of government financial policy.

David Ricardo and a number of other economists criticised in the works of Marx introduced great confusion into the theory of money circulation.

In his study of money circulation Ricardo was inconsistent and also confused credit and paper money. He rightly held that the quantity of circulation media in a country initially depends on the value of the unit of measurement of money and the sum of exchange values. Inasmuch as both are objectively determined magnitudes, mere paper tokens of the value of money, in his opinion, could replace gold if they were issued in a proportion corresponding to the value of the replaced money metal. But, according to Ricardo's theory, as long as at the given value of gold or the money tokens replacing it the quantity of money in circulation is determined by commodity prices, the discrepancy between media of circulation and the commodity mass subject to circulation arises at once as soon as the sum of exchange values and, consequently, also of commodity prices begins to decline or rise.

Given a decrease of exchange values owing to a reduction in the commodity mass or a decline in its price as a result of an increase in labour productivity and a cutback of production costs, the amount of money in circulation will be greater than is necessary. Given an increase of exchange values owing to a growth of the commodity mass or a rise in its price, the quantity of money in circulation will be smaller than is needed. In both cases gold, discharging the function of a medium of circulation, in accordance with Ricardo's views, will stand as a symbol of value either below or above its real value. Thus, the original exchange value of gold as a commodity determined by labour time and its value as a medium of circulation constantly diverge. Naturally, the gold substitute, paper money, must follow the movement of the price of gold. During a period of a decrease in value it must be depreciated for the same reason as gold and also as a result of the fact that it is issued in excessive quantities. Ricardo ignored the fact that, besides its function as a medium of circulation, gold has other functions, including the possibility of becoming a hoard.

Proceeding from his theory of the functional fluctuations of the value of gold in one country, Ricardo held that in different countries these fluctuations in the value of gold arising from different quantitative proportions of their functioning as money may go in opposite directions. This served as the basis for his theory of the migration of gold from country to country. According to Ricardo's theory, gold should flow out of countries with depreciating media of circulation as compared with the exchange values of other commodities into countries where a reverse tendency occurs, namely, a rise in the value of circulation media.

The function of precious metals as world money serving as a means of settling balances of payments was thus ignored. The movement of gold from country to country was not made dependent on the payment balances but was, as it were, deduced from internal functions of circulation in different countries and in different quantitative proportions. In the final analysis, Ricardo's theory, like that of his follower James Mill, did not go far beyond the quantitative theory of David Hume. Mill associated the value of money with the quantity of it directly circulating in a country.

Ricardo elevated the ebb and flow of gold between countries into a kind of absolute of money circulation. And since this ebb and flow of gold quite frequently jolts the economy, it follows that preference should be given to paper money. Preserving all the positive functions of metallic money, paper money, rationally combined with metallic money, had to "insure" the bourgeois economy against all the adverse phenomena of a purely metallic money circulation based on gold.

In the first half of the 19th century Ricardo's theory of money adversely influenced government policy in money circulation in some countries.

Proceeding from Ricardo's erroneous theory, Robert Peel devised his well-known system for regulating bank circulation in the 1840s. Peel was the most influential follower of Ricardo's theory of money. The initial premise was the theory's proposition that the metallic part of the totality of circulation media, gold, shifts, as it fluctuates in value, from countries where its value is low to countries with a high value. Thus the value of gold is, as it were, automatically regulated: it rises in the gold-exporting country and becomes cheaper in the importing country. A general level of the value of gold is thus established. From this followed the idea of linking the issue of bank notes with gold in such a way that the issue of bank notes should be automatically regulated by gold. For this purpose, as assumed by the authors of banking legislation in England, the issue of bank notes had to be secured by gold which, with the free exchange of bank notes for gold, guaranteed bank notes from depreciation as compared with gold. The laws of the circulation of credit money in its higher form of bank notes were thus ignored. It is this idea that was embodied in the Bank Charter Act of 1844 put through by Robert Peel.

The Peel Act is repeatedly mentioned in the works of Marx as a striking example of the failure to understand the essence and possibilities of properly regulating the issue of bank notes. We shall therefore examine this Act before analysing the theoretical aspects of the question.

Under the Peel Act, the Bank of England was divided into the two departments of issue and banking. The first represented a simple printery of bank notes, while the second was the bank proper with all the intrinsic functions of such an institution. The essence of regulating the issue of bank notes was resolved in such a way that the issue department could put into circulation, i.e., hand over to the banking department for its operations notes totalling £ 14 million without any gold backing because it was assumed that money circulation in Britain could not actually fall below this sum. As for the issue of bank notes over and above this amount, the issue department was to provide security in the form of gold and silver for the full amount of the issue, i.e., the notes handed over to the banking department. The latter could utilise them in its operations or keep them as a reserve.

If for some reason (e.g., if gold were exported to cover an unfavourable balance of payments) the amount of monetary metal in the department of issue decreased, then the sum of bank notes at the disposal of the banking department had to be reduced. If this reduction coincided with an increase in the needs for means of payment during the economic cycle, it could become the cause of serious complications in the circulation process.

Marx and other economists were highly critical of Peel's Bank Charter Act. The discussion went beyond the bounds of money circulation as such and was carried over into the sphere of bank capital, interest-bearing loan capital.

In the first half of the 19th century problems of loan capital became particularly important in view of the efforts to normalise money circulation upset in a number of European countries by the Napoleonic wars.

Some economists of the so-called banking school, including Thomas Tooke and John Fullarton, assuming the viewpoint of the banker, turned the difference of the money form of income from the money form of capital into a delimitation between circulation media and interest-bearing capital. Tooke and Fullarton equated the bill and the bank note and considered it possible to limit the issue of the latter to the amount secured by bills. They assumed that the circulation of bank notes completes the cycle of circulation of capital and proceeds without a direct connection with the circulation of money as such. Yet in both cases when money as a medium of circulation services in general the spending of incomes (for example, the expenditure of workers' wages during purchases in retail shops), just as when it is used in acts of purchase and sale between merchants themselves in converting the commodity form of capital into the money form and vice versa, circulation media remain as such. They only perform different functions: in the first case they service the spending of incomes, in the second the conversion of one form of capital into another. To put it differently, we have a distinction between the money form of income and the money form of capital, and not a distinction between the media of circulation and capital.

In the broad sense, circulation media can act as a purchasing or payment means during the realisation of an income or the transfer of capital. This circumstance was not of a strictly theoretical, but of practical, significance during the periodically recurring industrial crises. Starting in the sphere of capital circulation, such crises inevitably affected the realisation of the income, in particular the income of the most numerous class, the wage-earners. Today this is vividly displayed during inflation. Originating in the sphere of capital circulation, inflation, intentionally or otherwise, hits the real incomes of wage-earners hardest of all. Their fixed income in the form of the wages fund is the chief source capital used to mitigate in some way the adverse effect of the monetary crisis on capitalist production and capital circulation.

The epoch following the Napoleonic wars in Europe created particularly favourable conditions for studying the movement of capital with the object of laying a theoretical basis for the actual development of capitalism. The point is that during the constant expansion of real accumulation in the form of elements of capitalist production, the accumulation of money capital, money designated for loans, proceeded at an accelerated pace. The accumulation of loan capital presupposed the expansion of credit and ultimately had to facilitate the real accumulation of elements of capitalist production. But the latter ran up against the bounds of individual ownership of capital.

The growing scale of production did not allow one person to accumulate a sum of capital corresponding to the colossally increased size of enterprises. This became especially clear during railway construction, the building of canals and ports because of the transition from sailboats to steamships, and so on. The same also applied to the increasing scale of industrial machine-based production. This predetermined the wide development of the joint-stock form of capital.

Capitalist joint-stock enterprises facilitated the unusual concentration of production in the 19th century. At the same time the joint-stock form in banking promoted the concentration of money capital and the wide expansion of bank credit. Up to a certain time both these processes went in parallel, interacting and accelerating capitalist development through the multilateral credit system.

At a certain point the spreading concentration of production and loan or bank capital inevitably brought into being gigantic monopolies and led to the merger of bank and industrial capital and, on this basis, to the emergence of finance capital and a financial oligarchy. Linked with this was the transition of capitalism to its highest stage, imperialism, at the end of the 19th and the beginning of the 20th century. Thus, the development of pre-monopoly capitalism was completed towards the end of the 19th and the beginning of the 20th century. Thus, the development of pre-monopoly capitalism was completed towards the end of the 19th century.

Discussing the history of money circulation in general and in the last century in particular, Keynes painted a radiant picture. According to him, the high commodity prices of the period of the Napoleonic wars was replaced by the swift rise in the value of money. In the last 70 years of the 19th century, apart from brief interludes, commodity prices showed a tendency to decline and reached their lowest level in 1896. In his explanation of the phenomenon Keynes, in complete contrast to his general views of the role of money circulation, involuntarily stressed the role of gold: "The metal *gold* might not possess all the theoretical advantages of an artificially regulated standard, but it could not be tampered with and had proved reliable in practice."[1]

We cannot but agree with such a conclusion. What is characteristic is the author's mention of tampering with an artificially regulated monetary unit. It is precisely Keynes's supporters who most often resort nowadays to tampering with paper money.

Within 10-15 years after the Napoleonic wars, the European countries' deranged money systems were put in order. Capitalism as a whole, notwithstanding periodic crises, was in the ascendancy. This, on the one hand, demanded stability

---

[1] J. M. Keynes, op. cit., p. 12.

of circulation media. On the other hand, the development of capitalism itself provided the basis necessary for the stability of money circulation. Hence the general tendency to stabilise media of circulation in capitalist countries in the second half of the 19th century on the basis of the gold or silver standard.

Since national precious metal coins could not be used easily in international circulation owing to the difference in the content of the precious metal and the inconvenience of recalculation caused by big deviations from the decimal system in the parities of national coinage, it became the practice of international monetary circulation to remelt coins into bullion. Subsequently, bullion often had to be reminted into national coins. All this involved a definite economic loss and complicated the mechanism of international currency circulation.

Hence it is not surprising that the idea of unifying coin circulation in different countries spread among economists and political leaders in the second half of the 19th century. The question was raised of organising an international monetary system of circulation, of a more convenient decimal relationship between various national coins, and so on.

An international association for introducing a uniform decimal system of measures of lengths, weights and coins was organised in Paris in 1855. The association had a branch in Britain. In 1858 a proposal on the reciprocal conformity of currencies was made in the United States. International congresses on these questions were held in 1860 and 1863 in London and Berlin. A number of other steps could be mentioned demonstrating the tendencies to consolidate national currencies in the second half of the 19th century and the exploration of ways of internationalising monetary coin circulation.

The idea of such internationalisation was embodied in the convention on the formation of a monetary union in 1865, which came to be known as the Latin Monetary Union and consisted of France, Italy, Belgium, Switzerland and later also Greece. Subsequently many other countries of Europe and even Latin America tried to keep in step, in one way or another, with the monetary system of this union.

In brief, the monetary union aimed essentially to establish unified standards of minting for the purpose of the free convertibility of various national coins within the bounds of every state that was a signatory to the convention or acceded to it. A single standard weight of coins melted from a kilogram of an alloy of a definite grade of gold and silver and also brass was established. For uniformity the weight of coins was fixed in grams and the diameter in millimetres. Their nominal value was also established. For example 3,100 money units were to be minted from one kilogram of a gold alloy. Each coin had to be of 100, 50, 20, 10 and 5 units and correspondingly its weight changed. From one kilogram of silver 20 money units were to be minted. Moreover, each coin had to contain 5, 2 or 1 money units. Correspondingly the weight of the first coin had to be 25 g, the second 10 and the third 5 g of silver, with a certain difference in their diameter.

Thus, with strict observance of these rules, different national coins could be fully interchangeable in international settlements and circulate within the bounds of every member state of the Monetary Union.

For all its shortcomings the existence of the Monetary Union for several decades up to the end of the last century undoubtedly exerted a stabilising influence on money circulation in Europe. Under its effect some states put their monetary systems in order.

Owing to the depreciation of silver, a transition from bimetallism to gold monometallism emerged in the 1870s. Gradually the gold standard was, in one way or another, introduced even in countries (as, for example, in Russia) where for centuries silver had been used as the principal money metal and paper money at a lower rate than metallic money had circulated for more than 100 years. By a decree of December 17, 1885, gold imperials and half-imperials in denominations of 10 and 5 rubles were minted and put into circulation on January 1, 1886. The imperials and half-imperials corresponded to 40 and 20 francs; this clearly demonstrates the influence exerted by the idea of the Monetary Union.

But in Russia paper credit money in the last quarter of the 19th century was exchanged at the rate of 1.5 rubles per gold ruble. That is why, by the decree of January 3, 1897, the old imperials and semi-imperials were reminted with the same weight and gold content into coins with a nominal value of 15 and 7.5 rubles. This nominal value of gold coins corresponded to the actual rate of paper money at that time. Thus, a gold monetary standard in its pure form was introduced. One ruble contained 17.424 grains of pure gold. In view of the inconvenience for the population of the non-decimal system, gold coins were soon minted with a nominal value of 10 and 5 rubles but an unchanged content of gold of 17.424 grains. In August 1897 the transition to the gold standard was officially declared. At the same time as the declaration of the transition to the gold standard, the State Bank (transformed from the Commercial Bank in 1860) was entrusted with the issue of credit notes secured by gold. The issue of up to 600 million rubles was secured by gold to the extent of 50 per cent and above that amount by 100 per cent.

Since the bank of issue in Russia, in contrast to some West European banks of issue, was not a joint-stock company but a purely government institution, its credit notes were exchanged for gold and, as it were, represented gold certificates.

The comparative stability of money circulation in European countries during the second half of the 19th century favourably affected the development of credit. Internal and international private and state loans were furnished on an ever wider scale. The absence of sharp perturbations in money circulation facilitated the investment of the savings of all strata of the population in state and other securities with a fixed income. The stratum of *rentiers* among the middle classes increased. Savings and deposits in banks were of a stable nature.

Keynes had some basis for commenting: "Thus there grew up during the nineteenth century a large, powerful, and greatly respected class of persons, well-to-do individually and very wealthy in the aggregate, who owned neither buildings, nor land, nor business, nor precious metals but titles to an annual income in legal-tender money. In particular, that peculiar creation and pride of the nineteenth century, the savings of the middle class, had been mainly thus embarked."[1]

_____
[1] J. M. Keynes, op. cit., p. 13.

And so, the *rentiers* turned into the pride of the century. But it was at the end of the 19th century that capitalism entered its monopoly stage, one of whose features is the prevalence of the export of capital over the export of goods. The *rentiers'* capital, concentrated in powerful banks, was one of the preconditions for the gigantic increase in the role of the banks.

The coalescence of bank capital with industrial corporations led to the creation of powerful groups of finance capital which began to determine government policy aimed at a repartition of the world, which had been divided into colonies over the preceding 150-200 years.

A global war for a redivision of the world was imminent. Preparations for it were accompanied by an arms race and an unusual intensification of militarism. In this context a part of Engels commentary on the third volume of Marx's *Capital* merits special attention. It gives a by no means idyllic picture of capitalism on the threshold of the imperialist stage.

"Is it possible," Engels wrote, "that we are now in the preparatory stage of a new world crash in unparalleled vehemence? Many things seem to point in this direction. Since the last general crisis of 1867 many profound changes have taken place. The colossal expansion of the means of transportation and communication—ocean liners, railways, electrical telegraphy, the Suez Canal—have made a real world-market a fact. The former monopoly of England in industry has been challenged by a number of competing industrial countries; infinitely greater and varied fields have been opened in all parts of the world for the investments of surplus European capital, so that it is far more widely distributed and local over-speculation may be more easily overcome. By means of all this, most of the old breeding-grounds of crises and opportunities for their development have been eliminated or strongly reduced. At the same time, competition in the domestic market recedes before the cartels and trusts, while in the foreign market it is restricted by protective tariffs, with which all major industrial countries, England excepted, surround themselves. But these protective tariffs are nothing but preparations for the ultimate general industrial war, which shall decide who has supremacy on the world-market. Thus every factor, which works against a repetition of the old crises, carries within itself the germ of a far more powerful future crisis."[1]

The words of Engels were fully corroborated in the epoch of imperialism which set in before long with its world wars and socio-economic upheavals.

---

[1] Karl Marx, *Capital*, Vol. III, Moscow, p. 489.

MONETARY AND FINANCIAL PROBLEMS
AT THE IMPERIALIST STAGE

World capitalism entered the epoch of imperialism having relatively stable monetary and financial relations between the leading capitalist countries, relations based on the gold standard. Only a few economically backward countries like China, Iran, Afghanistan and Abyssinia, based their money circulation on silver.

The relative stability of currency circulation facilitated the export of capital and the development of international credit relations, which was one of the principal features of finance capital and the domination of imperialism. The export of capital both in the money and the commodity form was stimulated by the rapidly mounting construction of railways, which required a tremendous investment of capital and heavy industrial output (rails, rolling stock and equipment). Notwithstanding the customs barriers and other forms of the competitive struggle between the monopolies and among the major capitalist countries, world trade was expanding. The growing role of cartels, trusts and gigantic banks created the illusion that monopolisation in the sphere of production and circulation was capable of eliminating competition.

The development of international banking in the first decade of the 20th century made it possible to extend the use in international settlements of credit money—bank notes, drafts, promissory notes, cheques and cashless settlements by transferring sums from one current account to another in corresponding banks of different countries. All this furnished grounds for the revisionist theories about the conversion of the chaotic capitalist economy into an organised one under the aegis of the biggest monopolies. Fashionable concepts of organised capitalism, ultra-imperialism, appeared. The authors of these concepts, which proceeded from the possibility of eliminating competition by the monopolies, naturally called for a revision of the Marxist doctrine of the law of value and money. R. Hilferding, a leader of German Social-Democracy who wrote the book *Finance Capital* published in 1910, was especially outspoken in this respect. Paying tribute to the nominalist theory of paper money circulation, he put forward a concept meeting the far-fetched theory of organised capitalism—ultra-imperialism.

Evaluating the tendency towards cartelisation, which was under way at that time, Hilferding wrote that this process could lead to a situation when "together with the anarchy of production the objective semblance vanishes, the commodity as materialised value vanishes, and consequently money, too. The cartel distributes the products.... The circulation of money," he concluded, "ceased to be necessary, and the incessant cycle of money found its end in regulated society...."[1]

And all this, according to the author of *Finance Capital*, was to be achieved under organised capitalism.

Yet in Hilferding's time the entire system of international monetary circulation was based on the gold standard. Notwithstanding the enhanced role of banks and various types of credit money, the need for gold as world money rose. Gold invariably preserved its role in international payments. Capitalist countries tried not only to keep their gold stock but to extend it as much as possible. The biggest part of the world reserves of monetary gold was concentrated in the United States, France, Russia, Britain, Germany and Austria-Hungary—the principal capitalist countries at that time. Some capitalist countries were concentrating gold in expectation of military conflicts. Germany, which began financial preparation for aggression very early, was particularly active in this respect.

---

[1] Rudolf Hilferding, *Das Finanzkapital*, Wien, 1910, S. 295.

Benjamin Anderson, an American bourgeois economist, wrote on this score: "In order to take gold out of the hands of the people and carry it to the reserves of the Reichsbank, fifty- and twenty-mark bank notes were issued to take the place of the gold in circulation. German agents regularly appeared as bidders for gold in the London auction rooms."[1] While the accumulation of gold was the purpose of financial policy in expectation of war, it objectively reflected the existence of free money capital and was caused by the need for the capitalist countries to have gold security for the growing stock of bank notes in circulation. The accumulation of gold in gold-producing countries, e.g., Russia, was facilitated by the increase in its production. In other countries this was promoted by a favourable balance of payments.

The world gold stock as of December 31, 1913, i.e., less than a year before the outbreak of the First World War, was estimated at 20,600 tons. It is important to note that the gold reserves were mainly concentrated among the six leading powers of those days: the United States, Russia, France, Great Britain, Germany and Austria-Hungary; they held 68-69 per cent of the world stock of monetary gold.

Table 1

Gold Reserves at the End of 1913
(million dollars)

	Centralised gold	Gold in circulation	Total
United States	1,279.2	611.5	1,890.7
Russia	868.7	254.2	1,122.9
France	678.7	723.6	1,402.3
Britain	564.0	370.0	934.0
Germany	340.6	655.1	995.7
Austria-Hungary	257.5	44.0	301.5
Total	3,988.7	2,658.4	6,647.1

S o u r c e: F. I. Mikhalevsky, *Zoloto v period mirovykh voin* (Gold in the Period of the World Wars), Moscow, 1945, p. 15.

---

[1] Benjamin Anderson, *Economics and the Public Welfare*, New York, 1949, p. 8.

The table shows that the United States had the biggest gold reserves among future First World War belligerents.

London, however, was the world's undisputed financial centre, although New York, Berlin, Vienna, Paris and Amsterdam were also of great importance. It was the gold standard that enabled other centres of world trade to play a significant part. The accumulation of foreign exchange instead of gold was displayed as a tendency only in some economically underdeveloped countries or in countries dependent on the metropolitan states, e.g., India.

Professor Benjamin Anderson, who lived through the prewar period and the First World War, wrote in 1949: "In 1913 men trusted the promises of governments and governments trusted one another to a degree that is difficult to understand today."[1] He holds that war came as a surprise and a blow not only to the American people but also to the well-informed Europeans.

Possibly the First World War came as a "surprise" to the American people, but this was hardly the case as regards well-informed Europeans. Be that as it may, about a month prior to the outbreak of the war the stock exchanges in different countries, those highly sensitive barometers of the socio-economic climate, clearly pointed to the coming storm.

Thus, immediately after the assassination of the Austrian Crown Prince in Sarajevo on June 28, 1914 securities, especially state bonds, were sold wholesale on the Vienna stock exchange. In July a fever was racking the stock exchanges in the most important cities of the world. On July 23, a real panic broke out at the exchanges in Paris and Berlin and soon swept through London and New York as well. On July 27 the Vienna stock exchange was closed and the next day Austria declared war on Serbia. The tidal wave of panic engulfed the exchanges of Berlin, Toronto and Madrid. The St. Petersburg stock exchange was closed on July 30, two days before Germany declared war on Russia: on August 4, 1914 Britain declared war on Germany and the First World War began.

As was shown earlier, on the eve of the war all the great powers had considerable gold reserves. World economic ex-

---

[1] Benjamin Anderson, op. cit., p. 4.

changes proceeded smoothly on the basis of the gold standard and, therefore, it is important to ascertain, at least in general outline, what were the direct causes of the complications in this sphere.

Prior to the First World War London was the world's financial centre; foreign trade transactions, redemption of credits, especially bills of exchange discounted by British banks, were effected there in sterling on a large scale.

As the period of redeeming bills drew nearer the demand for pounds rose, but after the outbreak of the war it became increasingly harder to get them. The discount of new bills became more difficult. This was felt at once, at the initial stage of the war. The sterling rate rose from $ 4.86 to almost $ 7.00.

Military operations by the German navy on the sea routes presented a grave danger to world trade. The shipment of gold for international settlements became risky. This point could, incidentally, serve as some justification for those who were in no hurry to pay with gold for their liabilities. Anyway, gold transactions via London were abruptly curtailed. Foreign trade was also reorganised. The share of manufactured goods and raw materials for civil industries decreased in international trade, while shipments of strategic materials and foodstuffs for the enormous number of people under arms mounted.

The First World War made crystal-clear the fallacy of the theories about the advent of the era of organised capitalism.

In his work *Imperialism as the Highest Stage of Capitalism*, written at the height of the war in 1916, Lenin stated: "Monopoly under capitalism can never completely, and for a very long period of time, eliminate competition in the world market (and this, by the by, is one of the reasons why the theory of ultraimperialism is so absurd)."[1]

But the war which strained to the utmost the economy and finances of all the belligerents was perhaps the strongest factor which compelled all capitalist countries to intensify state-monopoly tendencies in the economy. The state was becoming not only the political instrument of the monopolies but also the mechanism of their competitive struggle. It was this

---

[1] V. I. Lenin, *Collected Works*, Vol. 22, p. 276.

struggle that ultimately led to the first imperialist war on a world scale.

But before world war broke out it might have seemed to some people that finance capital had found a way for the organised elimination of capitalist anarchic competition, if not in the economy as a whole, at least in world currency circulation.

A tendency towards the coalescence of banking by the leading monopolies with government financial institutions emerged prior to the First World War. The central banks of issue began to operate in closer contact with the state treasuries. These contacts were particularly extended in the issue of media of circulation and government securities. The apparatus and methods of financing war by robbing the working people through inflation was thus being practically prepared.

The banks became the agencies which ensured the placing of internal government loans. The latter assumed the form of interest-bearing bonds and other securities. State liabilities served as security for the issue of bank notes by the central banks.

The bank notes were handed over to the treasury for circulation every time the state had to cover its budget expenditure. In this case the bank notes represented liabilities of the bank payable to the holder issued instead of liabilities of the treasury of the bank. If such bank notes, as was the case before the war, were secured by gold in a definite ratio to their quantity in circulation and were freely exchanged by the bank (and the entire quantity of bank notes in circulation cannot in practice be presented for exchange), the bank notes preserved the nature of credit money. But if this condition was absent and the quantity of bank notes in circulation, as happened during the war, increased to a degree precluding their exchange for gold, such notes turned into ordinary fiat money.

Prior to the First World War bank notes in circulation preserved their function as credit money. The central banks of issue themselves engaged widely in discounting bills concentrated in the holdings of private banks. This was the main means of putting bank notes into circulation. From this it followed that the entire system of private banks was interested in the normal functioning of the central bank of the particular country. This interest of private banks and capitalist corporations in the normal functioning of central banks dictated the closest contact between the central bank and the treasury, on the one hand, and between central and private banks and corporations, on the other. This was the path followed by the development of finance capital in industrially developed countries, especially the United States.

The Federal Reserve System of banks was organised in the United States shortly before the First World War. During the war this system began to perform issue functions which in other countries are handled by central banks. Together with US Treasury the Federal Reserve System actually implemented the monetary and financial policy of the government in the interest of American finance capital.

The essence of the Federal Reserve System boils down to the point that the country's numerous banks have a centralised organisation capable of solving the most important questions of monetary and financial policy, discharging functions of issue, and so on. At the same time these banks preserve independence in purely banking affairs in the localities. After the 1913 Act the country was divided into 12 large regions in which regional Reserve Banks were set up. Local banks were the shareholders of the regional Reserve Banks.

The Federal Reserve System is headed by a Board of Governors approved by the President. This board, naturally, consists of persons who are trusted representatives of the US financial oligarchy. The Board of Governors of the Federal Reserve System is headed by a Chairman whose functions, in general, correspond to those of the heads of central banks of issue in other capitalist countries.

As for the directors of the regional Reserve Banks, two-thirds of them are elected by the shareholder banks and one-third is appointed by the Board of Governors of the Federal Reserve System. Such a selection of the leading officials of the Federal Reserve System ensures the best defence of the interests of US monopoly capital. The issue of bank notes called Federal Reserve notes, in denominations of $ 5 and higher, and of other securities is one of the principal functions of the Federal Reserve System.

The issue of Federal Reserve notes under the 1913 Act had to be secured fully by reliable bills of exchange which bank members of the Reserve System discounted in regional Reserve Banks. The Federal Reserve notes issued above the sum fully secured by reliable bills of exchange, under the original law, had to be secured by gold to an extent of not less than 40 per cent. Federal Reserve notes were to become the main form of credit money in the United States, but alongside them, notes of regional Reserve Banks, fully ensured by liabilities of local member banks and also treasury notes and coins, were allowed to circulate.

The Federal Reserve System actually started to function in the United States a month after the First World War began, when the regional Reserve Banks were set up in September 1914. Therefore, it could not play an essential part at the beginning of the war. When in expectation of the war US European creditors in the summer of 1914 began intensively to withdraw deposits from American banks and to export gold, the share of the American dollar sharply dropped in international payments.

But as the war disrupted European exports in world markets and American exports increased, including the shipment of US strategic materials to embattled Europe, the surplus in the US balance of trade mounted. This process is reflected in Table 2 which shows the trend of US foreign trade (million dollars).

Table 2

US Foreign Trade During
the First World War

Year	US exports	US imports	Balance of trade surplus
1913	2,483.9	1,792.5	691.4
1914	2,113.7	1,789.4	324.3
1915	3,554.7	1,778.5	1,776.2
1916	5,482.6	2,391.6	3,091.0
1917*	2,164.8	965.5	1,199.3

* January-April.

Source: Benjamin Anderson, *Economics and the Public Welfare* N. Y., 1949, p. 21.

In 1916, as can be seen in Table 2, US exports reached almost $ 5,500 million, or double the prewar level. Although imports simultaneously rose, the trade balance surplus multiplied several times.

The United States joined the war against Germany on the 6th of April 1917. This, naturally, changed the pattern of trade but the favourable balance remained. In 1916 and 1917 it amounted to about $ 3,000 million annually. Arthur Nussbaum, an American bourgeois economist, wrote that the USA, whose external liabilities had exceeded its assets abroad by at least $ 3,700 million, was swiftly changing from a debtor into a creditor.[1] Commercial credits to allies were granted on a large scale. On the other hand, it was necessary to make settlements in gold with neutral countries from which strategic materials were imported. The United States became, as it were, the financial centre of the allies fighting against Germany. It was the Federal Reserve System that played a big part in providing financial resources for the war.

It is not surprising that Anderson, assessing the role of the Federal Reserve System during the First World War, wrote that "it is difficult indeed, to see how we could have handled the financial problems of the war without it".[2]

The disorganising impact of the First World War on capitalism as a whole above all felt in the world currency circulation. It could not be otherwise because no belligerent imperialist country, except the United States, possessed financial resources sufficient to cover the astronomical military expenditure and maintain money circulation in a definite equilibrium. That is why during the First World War, as has always been the case in periods of big socio-economic upheavals such as wars and revolutionary crises, money circulation was disorganised. The war greatly undermined international trade and currency circulation as well.

The war once again demonstrated the correctness of the Marxist understanding of gold's function as world money because only it preserved this function unchanged. That is why the belligerent countries, renouncing the gold standard

---

[1] See Arthur Nussbaum, *A History of the Dollar*, N. Y., 1957, pp. 162, 163.
[2] Benjamin Anderson, op. cit., p. 44.

Table 3

**Principal Assets and Liabilities of the Federal
Reserve System During the War**
(million dollars)

	On 26 No-vember 1915	On 22 De-cember 1916	On 25 Oc-tober 1918
Gold reserves	492.1	728.4	2,045.1
Cash	529.4	734.5	2,098.2
Bills discounted:			
government war bonds			
all other	—	—	1,092.4
Bills bought in open mar-ket	327.9	323.0	453.7
US Government long-term securities	161.8	124.6	398.6
US Government short-term securities	129.2	435.0	282.5
Total earning assets	—	111.7	322.1
Liabilities	892.0	222.2	2,295.1
Paid capital	548.5	557.7	80.3
Government deposits . .	15.0	29.5	78.2
Reserve Member banks' deposits	398.0	648.8	1,683.5
Other deposits	—	—	117.0
Federal Reserve notes in circulation	165.3	275.0	2,508.0

S o u r c e: B. Anderson, op. cit., p. 31.

by refusing to exchange bank notes for gold in internal money circulation, tried to mobilise the national stock of gold
for its possible use as world money. In turn, the private hoarding of gold sharply mounted, constituting the reverse side
of the medal, the inflational derangement of national money
circulation. Bank notes secured by treasury bills were issued on a large scale, which was tantamount to the issue of
paper money of mandatory circulation by the treasury itself. Such money became the dominant category in internal
money circulation.

The belligerent countries, however, could not get along
without foreign trade, especially the import of strategic materials. Hence their desire to maintain the exchange rate of

their currency in international payments with the help of gold.

Since the increasing imports could not be paid for or covered by exports, the belligerent countries had increasingly to rely on their deposits in foreign banks and the stock of monetary gold. Those countries which had substantial investments abroad and gold reserves, like Britain and France, quite successfully maintained the rate of their currencies at a more or less satisfactory level, although considerably below parity (five-six per cent below parity at the New York exchange).

Russia was in a worse position. Since she had no big investments abroad, the rate of the Russian ruble, more than any other currency, depended on a favourable balance of trade. But the First World War affected Russia's exports more than those of other countries. While other countries in their overseas trade faced war dangers on the seas, Russia lost the possibility of sending its cargoes beyond the bounds of the Black and Baltic seas. The country's strategic position undermined exports, and this, in turn, affected the rate of the ruble in international payments, reducing it by half as compared with its parity.

Russia's financial weakness was also displayed by the fact that she had great difficulty in obtaining foreign loans even on onerous terms.

A big divergence between the internal position of a currency and its exchange rate in international markets was displayed in all countries more than ever before during the war. The purchasing power of national currency in internal money circulation was often below its purchasing power at the rate outside the country. One and the same currency, as it were, seemed to split: while in internal circulation, owing to inflation, it appeared in the form of fiat paper money, in foreign settlements it assumed various forms of credit money—drafts, cheques, various promissory notes, liabilities and so on, backed by exports, securities, or, lastly, by gold. This dual role of national currencies during the war also affected postwar currency circulation.

The postwar disorder in national currencies lasted for about five years after the war, but by no means owing to the shortage of gold necessary for stabilising internal money

circulation. With the abolition of the gold monetary standard internal money circulation was divorced from the gold
basis. It turned into paper money circulation subject to various degrees of inflation.

Towards the end of the First World War most of the belligerents still had a quite considerable stock of gold, although
some of the prewar reserves were repumped into neutral countries and the belligerents whose territory was not directly
affected by the war and exports did not substantially suffer
from the war and gained in some respects (exports of strategic materials and the like). The United States and Japan
could be regarded as such countries.

Table 4 gives an idea of the distribution of the gold reserves after the First World War.

Table 4

**Gold Reserves of the Principal Capitalist
Countries at the End of 1918**
(million dollars)

United States	2,657.9	Japan	225.6
France	664.0	Argentina	304.5
Britain	521.0	Holland	278.1
Germany	538.9	Italy	203.4
Spain	429.5	Canada	129.8

S o u r c e: F. I. Mikhalevsky, op. cit., p. 64.

In terms of actual gold stock after the war, the United
States stood out among other countries even more than before
the war, as is shown by Table 4. Its gold reserves exceeded
those of Russia, France, Britain, Germany and Italy combined. Other countries too steeply increased their gold reserves: Spain 4.6 times; Holland 4 times; Japan almost twice.
In a number of countries whose stock also considerably
rose it did not, however, exceed $ 100 million. Thus, Swit-
zerland's gold stock increased from $ 32.5 million to $ 80.4
million during the war; Sweden's, from $ 27.4 million to
$ 76.5 million and Denmark's, from $ 19.7 million to $ 52.2
million.

Though the United States greatly surpassed other countries
in its gold stock, it may be noted that on the whole the war
brought about a more even distribution of gold among the

belligerent and non-belligerent capitalist countries. In view of this situation the capitalist countries could have normalised internal money circulation on the basis of the gold standard and brought the international monetary system into balance. But this did not happen immediately after the war. The partial deflationary measures were aimed rather at curbing than eliminating inflation, which followed from the new conditions capitalism faced at that time.

The Great October Socialist Revolution in Russia struck a staggering blow at the formerly integral capitalist system. The belligerent countries were saddled with foreign and internal debts which could not be settled in the usual way. Small wonder that the ruling circles of the capitalist countries deliberately tried to preserve inflation as long as possible as the most effective source of budget revenue under certain conditions, as one of the mass indirect taxes whose brunt is borne by the working people, especially industrial workers. Inflation was regarded as a means of stimulating industrial production and exports with the object of improving the trade and payments balance and the financial position of the capitalist monopolies in general.

Quite a few supporters of so-called controlled inflation in internal circulation as a method for keeping business going with the help of the constant pressure of the inflationary indirect tax on consumption appeared among bourgeois economists after the First World War. Mention must be made of John Maynard Keynes, who this time was opposed to what he regarded as hasty measures for stabilising currency. He criticised Churchill's policy at the beginning of the 1920s designed to support the exchange rate of the pound sterling. "For we know as a fact," he wrote, "that the value of sterling money abroad has been raised by ten per cent, whilst its purchasing power over British labour is unchanged. This alteration in the external value of sterling money has been the deliberate act of the Government and the Chancellor of the Exchequer, and the present troubles of our export industries are the inevitable (and predictable) consequences of it."[1]

---

[1] John Maynard Keynes, *The Economic Consequences of Mr. Churchill*, London, 1925, pp. 5-6.

But Keynes saw the adverse aspect of raising the rate of sterling not only in export difficulties. He held that thereby "we increase the real burden of the National Debt by some £750,000,000 (thus wiping out the benefit of all our laborious contributions to the Sinking Fund since the war)".[1]

Keynes favoured a low exchange rate of the pound because this would stimulate British exports and, consequently, improve the balance of trade and at the same time ease the redemption of the public debt. In other words, he sought in the insufficient stability of currency a good way of eliminating the consequences of the war and making "laborious contributions to the Sinking Fund since the war".

But Keynes had no monopoly of such "wisdom". Other countries which had suffered from the First World War tried to utilise the same method for achieving the same ends. Thus, the prewar competition of capitalist countries in the world markets was supplemented after the First World War by new methods of monetary and financial struggle with the help of inflation within capitalist countries and lowering the foreign exchange rates of currencies or currency dumping. This is one of the essential symptoms of the decay and general crisis of capitalism.

It cannot be said, however, that this policy was applied without any hesitation by the ruling circles of all capitalist countries. While the financial bourgeoisie of a country had a class interest in such a policy, its individual groups who invested big capital in government and other public (municipal) bonds and other securities with a fixed income, were interested in getting this income in full-value currency. This contradiction was displayed both within individual countries and between creditor and debtor countries.

The United States became the principal creditor country after the First World War. It was naturally interested in stabilisation as the primary condition for normal credit relations. Such stability demanded a guarantee of the repayment of debts at a firm exchange rate of currencies or in gold.

---

[1] John Maynard Keynes, op. cit., p. 11.

Therefore, in their financial policy capitalist countries manoeuvred between preserving an inflationary situation within the country and maintaining the rate of their currency at a definite level in international payments. The latter demanded gold cover. But this cover did not signify a return to the gold standard in its classical form of the unhampered exchange of bank notes for gold.

The maintenance of the rate of a currency through monetary operations in the open foreign market began to be widely practised early in the 1920s. These operations, the purchase or the sale of one's currency, were aimed at regulating the supply and demand, which led to the desired alteration of the rate of exchange. But to engage in such operations not only gold but also foreign exchange or even broader foreign liquid assets were required. Such maintenance of currency rates with the help of gold and stable liquid assets came to be known as the gold exchange standard.

The gold exchange standard was acceptable to the United States because it enabled debtor countries to repay their debt to the United States on state and private liabilities punctually.

The monetary and financial policy of the United States was aimed at the deflation and stabilisation of West European national currencies, and primarily the German mark. This was the aim of American financial policy since the first days after the war, but its application began only after the revolutionary movement in Western Europe had been crushed. It was concretely embodied in what was called the Dawes Plan, so named after the American banker who headed the committee of financial experts which handled currency, financial and reparation questions. The Dawes Plan was adopted on August 16, 1924 at the London conference of the victorious powers. In effect it was the first claim of US imperialism to a directly dominant role in the monetary and financial affairs of the capitalist world.

What was the crux of the matter? The victorious powers which had fought against Germany could repay their debts to the United States and American financial corporations only if they received reparations from Germany in accordance with the Treaty of Versailles. For this it was essential to stabilise the revenue sources in Germany herself and her

disorganised money circulation.[1] The Dawes Plan was
designed expressly for this purpose.

Under this plan, Germany received a loan of 800 million gold marks (in round figures about $ 200 million) which
was to be used as gold backing of the issue of bank notes in
circulation. It was expected that stabilisation of money circulation would create the basis for economic stabilisation
and the influx of foreign capital. To make certain that the
"shot in the arm" given Germany in the form of a gold loan
was effective, the United States insisted on a temporary post-
ponement of reparation payments. In anticipation of this
move, France had occupied the Ruhr as early as January
1923 under the slogan: "The Boches must pay!" For our purposes we are interested not in reparation payments but in the
policy of stabilising money circulation, which the United
States wanted to achieve in Europe. The operation of the
Dawes Plan did in fact lead to measures which to varying
degrees helped to stabilise national currencies.

Keynes' opposition to Churchill's financial policy in Britain shows that these deflationary measures did not meet
with general approval. Like Keynes, many saw in prolonging
moderate inflation the main instrument for stimulating exports and easing the burden of the wartime public debt.
Nor was there any unanimity of opinion among the monopoly
bourgeoisie itself.

As is the case of any period of big economic changes, the
contradictions between the stratum of creditors and of debtors on questions of financial policy became most acute among
the bourgeoisie. The dividing line between them was deflation and inflation. But the inflational instability of money
circulation and the desire to preserve a low rate of national
currency remained the dominant factor in the general financial policy of most capitalist countries up to the outbreak
of the world crisis at the end of the 1920s and early 1930s.

While, on the one hand, inflation served as a means for
stimulating exports, on the other, it caused anti-inflation
tariff restrictions in importing countries, which ultimately

[1] To what extent money circulation in Germany was disrupted can
be seen from the fact that in 1924 the rate of the German mark in New
York was expressed in astronomical figures—4,000,000,000,000 marks
for one dollar.

impeded the expansion of foreign trade. This was also noted at the World Economic Conference held in 1927 because the relative stabilisation of capitalism was accompanied by an intensification of capitalism's organic vices and contradictions. This was particularly felt in the world monetary system.

Since the monetary system did not return to the old basis of the gold standard (meaning the securing of bank notes by gold clearly demonstrated by the exchange of bank notes for gold) and the gold exchange standard came into use, there was no need to hand over monetary gold into private hands. To maintain the rate of a currency, the necessary operations, including those involving gold, were conducted abroad by national banks or treasuries. That is why disposal of the gold reserves increasingly became an exclusively governmental function.

It goes without saying that government operations with gold and foreign exchange can be conducted only on a large scale and, consequently, any operations in gold were carried out primarily in bullion (the gold bullion standard).

The use of bullion as such in international settlements, in contrast to its use in coins in internal circulation, has always been practised. Marx drew attention to this point emphasising that gold thus changes its national uniform, as it were. "The different national uniforms worn at home by gold and silver as coins, and doffed again in the market of the world," Karl Marx wrote, "indicate the separation between the internal or national spheres of the circulation of commodities, and their universal sphere.

"The only difference, therefore, between coin and bullion is one of shape, and gold can at any time pass from one form to the other."[1]

Since in the 1920s full-value metallic money in coins (bullion or small change is not considered in this case) ceased to circulate, naturally gold remained only in the form of bullion in international settlements. The new actual change in the function of gold as world money was that gold stopped ensuring internal money circulation (and connecting the latter with the money circulation of other countries through

---

[1] Karl Marx, *Capital*, Vol. I, p. 125.

gold parity) and only maintained the external exchange rates of national currencies.

In other words, gold began to ensure liquid assets and foreign exchange in relations between states. From this it is possible to differentiate in effect two kinds of gold standard: the gold standard which ensures money circulation in general (internal and external) and the gold standard which ensures the external exchange rate of a national currency — the gold exchange standard.

Jacques Rueff, the prominent theoretician and proponent of the gold standard, a member of the French Academy who was an adviser to General de Gaulle when he was President, adheres to this viewpoint. In one of his articles on problems of the international monetary system he wrote: "The gold standard was used throughout the world until 1922 and then from 1933 to 1940.... A contrary system is the 'gold exchange standard'—as it existed in a number of European countries between 1922 and 1930, then again starting in 1945."[1]

Rueff does not single out the gold bullion standard as a special economic category. On the other hand, he in general outline sets the correct periodisation of the use of the gold and gold exchange standards.

Indeed, the separation of internal money circulation from external currency circulation in capitalist countries which began during the First World War was fully completed in 1922. Since then and up to the world crisis at the end of the 1920s and early 1930s, capitalist states, widely utilising the gold exchange standard for maintaining the rates of their currencies in international payments, widely employed inflational and credit stimulation for the recovery and development of their economies. This served as the basis for the so-called relative stabilisation of capitalism (1924-1929) and prepared the ground for an unparalleled economic crisis. It may be said that only a few years after the war, approximately at the beginning of 1924, monetary relations between capitalist countries became relatively stable and the gold exchange standard became dominant in the leading capitalist states.

---

[1] *The Wall Street Journal*, June 5, 1969.

Capitalism's relative stabilisation lasted for about five years. In the course of it the United States, exploiting its position as a creditor country, tried to reinforce the position of the dollar in international payments. This was done with comparative ease because, being a creditor, the USA had a favourable trade balance and the biggest gold reserves among the other principal capitalist countries. At the same time the US ruling element pursued a very rigid policy of protecting the home market against the importation of goods from countries with a depreciated currency. This was done chiefly through high tariffs.

The high American duties on imports impeded the development of world trade. They compelled other countries to pay for American credits not by the export of goods, but by the export of gold, by giving US capital participation in the industry of European countries, and so on. Naturally this was often done against the wishes of the European capitalists. Since it was impossible to pay in gold, capitalist companies gave American investors a considerable part of their shares and other securities. All this offered US capital substantial advantages in international currency circulation and credit.

It is not surprising that, during the period of capitalism's relative stabilisation in the 1920s, other big capitalist countries, too, even if they did not fully eliminate inflation in internal money circulation, began in one way or another to maintain the rates of their currencies in international payments close to parity. Britain, for example, tried to rally together round the pound the countries dependent on her. This, by the way, was Churchill's financial policy attacked by Keynes.

After the weakening of sterling in international payments, Churchill wanted to consolidate its position and to keep the countries of the British Empire within the orbit of the City.

Keynes counted on the inflational stimulation of exports and the easing of Britain's public debt by maintaining a lower rate of the pound. Ultimately both wanted to protect the interests of British finance capital. The whole point was how to combine both objectives without infringing the interests of individual groups of finance capital.

In contrast to the US monetary and financial policy, backed by high customs barriers, Britain's policy followed the line of expanding trade preferences in commerce with the countries of the sterling area, especially the dominions. But the position of the pound remained unstable, which prevented the British ruling circles from fully utilising the benefits of the relative stabilisation, as the United States did. The Dawes Plan tied Britain to the financial policy of the United States.

The desire to implant American capital in the industry of European countries represented the quintessence of US monetary and financial policy of the Dawes Plan period. Describing the financial policy of the United States after it entered the First World War and in the postwar period Benjamin Anderson wrote: "In World War I, between April 1917 and December 30, 1918, we expanded bank deposits by $5.8 billion, and bank loans and investments by $ 7 billion. This was enough.

"In the period from June of 1922 to April 11, 1928, we expanded bank credit by $ 13.5 billion in deposits, and by $ 14.5 billion in loans and investments. This generated our immense boom, our wide stock market, and our stock market crash of 1929."[1] This undoubtedly is a correct general evaluation of US financial policy in the 1920s which accelerated and intensified the world economic crisis of 1929-1933.

A characteristic feature of the period of capitalism's relative stabilisation was likewise the increased tendency towards forming and consolidating economic blocs and currency areas, which, on the one hand, added to the financial, economic and foreign trade difficulties of capitalism and, on the other, created the preconditions for new military conflicts and a new world war.

The foundations of the sterling area were laid in Britain. Imperialist Japan was creating a "co-prosperity" sphere in East Asia. This served as a cover for the usual colonial policy backed by Japan's armed forces.

---

[1] Benjamin Anderson, "The Road Back to Full Employment", *Financing American Prosperity*, A Symposium of Economists, New York, 1945, p. 45.

Out to gain a dominating position in the world monetary and credit system, Washington zealously guarded the Latin American countries from an invasion of capital from other imperialist states.

France tried to consolidate her positions in her African colonies with the help of trade and financial measures.

Germany, in a similar way and quite successfully, especially with the help of clearing settlements was tying the economically weaker countries of Eastern Europe and the Middle East to the chariot of her finance capital.

The possibility of a more or less complete break with the world market, autarky, was theoretically conceivable within the bounds of such blocs.

The tendency of the world capitalist market to split into individual economic blocs, in turn, adversely affected the stability of the world monetary system. From the socio-economic angle this was nothing but the exertions of world imperialism to insure itself against the disintegration of the obsolete colonial system. In these conditions the gold exchange standard helped to eliminate artificial partitions in the world capitalist economy, to smooth over market fluctuations of prices and to maintain world trade and credit relations. The world economic crisis of 1929-1933 shattered capitalism's relative stabilisation.

THE WORLD ECONOMIC CRISIS
AND ITS IMPACT ON CAPITALISM'S
MONETARY SYSTEM

The world economic crisis of 1929-1933 exerted a tremendous influence on the world monetary system. The crisis was not confined to the overproduction of goods. While some national markets were glutted with commodities that could find no buyers, others could have presented an effective demand for certain goods. What made the situation so complicated was the fact that the world market, which was the connecting link between national markets, was disorganised by the derangement of the credit system. One of the main causes of the latter was that creditor countries, and especially the United States, by their monetary and financial policy created a situation in which debtor countries could pay only in gold, and could not utilise their export potentialities in full measure.

Stimulated by dollar credits, the economic boom in the United States and some other capitalist countries in the long run ran up against the shortage of gold for the repayment of debts. Even if there had been much larger world reserves of monetary gold than there were at the moment of the crisis, mutual settlements on war and postwar debts could not proceed smoothly because the war debt arose under an entirely different level of commodity prices expressed in gold. A general re-evaluation of values was required, and in some cases also the full annulment of wartime debts to bring back stability to world trade and the credit system.

Yet the US ruling circles continued to stimulate economic development by easy credits right up to the time when the crisis broke. They also increased foreign loans with the object of further subordinating the economies of European countries to US finance capital. Thus, the issue of new securities for making additional investments in various sectors of the economy rose from $ 4,000 million in 1923 to $ 10,000 million in 1929. In the same year the United States had the smallest unemployment rate—only 0.9 per cent—during all the war and postwar years. It seemed as though the much-vaunted "prosperity" was functioning faultlessly and monetary and financial policy was following a correct course. But before the end of that year the American stock exchanges were overwhelmed by the crisis and the prices of securities dropped precipitously. Commodity prices in the world market, where disturbing fluctuations had been observed even earlier, began to decline swiftly.

In 1930, when no doubt whatsoever remained that the economy of the United States, like that of other countries, faced a serious crisis, and not just a slight recession, the American ruling circles continued their attempts to maintain business by artificial means. This was also expressed in President Hoover's calls to municipalities to increase the issue of bonds for financing public works to maintain employment and purchasing power. But these calls remained pious wishes.

In 1930 unemployment rose to 7.8 per cent or more than seven times as compared with the preceding year. In subsequent years it continued to mount, reaching the maximum of 25.1 per cent in 1933. In other words, one out of every four industrial workers employed before the crisis lost his job.

The credit system of the United States was so upset that many banks went bankrupt. In 1930 out of more than 24,000 banks 1,352 closed down. In 1931 this number increased to 2,294, and in the next year another 1,456 banks failed.

In view of the swift disappearance of gold from circulation, the exchange of bank notes for gold was stopped on March 6, 1933. All American citizens and corporations were ordered by the government to hand over to the Treasury monetary gold in their possession above $ 100. This was the first step towards the nationalisation of gold. Preconditions for the devaluation of the dollar were also created. The US ruling circles were in a hurry to receive payments in gold and dollars from US debtors prior to devaluation and to invest available money in foreign enterprises, to buy shares or invest capital in import operations.

The removal of gold from the private sector by the US Treasury through the issue to the owners of Treasury gold certificates was legalised at the end of January 1934. This action predetermined the devaluation of the dollar. The gold content of the dollar was reduced by 40 per cent under the law. The President's decision of January 31, 1934 fixed the gold content of $ 1 at 1/35 of a troy ounce (0.888671 g) or $ 35 per ounce of gold instead of $ 20.67 prior to devaluation. This sent up the value of the gold reserves of the USA after devaluation to $ 7,877 million instead of $ 4,652 million prior to devaluation. At the price of $ 35 per ounce of gold the new gold content of the American dollar amounted to 59.06 per cent of that prior to devaluation.

The principal European countries did not at once follow the American example. What was more, France, Belgium, the Netherlands, Italy and Switzerland formed the so-called "gold bloc" to preserve the gold basis of their currencies. The preservation of the old gold parity by a number of European countries was apparently dictated by economic considerations — the desire to keep foreign capital in their countries and to attract new capital as a way of saving the credit system from disintegration. In the long run, however, the gold bloc could not withstand the onslaught of the crisis. But for a certain time it played its part, hampering the repatriation of American capital from Europe in the form of gold. Highly indicative in this respect is the movement of the gold reserves of the principal capitalist countries during the world economic crisis. (See table 5.)

The table shows that the gold reserves in the United States began to rise after 1933 when the dollar was devalued and gold was concentrated in the Treasury. The situation was different in the gold bloc countries. It was during the first years of the period we are examining—prior to 1933 and 1934, i.e., prior to the devaluation of the American dollar, that the gold reserves in these countries rose. Subsequently this growth was either stopped or the reserves decreased somewhat. On the whole, however, the gold reserves in the gold bloc countries rose by 28 per cent from June 1931 to October 1935, while in the United States they increased by 24.6 per

Table 5

Gold Reserves of Major Capitalist Countries in the First Half of the 1930s (Millions of US Old Gold Dollars) at the End of the Month Indicated

	June 1931	June 1932	December 1933	June 1934	March 1935	October 1935	Percentage change between June 1931 and October 1935 (+ −)
United States	4,593	3,997	4,012	4,640	5,060	5,725	+24.6
Gold bloc countries	3,056	4,581	4,525	4,480	4,517	3,887	+27.8
Comprising:							
France . . .	2,211	3,183	3,015	3,117	3,238	2,830	+28.0
Belgium . .	200	372	380	369	314	345	+72.0
Netherlands	200	309	371	338	327	237	+18.5
Italy . . .	283	356	373	340	308	207	−26.9
Switzerland	162	361	386	316	330	268	+65.3
Britain . .	800	927	933	935	940	952	+19.0
Germany . .	354	62	109	34	36	38	−89.3
Japan . . .	424	212	212	227	235	247	−42.0
Spain . . .	468	436	436	437	438	436	−6.8
Argentina	349	248	238	238	238	238	−31.8
Other countries . . .	1,347	1,483	1,554	1,597	1,652	1,265	−6.3

Source: S. E. Harris, *Exchange Depreciation. Its Theory and Its History, 1931-1935, With Some Consideration of Related Domestic Policies*, Cambridge, 1936, p. 145.

cent during the same period. Losses of gold were sustained by Germany (89.3 per cent), Japan (42 per cent), Argentina (31.8 per cent), Italy, which was a member of the gold bloc, (26.9 per cent) and Spain (6.8 per cent). Moreover, the sharp decrease in Italy's gold reserves occurred in a brief period, from March to October 1935, when the gold bloc actually ceased to function and, moreover, the devalued American dollar became stable on the new gold basis.

The world economic crisis did tremendous damage to the capitalist countries, especially the United States. It put an

end to relative stabilisation and only memories remained
of the much-publicised "prosperity" in the USA. Chronic unemployment persisted and even in 1939 it amounted to 16.7
per cent of the labour force. It could not be otherwise because
of the general sharp decrease of business activity in the
United States in the 1930s.

After 1933 and up to the 1940s there was not a single year
in which the issue of securities, an indicator of business activity in capitalist countries, was above 50 per cent of the
1923 level. In 1934 the issue of new securities was only 7
per cent of that level; in 1935 15 per cent; in 1936-1937 it
rose to 46 per cent, but in 1938 and 1939 it again dropped
to 33 and 14 per cent respectively. It is not surprising that
stagnation in US industrial production continued. Free capital, finding no profitable employment in the country, hastened to migrate to countries where there were favourable investment conditions. As for the influence of the crisis on the
economy and money circulation of other capitalist countries,
all of them felt its impact to one extent or another. The gold
bloc gradually collapsed under the hammer blows of the crisis and even France, which was the bloc's mainstay, devalued the franc on October 2, 1936. France's example was followed by Italy three days later. Belgium had devalued its
currency even earlier, in March 1935. In September 1936
the Netherlands and Switzerland stopped exchanging bank
notes for gold; the export of gold for international settlements and the maintenance of the rate of their currencies
was kept up.

In effect, after a number of devaluations and the discontinuation of the internal exchange of bank notes for gold,
currency circulation was normalised to a certain extent in
the second half of the 1930s. A considerable part in this respect was played by the fact that instead of the indirect defence of the rate of national currencies practised prior to
the crisis, most countries began to employ gold on a wider
scale in reciprocal settlements. The United States, too, contributed substantially to normalising the situation. After
the devaluation of the dollar in 1934 it began to apply a rigid
policy of securing with gold both the Federal Reserve notes
put into circulation and also the deposits of its member banks.
Other countries followed the same line of enhancing the role

of gold in currency circulation. Thus, a temporary period set in when economic activity was not overstimulated through the excessive issue of liquid assets and credits as was the case prior to the world economic crisis.

On October 12, 1936 the US Treasury announced its intention of selling bullion gold at $ 35 per ounce (plus 0.25 per cent for operating expenses) if the banks of issue of other countries assumed a similar obligation to sell gold. Britain, France, Switzerland, Belgium and the Netherlands, as it were, officially legalised the extensive use of gold in settlements between states.

Countries with the gold exchange standard began to ensure the stability of their currencies with the help of the convertible currency of countries which entered into an agreement on interstate circulation of gold. The use of American dollars for these purposes became particularly widespread. Since payments in gold were made through international banking channels, the numbers of private capitalist businessmen in the sphere of foreign trade and economic relations were thus restricted. As a rule, a high ceiling for the total quantity of bank notes to be exchanged for gold bullion was set in international payments of private capital. This automatically made foreign trade ties more difficult for small-scale capital and intensified the monopolisation of foreign trade by Big Business.

There was a greater tendency towards state-monopoly control and regulation of foreign trade through various monetary and other measures: foreign exchange restrictions, the establishment of definite quantities of imported goods, the issue of licences for the import of goods, limits on the exchange of foreign currency, differentiation of customs duties according to countries, preferences, restrictions, and so on. Differentiation between capitalist countries themselves was deepened according to the degree of their monetary independence.

Big capitalist countries which possessed sufficient reserves of gold were able to maintain the rates of their currency with the help of gold (to prevent a drop in the rate of their currency by exchanging it for gold bullion). Countries which had no gold reserves had to be satisfied with setting up reserves of stable convertible currencies of countries more powerful financially and, with the help of these reserves, to maintain the exchange rate of their own currencies, i.e., to exchange their currency for that of the richer countries whenever necessary. Such mediated (through foreign exchange) regulation of the rate of national currencies by the economically weaker capitalist countries of itself made them dependent on the monetary and financial policy of the highly developed countries. Moreover, the economically weak countries with a gold exchange standard, wittingly or unwittingly, had to have some reserve of foreign exchange for maintaining the rate of their currency in international payments. From the economic point of view, this means that the economically weaker countries credit the richer states with the entire sum of foreign liquid assets in their reserves. But in the second half of the 1930s, after the world economic crisis, the economically less developed countries had no other choice.

In an effort to eliminate the consequences of the crisis at the expense of other countries the major capitalist powers stepped up the organisation of financial economic and trading blocs. This was the path taken not only by Great Britain, France and Japan, but also by fascist Germany and Italy.

The more intensified setting up of economic blocs, stemming from the changes in the trade and monetary and credit policy of the principal capitalist countries, curtailed multilateral trade, extended trade within the bounds of economic blocs and bilateral trade. This was undoubtedly a display of capitalism's general crisis. These tendencies threatened sooner or later to produce a new military explosion, a new world war. The crisis, as it were, spurred on inter-imperialist rivalry over colonies and the desire to extend the financial and economic blocs and areas. Thus, early in the 1930s imperialist Japan forcibly incorporated Manchuria into her Asian "co-prosperity" sphere. Italy was out to build up its own "area", including in it Abyssinia and some other regions of North Africa, ousting France and Britain from there.

Britain, employing diverse financial and economic instruments, extended and consolidated the sterling area. This was facilitated by the fact that during the 1929-1933 crisis the pound, relying on British capital's foreign investments and the stock of monetary gold, remained relatively stable and was widely employed in international payments. "For many countries which had previously based their currencies on sterling the choice was virtually automatic, their reserves were invested in London, the bulk of their trade was transacted with Great Britain, and there was no real alternative to keeping in step with sterling,"[1] *The Economist* wrote.

The United States and Germany were in a somewhat different position. Owing to economic stagnation, the US monopolies found no sufficiently profitable sphere for capital within the country. Therefore, they sought spheres for investment abroad, particularly in industrial countries of Europe. Germany was of particular interest from this point of view. Through Germany, which held a central place in Europe, US capital expected to obtain superprofits in other European countries.

International reactionary forces assumed that fascist aggression would be directed principally against the Soviet Union. Proceeding from such a prospect, international, particularly US, finance capital obviously regarded nazi Germany with favour, giving her a free hand in trade and financial relations with Southeastern European countries. Germany, in effect, formed a trade and financial-economic bloc with these countries.

Germany's specific monetary and financial policy became strikingly pronounced after Hitler's rise to power. It was marked by the inflationary stimulation of exports and the war industry, the separation of internal money circulation from world monetary circulation and the mobilisation of internal resources by non-economic methods, including the confiscation of gold. In Germany itself all measures were employed to mobilise foreign exchange and prevent its outflow from the country. Let us recall, for example, that on German ships sailing to other countries special ship money was used which could not be spent elsewhere, while on board ship ordinary marks were not accepted.[2]

Some foreign exchange restrictions were also applied in a number of countries in which Germany gained economic influence. But the function of gold "as a means of payment

---

[1] *The Economist*, May 1, 1948, p. 699.
[2] See Benjamin Anderson, op. cit., pp. 428-29.

in the settling of international balances" (Karl Marx) remained unchanged. Therefore, the accumulation of monetary
gold remained an object of special concern for capitalist
governments prior to the Second World War.

The role of the state in regulating currency exchange rates
increased. Treasuries and the central banks of issue began
constantly to participate in foreign exchange operations in
the open markets so as to regulate the rate of their own currency (to lower or raise it depending on the circumstances)
and to push the rates of other countries' currencies in a desired direction. This was achieved by the tried and tested method of intervention in the open market. Since the current
exchange rate of any currency, even with solid gold backing,
is determined by supply and demand at a definite period,
by easing or making more difficult the satisfaction of the
demand, governments sought to influence the exchange rate
of their own and other currencies.

The gold basis remained generally recognised. Moreover,
after the devaluation of the American dollar in 1934 the US
ruling element took special care to maintain the established
gold content of the dollar. This was comparatively easy to
achieve because the balance of US visible trade was invariably favourable. And although the balance of invisible trade
(freight, insurance, transfers of immigrants and tourist
travel) was invariably in deficit, this was compensated for
by the annual receipts of interest and dividends on investments abroad. Thus, the nature of the US balance of payments was ultimately determined by the movement of long-
and short-term capital. Before and during the 1929-1933
world crisis, owing to the excess of the export of capital over
its import, the United States usually had an unfavourable
balance of payments. But since the investments of capital
were made in various forms in dollars, this balance-of-
payment deficit was not accompanied by a big outlow of
gold.

The US balance of payments remained unfavourable during the five crisis years (1929-1933)—in three years gold was
imported and in two years (1931, 1933) exported.

From 1934 onwards the balance of the movement of long-
and short-term capital became positive and the USA im
ported gold to the value of more than $ 8,800 million ove

the five years (more than 3,000 million dollars in 1939). The war-fraught economic situation made itself felt in world currency circulation. After the second half of 1938 the war danger in Europe again caused a strong migration of capital to the United States. This also led to a big influx of gold which amounted to $ 1,657 million in 1938 and $ 3,018 million in 1939[1].

Indeed, during the second half of the 1930s the US gold reserves increased by leaps which cannot be explained by ordinary causes. Thus, in 1934 the gold reserves in devalued dollars amounted to $ 7,877 million, in 1935 to $ 9,116 million, in 1936 to $ 10,667 million, in 1937 to $ 12,487 million, in 1938 to $ 13,007 million, and in 1939 to $ 16,195 million. Particularly big was the leap in 1940 when the reserves reached $ 20,049 million.[2] This was no doubt caused by Hitler's attack on Poland on September 1, 1939, followed on September 3 by the British and French declarations of war on Germany. In this situation European money capital in the form of gold began to seek refuge across the Atlantic. Table 6 shows that direct American investments and investments in securities, bonds, loans and so on amounted in 1938 to about $ 11,500 million, while the liabilities were $7,000 million. Thus, US investments exceeded US liabilities by about $4,500 million, which characterises it as a creditor country. Of the $7,000 million of US liabilities, $4,500 million were portfolio investments, which is also characteristic of capital fleeing from Europe. Direct foreign capital investments in the USA were about $ 1,900 million. The US had direct investments abroad amounting to $7,100 million, i.e., 3.7 times greater than foreigners had in the United States.

In search of a quiet haven in which to weather the war storm, not only free European capital flowed to the United States from countries over which the armoured fist of nazi Germany was poised, but also repatriated American capital which

---

[1] See L. I. Frei, *Mezhdunarodnye raschoty i finansirovanie vneshnei torgovli kapitalisticheskikh stran* (International Payments and the Financing of Foreign Trade by Capitalist Countries), Moscow, 1960, p. 153.

[2] Ph. Cagan, *Determinants of Change in the Stock of Money, 1875-1960*, New York, 1965, p. 341.

Table 6

American Long-Term Investments
and Obligations Abroad in 1938
(million dollars)

	Investments			US obli-gations
	Direct	Portfolio	Total	
Europe	1,422	954	2,376	5,384
North America.	2,582	1,872	4,454	1,214
Central America and the West Indies	862	115	977	68
South America	1,551	968	2,519	40
Asia and Oceania	587	410	997	182
Africa	139	19	158	15
Not identified	—	10	10	104
Total	7,143	4,348	11,491	7,007

S o u r c e: C. Lewis, *Debtor and Creditor Countries*: *1938*, *1944*. Washington, 1945, p. 8.

had been in Europe in a liquid form. For these reasons the concentration of gold in the United States subsequently led to the shifting of the biggest part of the world stock to this country. The USA turned into the monetary centre of the capitalist world.

If we trace the movement of the US gold reserves since the devaluation of the dollar in 1934, on the whole it was on the ascendency up to 1942. The increased war spending and the purchase of strategic materials by the United States brought about a slow decrease in the American gold stock towards the end of the war. Then the United States again began to pump out gold in payment of war debts and for the export of goods to the markets of countries which had not yet recovered from the war. The end of the 1940s witnessed a record accumulation of gold in the United States.

This table shows that during the 15 years after the world crisis, notwithstanding some fluctuations, gold was accumulating in the United States. This was a result of the favourable balance of trade, the influx of capital frightened

Table 7

**Stock of Monetary Gold in the USA
After the Devaluation of the Dollar
and up to the End of the 1940s**

(at the end of the year)

Year	Million dollars*	Million dollars**
1934	7,877	4,652
1935	9,116	5,384
1936	10,667	6,300
1937	12,487	7,375
1938	13,007	7,682
1939	16,195	9,565
1940	20,049	11,841
1941	22,713	13,414
1942	22,759	13,441
1943	22,339	13,229
1944	21,194	12,517
1945	20,294	11,986
1946	20,341	12,013
1947	21,417	12,649
1948	23,740	14,021
1949	24,637	14,551

* In devaluod dollars: $35 = 1 troy ounce of gold.
** In dollars prior to devaluation: $20.67 = 1 troy ounce of gold.
S o u r c e: Ph. Cagan, op. cit., pp. 340-41.

by the war (including that from countries which underwent socio-economic changes owing to the war which ruled out its repatriation), the return of American capital to the USA and gold production in the United States itself.

The total sum of centralised gold in the banks of issue and treasuries of the capitalist world reached $23,815 million in mid-1938, of which $12,963 million was in the United States. In other words, even prior to the Second World War more than half of the centralised gold stock of the capitalist world was concentrated in the USA. At the end of August 1939, when the war became inevitable, 62 per cent of the world stock of monetary gold ($28,483 million) was in the United States. Subsequently this proportion further changed in favour of the USA. Its reserves were swelled by the previously mentioned sources during the war not only absolutely, but also relatively, rising to 70 per cent of the world stock.

It was natural that the American dollar, based on such reserves, was becoming the most reliable reserve currency for countries with the gold exchange standard. While during the war many countries in their internal money circulation were compelled to resort to inflation to one degree or another, they sought to utilise the American dollar as a reserve currency for maintaining the exchange rate of their liquid assets in external payments. The dollar started to be used in so-called stabilisation funds.

It was this new role of the American dollar during the war that was taken as a model in transforming the world monetary system.

The situation in Germany was different. The nazi state machine placed the financial resources of its allies under its control. Since settlements between Germany and her allies were made by way of clearings, the gold and exchange reserves controlled by the nazi Government were utilised to pay for the goods and services of neutral states. Only paper money circulated in nazi Germany and the countries under her military and political control during the war. Owing to uncurbed inflation, money circulation was completely disordered towards the end of the war.

The postwar currency system was built up without the participation of the countries which fought on the side of German fascism. The main role in creating it was played by the Anglo-Saxon countries. Moreover, the leading part was played by the United States, whose finance capital received stimuli for broad expansion during the war.

US finance capital played an important part in financing the war. Internal loans given the Federal Government by the American banks enabled the state not only to build up and technically equip land, naval and air forces many times larger than in peace-time, but also to render material assistance to the allies, and so on. Naturally, what happened was that, in financing the Government's military spending, the US monopolies gave credits with one hand and with the other received profitable war contracts. Ultimately it was the tax-payers of the United States and other countries who had to foot the war bill. But during the war this socio-economic question was not probed.

The following figures illustrate the gigantic mobilisation of resources for war: between June 30, 1939 and December 31, 1944 holdings of government securities by commercial banks grew by $ 59,500 million (from $ 18,000 million to $ 77,500 million). Correspondingly government security holdings by the Federal Reserve banks increased by $ 16,500 million over the same period.[1]

During the war the amount of media of circulation, chiefly Federal Reserve notes, was unusually expanded. At the end of June 1939 the total quantity of them in circulation was $7,000 million, while in April 1945 it reached $ 26,000 million.

The credit expansion of American capital during the war could not be confined to national boundaries. But during the war private American capital could not take the risk of furnishing loans without Government guarantees. That is why the Government, which drew resources for waging the war from internal state loans, often assumed the role of cred-itor with regard to other states. Thus, large amounts of Federal Reserve notes given to the Government under its loan obligations were used not only in internal circulation, but entered along different channels (loans, payments for imported strategic materials, and other Government spend-ing abroad) into world monetary circulation and the foreign exchange reserves of other countries. During the war the Amer-ican dollar as currency of the chief creditor country, the United States, became the principal international medium of circulation, in a certain way more convenient than gold (the transportation of the latter in wartime involved high risk and expense). It is not surprising that already in wartime the US ruling element, with the help of countries within the orbit of American financial influence, began to work for the establishment of a united world monetary system in which the American dollar would dominate. The foundations of this system were laid in the Bretton Woods Agreements prior to the end of the Second World War.

---

[1] Benjamin Anderson, op. cit, p. 45.

THE POSTWAR WORLD MONETARY SYSTEM
OF CAPITALISM AS A PRODUCT
OF US FINANCE CAPITAL

In examining the world monetary system in its historical aspect, mention must be made of the decisions made at the financial and economic conference held in Bretton Woods (USA) in June 1944. The decisions of this conference, convened on the initiative of the United States and held under its aegis a year prior to the end of the war, were an international action which consolidated the emergent dominating position of American finance capital in international monetary circulation and financial and credit relations. By that time the United States had succeeded in accumulating the main part of the world's gold stock ($23,400 million at the end of 1943), and the further development of financial and economic relations in the capitalist world depended on how the USA intended to use them. But even before the conference, during the preliminary work of financial experts it had become clear that the United States wanted to utilise the existing situation for consolidating the hegemony of American capital.

At the conference the United States very definitely sought to weaken the former tendencies to consolidate economic blocs and currency areas, putting up against them its monetary policy designed to secure the hegemony of the dollar. Moreover, as a result of the Second World War and the defeat of fascist Germany and Japan, the blocs in Southeastern Europe and in Asia headed by these countries collapsed. A number of the countries belonging to these blocs fell away from the capitalist system embarking on the socialist road. This naturally led to the mutual drawing together of these countries and their economic co-operation on a mutually beneficial basis.

The US ruling circles which called the tune during the conclusion of the Bretton Woods Agreements did not expect that the defeat of fascist Germany and Japan would lead to the breaking away of a number of European and Asian countries from capitalism. They confidently projected the shaping of the postwar capitalist system on the establishment of American hegemony in capitalist financial and economic relations after the war. Thus, the Bretton Woods conference decided to set up two international financial organisations with special functions: the International Bank for Reconstruction and Development (IBRD) and the International Monetary Fund (IMF).

The aims and tasks of the IBRD were to a certain extent revealed in its name. But some provisions of its charter show in what ways it was contemplated to achieve them. Thus, according to Article 2 of the charter, the bank was designed to promote private foreign investments by guaranteeing and participating in loans and other private investments. From this it followed that the IBRD had to not only discharge the functions of a bank for the long-term financing of its member states from its paid-in capital and mobilised resources, but also to act as mediator and guarantor between private capital of creditor countries and the respective loan-receiving countries or countries in which private capital would be invested. It is easy to understand that such capital could only be private capital from countries which had not been weakened by the war, above all the United States. For the convenience of the borrowers bank loans were to be given in the currencies of different countries as needed by the borrowers. But all these details could not alter the cardinal function of the Bank—to serve as guarantor and mediator in investments of private capital. The share of different countries in the Bank's capital was determined by the financial potential of the countries themselves. In keeping with this principle, the United States assumed a dominant position in the leading bodies of the IBRD, which began to function in 1946.

When the Bretton Woods Agreements were concluded, it seemed to many that it was the IBRD which was destined to play the most important part in the restoration and development of the postwar economy. But this was far from being the case. The postwar situation demanded of US finance capital the wider use of other ways and means of struggle for world supremacy. In this context greater attention is merited by the other international organisation set up under the Bretton Woods Agreements—the International Monetary Fund.

From the formal viewpoint, the International Monetary Fund can also be regarded as an organisation of the banking type. At the same time it is a specific organisation. It is radically different from former monetary organisations. Even such a body as the Latin Monetary Union which existed in the 19th century only remotely resembles the IMF. The main purposes of the IMF are to promote international monetary co-operation and extend international trade.

The International Monetary Fund was designed to facilitate stability of circulation and understanding between members of the organisation, and to prevent competitive depressions in monetary circulation (i.e. currency dumping, etc.). Lastly, this organisation had to help build up a system of reciprocal payments on current accounts between IMF members and the limitation of any restrictions in foreign circulation which could hamper world trade. The enumerated propositions, as it were, admitted the fallacious nature of all preceding practices in inter-capitalist financial and commercial relations, including economic blocs, preferences, currency, customs and other restrictions. New ideals of organised capitalism were put to the fore which, as always, were destined to remain mere paper declarations.

The interstate nature of this organisation was recorded in the statutes of the IMF. In contrast to the IBRD, the tasks of the IMF did not include business relations with private capital. The IMF, the way it was conceived, may at first glance be compared with some kind of an interstate mutual aid organisation, the purpose of which is to help regulate the balances of payments of the Fund's member countries, and maintain the exchange rates of national currencies in international markets. This greatly appealed to financially weak countries.

According to the statutes, the International Monetary Fund was regarded as legally formalised on December 27,

1945, when, in accordance with the decisions of the Bretton Woods Agreements, 80 per cent of its capital was paid in. It was made up of subscriptions by the countries which had decided to set up the organisation.

IMF membership was not limited to the founding countries. Accession to the organisation was envisaged, with a subscription commensurate with the financial potential of a country.

At present 126 countries are members of the IMF, while in 1956 there were only 60. The capital of the Fund has also risen substantially through both subscriptions of new members and an increase in the subscriptions of old members, primarily the financially leading capitalist countries.

At present the capital of the fund in currencies of different countries amounts to about $ 21,000 million as against $ 9,200 million at the end of 1958. Part of the capital is in gold. In January 1969 it amounted to $ 2,288 million.

To give some idea of the IMF and its functions, it should be emphasised that the influence individual countries enjoy in it depends on the size of their subscriptions. From this standpoint too the United States (whose subscription exceeds $ 4,100 million), Britain ($ 1,950 million), and France and the Federal Republic of Germany ($ 785,5 million each) are prominent. The subscriptions of other countries are much smaller. They are paid in national currencies and partly in gold.

Votes in the policy-making bodies of the IMF are distributed depending on the size of the subscriptions, i.e., as in corporations, depending on the number of shares (each $ 100,000 of the subscription gives a country one vote plus 250 votes irrespective of the size of the subscription). Under this system, the United States had 26.6 per cent of the vote, Britain 12.7 per cent, and the other countries, correspondingly, a much smaller number.

The executive body of the IMF is the Board of Governors, consisting of the most authoritative financial representatives of member countries, who meet at annual sessions. More than 29 such sessions have been held so far.

The Executive Board of Directors, in which the main place is held by US representatives, is the standing agency of the IMF which actually determines the current activity of the organisation. Its headquarters are in Washington, D.C.

What is the meaning and purpose of such an intricate organisational set up? It represents an attempt to introduce elements of organisation into the capitalist monetary system.
American financiers and political leaders missed no chance
to prove the objective necessity for precisely such an organisation of the monetary system which is supposedly beneficial to all countries.

The question of returning to the gold standard was not
raised, but even so it was clear that in a situation in which
more than half of the world gold stock was concentrated in
one country, the United States, it was not so easy to return
to the gold standard of the former type with the free exchange of bank notes for gold. In this case it seemed natural
that the country possessing the biggest reserves of gold and
which had become the creditor of many other countries should
furnish its currency as an international medium of circulation. The question arose, how could this currency preserve
its stability if it were not based on the gold standard with
a free exchange of bank notes for gold? This was the question
that was decided in Bretton Woods. It was found necessary
to preserve unchanged the so-called dollar price of gold, the
exact relation of the American dollar to gold: 35 dollars equal-
led one troy ounce of pure gold (a troy ounce is equal to
31.10348 grams, and from this it followed that one dollar was
equal to 0.888671 g).

The United States confirmed its obligation to sell gold to
other countries for dollars at this price with an addition of
0.25 per cent for covering commercial expenses. It agreed to
buy gold from other countries on the same terms.

After the war it was a matter chiefly of buying gold in the
United States (the gold stock in other countries was insignificant). Therefore, the question arose, would other countries
not resort to the massive buying of American gold in an indirect way? Such a possibility was not ruled out. By buying
dollars with their currency and presenting them to the US
Treasury in exchange for American gold, the capitalist countries could very swiftly exhaust the American gold reserve.
To prevent this, Article 4 of the IMF agreement stipulated the
obligation of IMF member countries to maintain the price
of gold at the indicated level and to prevent its upward and
downward fluctuations by more than 1 per cent. The coun-

tries which assumed this commitment under Article 4 of the IMF agreement also recognised that their currency was convertible into gold. And this implied their obligation to exchange their currency for gold on the same terms as the United States. From this it followed that all currencies of IMF member countries had to have a fixed gold parity.

Since the relation between gold and the dollar had already been given a constant value, in practical terms the gold parity of other currencies began to be expressed as their relation to the dollar. Thus the West German mark had a 4 : 1 ratio to the American dollar. In other words, the gold content of 4 marks corresponded to the gold content of one dollar.

In practice, however, it rarely happens that the current market rate of a currency fully coincides with its parity. The rate usually deviates from the parity under the influence of supply and demand. If a country's balance of payments is favourable and it has to receive the difference from abroad in gold or hard currency, the rate of its currency rises. If, conversely, a country's balance of payments is unfavourable and it has to make payments abroad, the rate declines.

It is expected that to pay for a deficit in the balance, a country will have to buy either gold or the liquid liabilities of other countries, e.g., bills or foreign exchange, at times paying even considerably more than the parity rate.

These fluctuations of the exchange rates could also harbour a threat to the gold base of the dollar. For example, a country could deliberately buy dollars during a period when there was a high exchange rate for its currency and then exchange them for American gold. To preclude such a possibility, it was laid down in the IMF agreement that just as all Fund member countries had to maintain the fixed price of gold within the bounds of a fluctuation of not more than 1 per cent, the rates of the currencies of these countries must not deviate from parity or in relation to the dollar by more than 1 per cent. How can this be achieved by the IMF countries? For this purpose, depending on the circumstances, one of two things can be done: either a country has to buy part of its currency for gold or foreign convertible currency and then the demand for it will have a raising effect on the exchange rate or, on the contrary, to increase the influx of its own currency in the money market by exchanging it for other currencies, buying securities in stock exchanges, and so on, and then the bigger supply of the given currency will lower its rate.

All these examples show that the entire system for regulating currency rates was compelling central banks as the financial agencies of IMF countries to constantly intervene in money markets, orienting themselves on the dollar. Formally these countries exerted efforts and quite often spent gold or foreign convertible currency in order to maintain the exchange rate of their currencies but at the same time each of them individually, and all of them together, maintained the exchange rate of the dollar, the "key currency".

Indeed, if, in order to raise the rate of its currency to the fixed parity with the dollar, the government of some country spent gold for its purchase, it thereby maintained the dollar as the monetary standard. But this standard, according to the IMF rules and the commitments of the US Government, must itself have a stable relation to gold.

Thus, gold was ultimately the foundation of the postwar monetary system but the latter relied on gold through the American dollar. The excessive issues of dollars as a national US currency, causing inflation within the country, could drag onto this path other countries, whose currencies are linked to the dollar through the general system of regulating exchange rates.

The Bretton Woods Agreements also gave rise to one more circumstance which made the national currencies of many countries dependent on the US dollar. Whenever regulation methods nevertheless failed to maintain the rate of a currency within the bounds of the permitted fluctuations from parity or the relation to the dollar, the IMF rules demand an official change in the parity of the given currency.

Depending on the circumstances, such a change of parity may either be its decrease, devaluation, or increase, revaluation. This still more increased the dependence of national currencies of other capitalist countries on the American dollar.

But during the Second World War and the postwar derangement of international markets capitalist countries had to reconcile themselves to this dependence.

What was the meaning and purpose of this monetary system for the United States? Thanks to it the national American currency simultaneously became a world currency which replaced gold. This offered American finance capital great advantages in the struggle against rivals and turned the dollar into a weapon for gaining domination in international monetary and financial relations.

The most important thing was that the issue of American bank notes in dollars, which became a legal international medium of exchange, remained uncontrolled in the hands of the American ruling circles. This enabled them to utilise the issue of bank notes and other liquid assets for the expansion of credit, just as in internal circulation. In fact, American dollars became world credit money, the issue and circulation of which were subordinated to the laws we examined earlier. Washington, however, embarked on the path of their unlimited issue.

Taking this path the US financial agencies were pursuing a seemingly noble aim—to supply the postwar capitalist world with reliable liquid assets instead of the gold concentrated mostly in the United States. They were doing it with real American sweep, rightly considering that, in view of the acute shortage of gold and other reliable international liquid assets in other countries, the dollars issued in circulation in postwar conditions could not be presented to be exchanged for American gold. Even if this should happen as an exception, it would not greatly influence the money market. It was also held that, with the favourable trade balance of the United States, there would be an increased demand for American dollars abroad to cover the trade deficit of other countries. Dollars or US Federal Reserve notes, as it was assumed, would be required merely as a means of international circulation—a substitute for gold. Moreover, it was expected that reliable bank notes or credit money, backed by short-term bills and other securities, within definite bounds would also function independently of a link with gold. After the war American banks had in their safes sufficient foreign liabilities to serve as security for the Federal Reserve notes. The calculations of the US ruling circles when this monetary system was created were based on the sum total of these factors.

True enough, the demand for dollars abroad enabled the United States for a long time to play the role of a bank in relation to other countries of the capitalist world. The United States was compared with a bank by US financiers, e.g., William Martin, Chairman of the Federal Reserve Board, at a conference on financial questions held in New York in the summer of 1968. He even regarded it as a service provided by the United States that it, like a bank, through the Marshall Plan and in other ways, supplied the capitalist world with liquid assets.

Indeed, the United States furnished credits to other countries in different forms, and in this way American capital penetrated their economies. The methods and forms of this penetration were diverse: direct investments in foreign industry, the purchase of shares in foreign companies, participation in mixed enterprises, deposits in foreign banks, loans issued for definite purposes and marketable bonds.

Lastly—and this was particularly important to the US Government—the status of the dollar as an international monetary unit enabled the US Treasury to utilise American currency for covering the military expenditure abroad, instead of gold. It became possible, through the wide issue of liquid liabilities, bank notes and so on, or, as it is customary to say, of dollars, to render "aid" and credits for arming other states, disregarding the unfavourable balance of payments of the USA. Since this "aid" was supplemented by credits at high interest rates and involving economic and political concessions, in the long run American finance capital could not complain that its role as banker to the capitalist world was not advantageous to the United States. It was just as advantageous as that of the banker, of whom Karl Marx wrote: "Those of his notes... cost him nothing, save the cost of the paper and the printing. They are circulating certificates of indebtedness (bills of exchange) made out in his own name, but they bring him money and thus serve as a means of expanding his capital."[1]

An easy way of making money with the help of financial machinations has always tempted not only private capitalists and capitalist corporations but also the governments of capitalist states. It is therefore natural that not only individual capitalists and big financial corporations but also central state banks, treasuries and other government agencies

---

[1] Karl Marx, *Capital*, Vol. III, pp. 444-45.

take part in large-scale speculation on the stock exchanges.

Government financial agencies engage in currency intervention, different combinations with state securities, and so on. Hence it is not surprising that, relying on the special position of the dollar, the United States quite frequently allowed itself to expand foreign credits too lavishly, disregarding its balance-of-payments deficit. There was fundamentally nothing new in all this.

It was thus effecting its financial and economic expansion in other countries.

It goes without saying that we are not inclined to regard the financial invasion of American capital in other countries as mere speculation. But much of what has been done in postwar years in this sphere is not as idealistically motivated as the apologists of US finance capital claim. The capitalist economy is indebted for its postwar recovery and development not to American credits but to the exploitation of the working class, especially through the extensive use of inflation.

The US ruling circles, of course, not out of ethical but purely practical considerations sought to remove the inflational derangement of national currencies because this prevented the full operation of the world monetary system based on the Bretton Woods Agreements and hindered the expansion of American capital in the form of credit and various investments. Moreover, the dumping of commodities in the world market as a result of inflation impeded American exports and threatened the US home market, although it was protected by high customs barriers.

A great deal has been, and is being, written about inflation in the world press. Some economists, paying tribute to Keynesianism, praise it as the only way to ensure full employment and as a stimulant of exports. Others condemn it because, by artificially stepping up exports, it leads to keener competition and disorganises world trade. The Bretton Woods Agreements, had they been strictly applied, would have been incompatible with inflation (this by no means proves the merits of the system as such).

Let us examine the meaning of inflation. It offers advantages to export goods because it cuts the labour costs. It reduces

the real wages of the total working class and this is a gain
for the total class of capitalists in a given country. In other
words, since nominal wages remain unchanged, during inflation workers producing one and the same quantity of
commodities are themselves able to buy much less because
inflation reduces the purchasing power of money. What the
workers are unable to buy in the home market, can be exported by the capitalists abroad. But the stimulating action of
inflation on exports is not limited to this point.

It spurs on exports by diverting commodities from the
home to the foreign market through the reduced currency rate.
Let us assume that for a certain period an industry sells its
output in the home and foreign markets in equal parts and
obtains in the home market 1,000 national money units and
in the foreign market X foreign money units which, according to the fixed rate, are equivalent to the selfsame 1,000
national units. In such a case it makes absolutely no difference to the given industry where it sells its output—in
the home or foreign market (though preference will be given
to the home market because it is closer and better known).

Now, let us assume that inflation cuts the exchange rate
of the given national money unit by 25 per cent. Then for the
goods sold in the home market the receipts will be the
same—1,000 money units; for the goods sold in the foreign
market the same X. But in exchanging the foreign currency
for the national currency the exporter will receive an additional 25 per cent or the difference in the exchange rate
$\frac{1,000 \cdot 25}{100} = 250$. It is this difference that will stimulate the
exports of the given commodities. Moreover, exports to for-
eign markets will be expanded by reducing their sale in the
home market. This mechanism of stimulating exports with
the help of a lowered exchange rate is known as monetary
dumping.

After all that has been said about the role of inflation as
a factor in stimulating exports, it becomes clear why the
US ruling circles acted to curb it in capitalist countries.
Under the Bretton Woods Agreements the US currency had
to remain stable, while other capitalist countries after the
war resorted to stimulating their exports through monetary
dumping. This was the main reason why in the initial postwar

years the United States took measures to restrict inflation in the capitalist world. West Germany, Italy, Japan, and other countries began to stabilise their currencies under the direct pressure and with the "aid" of Washington. Thus, on April 25, 1949, by way of implementing the so-called Dodge line, the Japanese yen was stabilised at the level of 360 yen to the dollar. This ratio remained unchanged until December 19, 1971, when the yen was revalued.

Relying on the Bretton Woods Agreements and the International Monetary Fund, the US ruling element in one way or another extricated the economy of capitalism from the wartime stagnation. But it also drew it into the channel of American monetary and financial policy, which suited the interests of US monopoly capital.

Big changes in the currency circulation of the capitalist countries began four years after the end of the war. They were linked with the monetary and financial policy of the USA, particularly the Marshall Plan and the formation of the Organisation for European Economic Co-operation (OEEC). This plan pursued the same ends as the entire monetary system.

The Marshall Plan was a specific programme of "aid" to, and pressure on, the European countries designed to consolidate US monetary and financial hegemony in Europe. As the first prerequisite it was necessary to stabilise the currencies of West European countries and to link them to the American dollar in accordance with the Bretton Woods Agreements. It was this purpose that was to be promoted by American loans and "aid" under the Marshall Plan.

Outlining the basic principles of this plan in a speech delivered on July 5, 1947, in Harvard University, US State Secretary Marshall expounded the idea of the need for the economic unification of the capitalist countries of Western Europe so as to guarantee the efficient use of the financial resources of the United States for the accelerated shifting of the economy of the former belligerent countries on to peaceful lines.

The West European countries could not but heed this demand of the US ruling circles and as a result of the convention signed in Paris on April 16, 1948, by 17 West European countries, including Britain, France, West Germany and

Italy, the OEEC was set up. Through this organisation about $ 30,000 million dollars came to Western Europe under the Marshall Plan and other programmes in the form of "grants" and loans in order "to help put the economies of Europe back on their feet again", as claimed by Henry H. Fowler, former US Secretary of the Treasury.[1]

But this official statement was made many years after the end of the Marshall Plan. Actually, through the OEEC the US ruling circles succeeded in stabilising the West European currencies, considerably liberalising the foreign trade of Western Europe, eliminating various quotas and tariff barriers which hindered the successful spread of American goods in the West European market. The OEEC facilitated the introduction of a system of multilateral payments, reorganised in September 1950 into the European Payments Union (EPU). This facilitated the introduction of the US dollar as a substitute for gold in the currency circulation of the Old World.

The monetary and financial policy of the United States was one of the causes for the wave of devaluations which swept the capitalist countries in 1949. This wave was set rolling by the devaluation of the pound as a result of Britain's foreign trade difficulties arising from the weakening of the sterling area and the system of trade preferences.

The difficulties of British exports worsened the country's trade and payments balances, which led to an outflow of the gold reserves. That is why even after the formation of the OEEC the ruling circles of Britain sought to expand exports with the help of the methods of inflation described earlier.

In the summer of 1949 the rate of the British pound dropped very sharply, and the Government was unable to control the rate even at the lower level. The Labour Government pressed the United States to carry out measures which could eliminate Britain's dollar deficit, specifically to admit more British goods into the United States, to furnish dollar loans on easy terms, and so on. But the attempts to normalise the country's finances were unsuccessful. At the IMF session, held in Washington in September 1949, the US Government,

---

[1] *The Department of State Bulletin*, August 2, 1965, p. 210.

on the strength of the IMF rule about coordinating the rates of exchange in relation to the dollar, raised the question of devaluing the pound sterling. The Labour Government, seeing no possibility of waiting for a more favourable economic situation, resorted to a substantial devaluation of the pound on September 18, 1949. Instead of the rate of $ 4.03 per pound which existed hitherto, a rate of $2.80 per pound was introduced. Thus, the new parity of sterling to the dollar decreased by 30.5 per cent. The price of gold in British currency rose from 248 shillings per ounce, instead of 172 shillings 3 pence prior to devaluation.

The devaluation of the pound triggered off a chain reaction in the countries of the sterling area—from Australia and New Zealand to Norway and Sweden.

What is important for us is not a description of the process of currency devaluation by countries as such but the impact that the massive devaluation of national currencies had on the capitalist economy.

From the economic viewpoint, what happened, as it were, was the simultaneous reduction to a common denominator of the devalued currencies and the establishment of a strict correlation of parities to the dollar in accordance with the IMF rules. The role of the American dollar was enhanced under the aegis of the IMF. A new stage in the monetary and financial policy of the United States was opened in September 1949. It was marked by the further purposeful introduction of the dollar into world currency circulation. Moreover, the accumulation of foreign exchange reserves in dollars was intensified in countries which were unable to increase their gold stock.

This process of raising the role of the dollar in world circulation led to a change in the quantitative indices characterising the position of the United States itself from the viewpoint of international liquid assets. It is not by chance that in 1949 the gold reserves of the United States reached their maximum, $ 24,600 million, or almost 70 per cent of the world stock of monetary gold.

The dollar, it seemed, solidly rested on a huge gold basis. But quantitative changes occurred in the world monetary reserves after 1949. The sum of dollars in circulation increased relatively swiftly and the US gold reserves began to

decline, although slowly. The USA turned into a supplier
of liquidity for the world monetary system. This exerted a
corresponding influence on its own monetary position.

The monetary assets of the United States in the form of
reserves of gold and foreign exchange either remained unchanged or were slowly shrinking, while their "liabilities"
abroad, especially notes of the Federal Reserve System and
Treasury bills were increasing. The gap between the available assets and foreign liabilities was widening. Thus, the
introduction of American dollars into world circulation and
the exchange reserves of other countries led to a decline in
the gold backing of the dollar. The discrepancy between the
gold stock in the USA and the liquid liabilities to other
countries (bills of exchange, Federal Reserve notes and so
on) was increasing. In 1938 the liquid liabilities of the USA
to other countries amounted to $ 2,200 million and the
country had a gold stock of $ 14,600 million; in 1949, with
a gold stock of $ 24,600 million, the liquid liabilities rose
to $ 8,200 million[1]. In other words, in 1938 the liquid liabil-
ities were only about 15 per cent of the gold stock, while
in 1949 they amounted to 33 per cent. Thus, the absolute
and relative growth of liquid liabilities, chiefly American
short-term bills and bank notes abroad, was much in evidence.

This process of the introduction of American liquid liabilities into international circulation was further accelerated
when US imperialism launched its military venture in
Korea in the summer of 1950. The temptation to cover the
military expenditure abroad by dollars and other liquid
liabilities instead of gold was so great that already in 1952,
with the US gold reserves cut to $ 23,300 million, the liquid
liabilities had increased to $ 11,700 million.[2]

The war in Korea marked a turning point in the extensive
use of the postwar monetary and financial system of capitalism in the interests of US finance capital. The dollar
became an instrument for the wide investment of US capital
in other countries, a means of financing the Pentagon's
military ventures.

---

[1] Robert Triffin, "International Monetary Position of the United
States", *The Dollar in Crisis*, New York, 1961, p. 228.
[2] Ibid., p. 229.

THE MONETARY SYSTEM
AND THE CONTRADICTIONS OF CAPITALISM

The beginning of the 1950s may be regarded as a new stage in the history of the postwar monetary and financial system of capitalism. By that time the quite prolonged period of its build-up had ended, international financial organisations had begun to function and the financial might of the United States had reached its zenith. At the end of the 1940s the American stock of monetary gold reached its maximum level, about $ 25,000 million, or 8 times greater than that of the six European countries which later formed the Common Market and Britain combined.

World currency circulation needed liquid assets and presented a mounting demand for American dollars, which replaced the gold that the capitalist countries were short of owing to its concentration in the United States. The uneven distribution of gold between the capitalist countries was greater than ever before in the history of world circulation. Here are the relevant figures. World monetary gold (exclusive of socialist countries) in 1949 totalled $ 35,055 million, of which $ 24,563 million, or 70 per cent, were in the United States; $ 9,041 million, or about 25.8 per cent, was held in other capitalist countries, and $ 1,451 million, or about 4.2 per cent, was at the disposal of international institutions.[1] There is nothing surprising in the fact that under these conditions more than $ 8,200 million of liquid dollar holdings remained firmly in the foreign exchange

---

[1] Robert Triffin, *Gold and Dollar Crisis. The Future of Convertibility*, New Haven, 1960, p. 5.

reserves of other countries and at the disposal of internation
al institutions.[1] Nevertheless world currency circulation
ran up against huge difficulties, which US financial circles
tried to exploit. It is during this period that the vaunted
formula "the dollar is as good as gold" gained wide acknowl-
edgement.

Awareness of its financial and economic might impelled
US imperialism to military and political adventures, the
first of which was the war in Korea started in the summer
of 1950.

During the Korean War (1950-1953) the monetary and
financial system of capitalism, based on the Bretton Woods
Agreements, was for the first time extensively utilised in
the interests of US capital as a weapon of its aggressive
policy.

The war in Korea, despite the expectations of the Pentagon strategists, was by no means a triumphant march to
the sound of drums and pipes. It demanded great exertions,
big budget expenses and much foreign exchange to cover
military spending abroad. Suffice it to say, for example,
that the expenditure of foreign currency through the channels of the US military establishment in Japan during the
Korean War increased fourfold. According to figures provided by the Bank of Japan, in three years (1951-1953) receipts
of foreign exchange through the channels of the US military
establishment (military purchases, spending by US service-
men and so on) contributed about $2,000 million to Ja-
pan's balance of payments. US military spending in Japan
continued to remain at a high level, exceeding on the average $ 500 million annually up to the 1960s. At the begin-
ning of the 1950s the American military expenditure in
Western Europe and other countries likewise increased.
This was linked with the formation of the aggressive NATO
bloc (April 1949) under the aegis of American imperialism
and the intensive setting up of US military bases in capitalist countries. That is why the so-called military expenditures abroad by the United States, i.e., the sums spent
minus the income from the sale of war surplus stocks, etc.,
amounted on the average to $ 2,100 million annually in

---

[1] Robert Triffin, *Gold and Dollar Crisis. The Future of Convertibility*,
p. 5.

1950-1956, to $ 2,800 million in 1956-1960, and reached
$ 3,100 million in 1958[1]. As a result of the existing inter-
national monetary system all these expenditures were covered not by gold but by liquid liabilities of the United States
or, to put it in more general terms, by dollars.

In postwar years, seeking to tie other capitalist countries
as strongly as possible to the chariot of American imperialism, the US ruling circles rendered so-called military aid
to those of them which were of special interest from the
viewpoint of Pentagon strategy.

Thus, in the period between 1946 and 1949 military aid
amounted to $ 206 million annually on average, while in
the 1950s it exceeded an average of $ 2,400 million.[2]
In addition to investments of American capital abroad
the expenditure for government "aid" and credits of a non-
military nature were added during this period. In 1951-
1957 they averaged annually almost as much as military
aid— $ 2,358 million. After the end of the Second World
War and up to 1957 the expenditure of the US Government
on military and other aid exceeded $ 5,100 million annu-
ally in round figures.[3]

One may ask why the US ruling circles were so generous?
It undoubtedly stemmed from the assumption that, with
the help of broad trade and credit expansion and direct
investments abroad, US capital would succeed in attaining
a position in which the favourable balance of visible and
invisible trade, together with the profits on capital abroad,
would make the balance of payments favourable and then
any danger of an excessive increase in liquid liabilities to
foreign states would be eliminated.

Proceeding from these calculations, private American
capital in all forms was widely invested abroad. Direct
investments, loans and deposits of American capital in West
European banks were rising. This was also facilitated by
the fact that the rate of return on capital abroad, as a rule,
was substantially higher than in the USA. It is for this

[1] *Economic Report of the President Transmitted to the Congress,
January 1962*, Washington, 1962, p. 149.

[2] Shigetsugu Okumura, "The 'Dollar Crisis' and the United States
Economy", *Osaka City University Economic Review*, Osaka, No. 4,
1968, p. 13.

[3] Ibid.

reason that American deposits in West European banks, which came to be known as Eurodollars, gradually began to circulate between European banks and trading and industrial companies in the form of short-term loans which brought in a higher income both to the initial depositors and to those who borrowed Eurodollars. The rise of Eurodollars no doubt most conclusively corroborates the Marxist proposition about capital's search for superprofits regardless of national boundaries.

This is the only proper explanation for the origin and economic essence of Eurodollars, but, instead of this, Prof. M. Wasserman, an American economist, resorts to a long discourse, and hints that Eurodollars appeared because some banks of the East European socialist countries found it more convenient to keep their operational foreign exchange reserves in West European banks in dollars. But apparently sensing that his arguments carry no weight, he eventually admits that the deficit of the US balance of payments after 1950 and particularly beginning from 1958 onwards brought about a situation in which US "trading partners" were "gradually well supplied with dollars". This, in his opinion, "contributed to the development of overseas dollar markets".[1] But this is exactly the penetration of American dollars in world circulation that is examined in this book. The only difference is that Wasserman repeats the official explanation of American monetary and financial policy in this period. In his opinion, the appearance of dollars in Europe was, as it were, some kind of a service to trading partners. Hence the use of the term "supplied" when "implanted" would have been more correct.

In this connection it is interesting to cite the view of the nature of Eurodollars which appeared in the press. Thus, Richard Mooney wrote in the Paris edition of *The New York Times*: "Eurodollars are a relatively new medium of international credit, in existence only a half-dozen years. Roughly defined, they are dollars deposited in foreign banks, mostly in Europe, and loaned from bank to bank and eventually to business customers.... They exist because they

---

[1] M. Wasserman and others. *International Finance*, New York, 3, p. 46.

make extra money for lenders and borrowers. The lender, or original depositor of the dollars, earns higher interest than by depositing in the United States. For the borrower, the higher interest rates are still not so high, as he might have to pay for local funds."[1]

The search for higher profit than could be obtained in the United States is connected with Eurodollars, as in general with American investments abroad. It is not surprising that, notwithstanding the continuous increase of investments of American capital abroad, the net repatriation of profits and interest on capital during the 1950s, according to the data of the Economic Report by President Kennedy to Congress, amounted annually to about $2,200 million. Instead of repatriating the profits on capital the financial tycoons preferred to reinvest them abroad.

Yet, after the Second World War, particularly in the 1950s, big changes took place in the position of the United States as a creditor country. This may be seen in Table 8.

Table 8 discloses the essential aspects in the changes of the international financial position of the United States which occurred from the end of 1949 to 1960.

What stands out above all is the steep increase of direct investments of American capital abroad, from $10,700 million to $32,700 million, or three times. This results from the financial and economic expansion based on the privileged position of the dollar in the postwar monetary system of capitalism. The need for working capital compelled West European businessmen to allow the direct participation of US capital in their industrial companies, to give Americans a big part of the shares, and so on.

For the very same reason other long-term private investments of American capital abroad also increased from $4,900 million to $12,600 million. These were mostly special-purpose loans, investments in securities known as portfolio investments.

Foreign long-term investments in the United States grew at an incomparably smaller rate both in absolute and relative terms, and it is not they that called the tune. The main thing that characterises the weakening of US positions in

---

[1] *The New York Times*, Paris, June 23, 1964.

Table 8

International Investment and Gold Position
of the United States in 1949 and 1960
(millions of dollars, end of year)

	1949	1960
Assets	55,200	89,200
of which:		
gold and short-term liquid assets	28,600	26,800
of which:		
Gold	24,600	17,800
IMF subscription	2,800	4,100
Short-term private liquid assets	1,300	4,900
Long-term assets	26,600	62,400
of which:		
Direct investment	10,700	32,700
other private investment	4,900	12,600
US Government claims	11,000	17,000
Liabilities	16,900	44,700
liquid	9,800	26,200
of which:		
Foreign official organisations	2,900	10,300
IMF	1,300	2,600
Other international organisations	400	1,400
Private	4,600	9,600
Foreign and international holdings of US Government bonds and notes	600	2,300
Long-term	7,100	18,400
of which:		
Direct investment in USA	2,900	6,900
Other private investment	4,200	11,500
Excess of assets over liabilities	38,300	44,500

Source: *Economic Report of the President Transmitted to the Congress, January 1962*, Washington, 1962, p. 151.

the monetary and financial system of capitalism was that in the period we are examining the short-term liquid liabilities of US official and private institutions held by central and private foreign banks increased from $ 9,800 million to $ 26,200 million or 160 per cent. A considerable part of these liabilities were bank bills of exchange and bank notes, i.e., precisely the liabilities which could be presented, and actually were later presented, to be exchanged for American gold.

The US Administration sought solace in the fact that on the whole the country's assets exceeded its liabilities by

$ 40,000 million. But this excess proved of no avail in rectifying the situation. With a higher rate of return abroad a more or less sizeable repatriation of American capital was out of the question. Moreover, the repatriation of long-term investments, especially direct investments in industry, is not an easy matter because they are in the form of fixed capital, industrial equipment, real estate, and so on. But utilising short-term liabilities, foreign financial circles mounted attacks—and not without success—on fort Knox, where the gold stock of the United States is kept. This led to a multifaceted process of changing the financial position of the United States in the capitalist world. The nature and movement of this process are shown in Table 9.

Table 9

Movement of World Gold Stock and Dollars Abroad
(million dollars, end of year)

Year	World gold stock	Gold stock of the USA	Gold stock of other countries	Dollar holdings abroad
1949	35,055	24,563	9,041	8,226
1950	35,498	22,820	11,184	10,197
1951	35,664	22,873	11,261	10,173
1952	35,968	23,252	11,024	11,719
1953	36,396	22,091	12,603	12,739
1954	37,056	21,793	13,523	14,019
1955	37,716	21,753	14,155	15,230
1956	38,246	22,058	14,496	16,433
1957	38,960	22,857	14,923	16,600
1958	39,851	20,582	17,937	17,637
1959*	40,332	19,746	18,677	20,055

* June.

Source: R. Triffin, *Gold and Dollar Crisis. The Future of Convertibility*, New Haven, 1960, p. 5.

Table 9 shows that during the 1950s the world gold stock steadily increased. Between 1950 and 1958 it rose by $ 4,796 million. In the first half of 1959 it grew by $ 481 million. Yet the movement of the gold reserves of the Unit-

ed States and of other capitalist countries was proceeding
in opposite directions: the gold stock in the United States,
notwithstanding fluctuations, decreased during this period
by $3,981 million and in June 1959 by even $4,813 million, while the reserves of other capitalist countries rose by
$8,896 million at the end of 1958 and by $9,636 million
in June 1959.

A comparison of these figures shows that the gold stock
of other capitalist countries increased not on account of
American gold but chiefly due to the annual increase of production and its influx into monetary state reserves. American dollars which were kept in the official reserves of capitalist countries were also to a certain extent used for buying
gold. For this reason, with the continuous increase of dollars abroad, chiefly in the official reserves and in banks,
the gold stock in the United States also fluctuated. In 1956
and 1957 it even considerably increased as compared with
the preceding two years. This brief rise gave way to a steep
decrease at the end of 1958 and the beginning of 1959 which
became continuous.

This turn was so threatening that the Eisenhower Administration tried to stop the outflow of American gold by
administrative measures. But, naturally, this could not
be successful, since the changes were a result of deep economic causes operating not only in the United States. Economists in the USA and other countries naturally sought to
discover the reasons for the monetary crisis and to find a
way out of the entangled situation. These were the motives
that prompted Professor Robert Triffin to write the book
Gold and Dollar Crisis. He was one of the first to understand
"the absurdities associated with the use of *national* currencies as *international* reserves".[1] Triffin reproached his "bright
colleagues" for not fighting "with an opposite, and equally
absurd, theory of a permanent and untractable dollars
glut."[2] He was referring to the dollar shortage, a notion
which had dominated economic and political thinking in
the United States and abroad for more than 10 years before
he wrote his book. He suggested as a way out the interna-

---

[1] Robert Triffin, op. cit., p. 10.
[2] Ibid., p. 3.

tionalisation of money circulation, in fact, the creation of a world currency. As for Professor Triffin's reproaches against his "bright colleagues" and hints at the one-sidedness of economic and political thinking in the United States and other countries, they were correct in the main. This particularly applies to the US ruling circles.

It would be wrong to examine the monetary crisis only from the viewpoint of the financial and economic policy of the USA, however great its importance in this respect. Other factors too played quite a significant part in the development of the monetary crisis in postwar years into the trend that we are witnessing now. These factors were: expansion of world trade and other forms of economic relations on the basis of the increased industrial output of capitalist countries and a change in the alignment of forces in the capitalist world in general. These factors affected the world monetary system indirectly. They were mediated by foreign trade, the international movement of capital, internal money circulation and, lastly, the political situation in the capitalist world at the beginning of the 1960s. For example, quite a significant role was played by the militarist aspirations of some capitalist countries. Mention should first of all be made of the fact that in the 1950s, especially after the war in Korea, the militarist course of the US ruling circles had a clearly adverse effect on American exports, the most stable mainstay of the balance of payments. Thus, in 1953 world exports totalled $74,300 million, with US exports amounting to $15,782 million, or 21.2 per cent; in 1960 world exports were $113,600 million, the United States accounting for $20,584 million, or 18.1 per cent. In other words, the growth of US exports lagged behind the world average. In the period we are examining world exports increased by 53 per cent and US exports by 30.4 per cent. During the same period exports from West European countries, notwithstanding the obvious lag of Britain, grew by 81 per cent. Even exports from Britain rose higher than the American figure—by 45 per cent.

If we compare US exports with those of the Common Market countries, the relative weakening of US positions stands out even more clearly. In 1953 the EEC countries accounted for 19 per cent of world exports, while in 1960 they surpassed

US exports both in absolute and relative terms, reaching
$ 29,733 million or more than 26 per cent of the total.
The export position of the USA was considerably weakened
by the war in Korea and the aggressive aspirations of American imperialism in general. The same reasons cut the
favourable foreign trade balance, which provided the basis
for the balance of payments. The upshot of it has been a permanent balance-of-payments deficit.

Thus, while the favourable US balance of trade reached
$ 6,892 million annually between 1946 and 1949, in 1950-
1954, (the period which included the war in Korea), it
averaged $ 2,029 million, i.e., was cut by about 67 per
cent. In 1955-1957 it rose to $ 4,476 million and then
steadily declined up to the end of the 1950s. In 1959 exports
exceeded imports by only $ 985 million. In view of this during
the seven years prior to 1957 the US balance-of-payments
deficit amounted to $ 1,500 million annually. In the
next three years it averaged $ 3,700 million and in 1960
rose to $ 3,900 million.

It is no exaggeration to say that at the beginning of the
1960s the results of the US financial and economic policy
offered no grounds for optimism. There was every reason for
pessimistic forecasts, and the American press began to
feature them.

The change in US exports and the deterioration of the
balance of payments in the 1950s also altered the position
of the United States in the world monetary system. The
most general indicator in this respect are a country's
reserves of gold and foreign exchange reflecting its payment
position vis-à-vis the rest of the world and its financial and
economic situation. Under capitalism a nation cannot have
stable reserves of gold and convertible currency unless it is
able to make ends meet in its external economic payments.
This applies all the more to countries which joined the IMF
and, as pointed out earlier, undertook to regulate the rate
of their currency, not allowing any substantial deviation
from the agreed parity in relation to the dollar. Without
gold and exchange reserves such regulation is impossible
without loans, including borrowing from the IMF. If the
situation in the capitalist world is examined from this
viewpoint, one cannot fail to notice the striking changes

which occurred during the 1950s, namely, the weakening of the position of the United States and strengthening of the positions of some West European countries.

In 1951 the United States had a stock of monetary gold amounting to $ 22,873 million, or 64.3 per cent of the world total ($ 35,575 million).

In 1960 the world gold stock rose to $ 40,525 million while in the United States it decreased to $ 17,804 million, or 43.9 per cent of the total.

These figures show that in the 1950s the United States lost more than $ 5,000 million of its gold reserves. The weakening of its position in the currency circulation of the capitalist countries was all the more dangerous for the United States because the economy of other countries was growing at a faster pace. Some of them, especially the Common Market countries, on the contrary, during this time substantially increased their stock of gold and convertible currency, the selfsame dollars. Subsequently the Common Market gave considerable trouble to the US financial circles.

Before presenting the respective comparative data, one essential reservation should be made. When comparing monetary reserves, gold and foreign exchange in capitalist countries, it should be borne in mind that the United States as the "key currency" country formerly had only gold. It did not need foreign exchange because its own national currency could be used, if need be, for international settlements. This often enabled US financial agencies not to resort to gold in making such settlements, while other countries could not manage without gold. These countries, apart from Britain, enjoyed no such advantage. They could make external payments in their own currency if the partner wanted it; this, however, was not the rule but the exception. Therefore, the gold and exchange reserves of capitalist countries prior to the crisis always included convertible currency, dollars and pounds, and were actually equal to gold. Some of them, Japan, for example, had almost no gold and kept only foreign exchange in reserve.

As the position of the United States in the world monetary system weakened, its former advantage as the "key currency" country began to turn into the opposite: the United States had to spend a lot of gold to maintain the rate of the dollar. But the US ruling circles considered this to be a temporary phenomenon. Mistaking the wish for reality, they continued to use dollars extensively as an instrument of economic and political expansion.

Table 10, which shows the gold and foreign exchange reserves of the principal capitalist countries, gives a clear picture of the growing quantitative changes in the monetary sphere which were about to turn into a new quality.

During the 1950s the gold and exchange reserves increased quite swiftly on the whole. During the entire decade there was not a single year without a noticeable growth both in gold and other liquid assets. It is characteristic that the world gold stock in 1960 rose by $4,950 million as compared with 1951. If we add to this more than $5.000 million (the decrease in the gold reserves of the United States during this period) the conclusion may be drawn that other capitalist countries received at their disposal additional gold amounting to about $10,000 million. Newly-mined gold and that from the shrinking US reserves increased the gold stock in West European countries.

At the beginning of the 1950s the gold and exchange reserves of these countries were insignificant. The gold stock of the United States was several times greater than its reserves of gold and foreign exchange combined. In 1960 the difference was only $2,800 million. Moreover, it continued to decline; the American gold stock kept flowing out of the country, while the gold and exchange reserves of the Common Market countries were going up.

Britain, whose currency was devalued in 1949, noticeably increased its gold and exchange holdings. As a creditor country, it tried to stabilise its currency and rally together, on this basis, the sterling area countries; hoping to extend commerce in this zone with the help of trade preferences. The special position of the pound in this area offered Britain the privilege of utilising her currency in many cases for regulating the balance of payments, credits and so on. Moreover, in the 1950s London again became a big financial centre. A considerable part of the international gold, foreign exchange and credit operations were transacted via London. But the international brokerage functions of the British banks even in the 1950s were not reinforced by adequate

Table 10

Change in the Gold and Exchange Reserves of the Financially Leading Capitalist Countries
(million dollars)

Country	1951			1955			1960		
	Gold	Foreign exchange	Per cent of gold	Gold	Foreign exchange	Per cent of gold	Gold	Foreign exchange	Per cent of gold
World Reserves*	35,575	20,950	63.0	37,620	24,970	60.1	40,525	33,700	—
United States	22,873	—	100	21,753	—	100	17,804	—	100
Britain	2,200	135	94.2	2,050	70	97.0	2,800	431	86.6
France	597	19	96.9	942	970	49.2	1,641	429	80.0
Federal Republic of Germany	28	427	6.1	920	2,015	31.3	2,971	3,766	44.1
Italy	333	441	43.0	352	815	30.1	2,203	876	71.5
Belgium	635	419	60.2	928	219	81.0	1,170	252	82.3
Netherlands	316	...	...	865	358	70.7	1,451	291	83.3
EEC	1,909	1,306	59.3	4,007	4,377	47.7	9,396	5,614	62.3
Switzerland	1,451	193	88.4	1,597	250	86.5	2,185	139	96.0
Canada	842	984	46.2	1,134	776	59.3	885	951	48.2
Australia	112	1,022	10.0	144	691	17.2	147	696	17.4
Republic of South Africa	190	197	49.0	212	154	57.9	178	66	73.0
Sweden	152	332	31.4	276	194	58.9	170	318	34.9
India	247	1,698	12.7	247	1,619	13.2	247	423	37.0
Japan	10	...	...	23	746	3.0	247	1,577	13.5

* Including reserves of international organisations

S o u r c e: *United Nations Statistical Yearbook*, 1961, N. Y., pp. 521-22.

economic growth and the expansion of commodity exports, which potentially threatened with financial and economic difficulties.

Switzerland held a special place. This country, which formally did not join the IMF, has played, and is playing, an important role in the financial affairs of the capitalist world.

The setting up and consolidation of the European Economic Community, or the Common Market, was an important event in international relations during this period. When this organisation was established, neither its organisers nor the US ruling circles could foresee the influence it would be able to exert on international currency circulation and credit relations. The emergence of the Common Market as a regional organisation ran counter to the global tendencies of American financial policy and, moreover, it created prerequisites for current reciprocal crediting of the Common Market countries in trade and other transactions, which reduced the need for circulation media. More favourable opportunities were created for settlements without cash. All this could not but reduce the need for liquid assets, including American dollars and Eurodollars, in relation to the growing circulation of goods. In their reciprocal financial and economic relations Common Market countries could manage without the London and New York financial centres. They resorted to their assistance in their relations with non-European countries.

France, not without success, whipped together her franc area, consisting of the formerly dependent African countries. This led directly to a decrease in the need for American dollars, which, as shown earlier, became firmly entrenched in Western Europe. Here is the crux of what is called the "dollar crisis" problem, around which discussions flared up among bourgeois economists and political leaders. In these discussions which assumed an international character the initiative was grasped by official representatives of the US ruling circles grouped around the White House. Considerable initiative was also displayed by President John F. Kennedy. The American approach was supported by international organisations.

The point of departure was the Keynes doctrine that it was possible and necessary to control the movement of capital in order to steer economic growth in the direction required, to accelerate or slow it down with the help of such instruments as the discount rate. Special significance was, and is, attached to the latter from the viewpoint of stimulating or curbing inflation tendencies. This, as will be subsequently shown, was a case of the unfulfilled good wishes to escape from the sphere of operation of capitalism's objective laws governing world currency circulation which began to exert an adverse influence.

THEORY AND REALITY.
PRESIDENT KENNEDY'S POLICY

Notwithstanding the obvious symptoms of an imminent derangement of the capitalist monetary system, which became visible at the end of the 1950s and early 1960s, the US ruling circles kept to their former policy of economic and political expansion. They also called the tune in international financial and economic organisations. The main thesis they employed to justify the need for further maintaining the existing dollar-based monetary system was resolved to the point that the expansion of international trade demanded an increase in liquid assets. From this the conclusion was drawn that it was necessary to put more dollars into world circulation. Attempts were made to demonstrate the direct quantitative link between the world commodity turnover and the world gold and foreign exchange reserves. R. Triffin in his *Gold and Dollar Crisis* presented long columns of figures showing the correlation between monetary reserves and import since 1913, trying to deduce some regularities. But, as was to be expected, nothing came of it. World commodity turnover is too diverse and the means of mutual settlements, from cash to the deferred payment and clearings are too varied to allow of the establishment of any definite quantitative relationship between world imports and liquid assets as they are understood by contemporary Western economists. The so-called international liquid assets in 1961 amounted to about $ 62,300 million and world imports (cif) to $ 124,500 million.[1] Conse-

---

[1] *Monthly Bulletin of Statistics*, April 1969, pp. 110-114.

quently, the ratio between international liquid assets and world imports was 1:2. In 1968 international liquid assets amounted to about $ 76,300 million, while world imports rose to $ 223,300 million; consequently, the ratio became 1:3.

During this period the sum of world liquid ⌐assets increased by about 22.6 per cent, while world imports rose by 79.3 per cent. Consequently, the slower growth rates in world liquid assets did not prevent a considerable expansion in world imports. The world gold stock which was part of the liquid assets was more than ever in no definite quantitative relation to world imports. In 1961 the world gold stock amounted to $ 41,100 million, in 1965 it increased to $ 43,200 million and in 1968 (end of September) decreased to $ 40,600 million.[1]

As world money, gold functions as a universal means of payment, a universal purchasing medium. At present gold discharges its function as a means of payment chiefly during settlements of international balances. The days when merchants paid in gold for goods purchased at international fairs, or during bilateral commercial transactions are a thing of the distant past. Therefore, it is hardly proper to place the gold stock in some kind of direct relation to world imports. Nevertheless, the role of gold in the capitalist world has not diminished. As formerly, it embodies the absolute social materialisation of wealth, which cannot be said about dollars. Dollars in the form of bank notes, bills of exchange, and so on, are no more than liquid liabilities of the United States to countries which for one reason or another keep them in their reserves. In contrast to gold, which is world money because of its intrinsic value, dollar liquid liabilities, like any credit money, begin their path as a means of payment and complete it in one and the same bank. And if American financial circles like to compare the United States to a bank in relation to the rest of the capitalist world, they also ought to draw the appropriate conclusion as regards their liabilities or dollar assets held in other countries in dollar accounts belonging to foreigners. The sum of these liabilities in 1960 was quite imposing.

---

[1] Ibid.

Table 11

International Liquidity Position of the United States
(million dollars)

	1938	1949	1952	1957	1958	1959	October 1960
I. Gross assets	15.2	28.1	27.1	27.8	25.9	26.3	25.9
A. Gold	14.6	24.6	23.3	22.9	20.6	19.5	18.4
B. Foreign exchange	0.6	0.8	1.0	2.2	2.5	2.6	3.3
C. IMF quota		2.8	2.8	2.8	2.8	4.1	4.1
II. Gross liabilities	2.2	8.2	11.7	16.6	17.6	21.6	23.5
A. Foreign countries	2.2	6.4	9.9	14.9	15.6	17.7	19.2
1. Official . . .		3.1	4.9	7.9	8.7	9.1	10.3
2. Banks		}2.9	2.4	3.5	3.5	4.7	5.2
3. Others . . .			1.7	2.2	2.4	2.4	2.3
4. Bonds and notes		0.4	0.9	1.2	1.0	1.5	1.4
B. International		1.8	1.9	1.7	2.0	3.8	4.4
III. Net Assets							
A. I-II	13.0	19.9	15.3	11.2	8.2	4.7	2.3
B. IA-IIA . . .	12.4	18.2	13.4	8.0	5.0	1.8	—0.8

S o u r c e: R. Triffin, "International Monetary Position of the United States", in *The Dollar in Crisis*, 1961, pp. 228-29.

Table 11 conclusively shows that the main thing in the monetary relations of the United States with other countries was that its liquid liabilities in dollars, mainly treasury bills and bank notes and dollar accounts in foreign banks, gradually exceeded the sum of the national gold stock. While in 1949 the gold reserves exceeded all the liquid liabilities of the United States to foreign states by $ 18,200 million, in October 1960 these liabilities topped the gold stock by $ 800 million. The gap between the gold stock and US liquid liabilities increased very swiftly after the war in Korea.

During the Korean War the United States for the first time began to cover military spending abroad on a wide scale through the issue of Federal Reserve notes, short-term

Treasury bills and other liabilities. This easy way of covering the war expenditure abroad not by gold but by its
national currency, dollars, suited the US ruling circles and
they continued with it in the second half of the 1950s. They
used the same method when rendering the much-publicised
American "aid" to other countries. This made it possible to
picture US financial policy as sacrifices made to save capitalism from the postwar financial and economic breakdown.

But it is a fact that these "sacrifices", as shown in Table 8,
did not prevent the United States from increasing direct
investment and long-term assets abroad from $ 26,600 mil-
lion in 1949 to $ 62,400 million in 1960—almost 2.5 times.

The credit expansion and the policy of investment through
the issue of credit money and other liabilities upset
the equilibrium between the current assets of the government, gold reserves included, and short-term liabilities,
including Federal Reserve notes. This created an exceptional
situation: the creditor country, whose long-term capital
often dominated the important industries of other capitalist
countries, found itself in an extremely difficult position,
being unable to repay its short-term liabilities.

There is nothing surprising in all that, however. In this
case American monopoly capital utilised the issue by the
state of credit money (we refer not only to the US Treasury
but also the Federal Reserve System, which performs the
function of the country's central state bank) for capturing
important positions in the economies of other countries.

It cannot be claimed that the financial agencies of the
United States acted fully in contravention of the financial
policy of the central banks of other countries. The point is
that under the gold exchange standard, in contrast to the
gold standard *per se*, central banks issue notes covered not
only by outstanding debts or commercial bills and gold
but also by foreign exchange, foreign liabilities. Banks in
other countries, receiving dollars through one channel or
another, were in no hurry to exchange them for American
gold. Leaving them on their balances as security for their
bank notes put into circulation, they used them in the American money market, deposited them, buying Treasury bills,
and so on. Thus, the sum of the unpaid accounts of US finan-

cial agencies snowballed: the gap between their liquid liabilities and the American gold stock continued to widen.

Monopoly corporations enjoyed the advantages accruing from the policy of dollar expansion, while the US government had to foot the bill for the whole cast of this policy.

Debts of a state in other countries, too, often directly or indirectly help to enrich the capitalist monopolies. In the given case the situation in the USA was complicated by the fact that in the early 1960s the Administration was faced with the difficult task of redeeming foreign liabilities, while private capital continued to flow out to other countries.

In his message to Congress in January 1961 President Kennedy had to state not without anxiety: "It is true that, since 1958, the gap between the dollars we spend or invest abroad and the dollars returned to us has substantially widened. This over-all deficit in our balance of payments increased by nearly $ 11,000,000,000 in the last three years—and holders of dollars abroad converted them to gold in such a quantity as to cause a total outflow of nearly $ 5,000,000,000 of gold from our reserve."[1]

This official admission by the President that all was not well in the United States' financial relations with other countries clearly revealed the advent of the monetary crisis. In the circumstances it inevitably had to develop from the crisis of the dollar into a general crisis of the monetary system, which entailed the strongest jolts to capitalism in the second half of the century. The ruling circles of the United States and other capitalist countries naturally could not remain passive onlookers.

President Kennedy's message to Congress which paid great attention to monetary problems opened up a new phase in the search for a way out. Not only official government agencies and officials whose duty it was to handle these matters but also many economists in universities, colleges, banks and corporations joined in tackling the problems.

What was the policy of the United States, i.e., the policy of President Kennedy himself and his closest associates? The Kennedy Administration undertook actively to defend the dollar. Striving to gain "understanding" and "support"

---

[1] *Vital Speeches of the Day*, February 15, 1961, p. 258.

of the governments of other capitalist countries, Washington advanced its programme for defending the dollar. It called for persuading NATO allies to assume a considerable part of the expenditure on joint military measures, requesting the principal trading partners of the United States to refrain from restrictions with regard to American exports. The intention was announced of reducing the expenditure of the US armed forces abroad and foreign military "aid".

As for support by the governments of other countries in defending the dollar, on the whole the hopes were not justified. The Federal Republic of Germany agreed to repay in advance small sums owed to the United States and Japan consented to begin payment over 15 years of $ 490 million for food aid during the years of occupation.

Notwithstanding a policy of economy in the spending of foreign exchange along military and other channels, the result was insignificant and unstable, which US Secretary of the Treasury Dillon was compelled to admit at a meeting of the Boards of Governors of the International Bank for Reconstruction and Development and the International Monetary Fund on October 1, 1963. According to Dillon, the deficit in the US balance of payments was reduced in 1962 to $ 2,200 million as compared with $ 2,400 million in 1961 and $ 3,900 million in 1960. But the deficit "grew markedly larger during the first half of 1963".[1]

That is why the Kennedy Administration from the very outset concentrated effort on expanding exports so as to increase the favourable trade balance and reduce the deficit of the balance of payments. Special attention was paid to the fight against the tariff and trade barriers of the European Common Market, which hampered American exports to Western Europe. Such a connection between the policy of defending the dollar and attempts to stimulate American exports was part of the general line of the Kennedy Administration; it sought, without introducing changes in the existing international monetary system, to reinforce within it the position of the American dollar by increasing the favourable trade balance. It was assumed that this would make it possible to achieve an equilibrium in the balance of

---

[1] *The Department of State Bulletin*, October 21, 1963, p. 616.

9—0247

payments even if a high level of US capital exports abroad were maintained. This was the premise from which President Kennedy proceeded when he introduced in Congress the Trade Expansion Bill early in 1962. To stimulate American exports, the bill provided that the President be empowered to reduce custom duties by mutual agreement with other countries.

In his message to Congress on this question (of January 25, 1962) Kennedy expounded a big programme which could promote the unification of the West. The concept "West" implied Western Europe and chiefly the countries of the Common Market. "Free movement of trade between America and the Common Market would bolster the economy of the entire free world (meaning the capitalist world.— *A.S.*), stimulating each nation to do most what it does best."[1] In other words, the purpose was to compel countries to specialise and to trade more. In this light the monocultural pattern of colonial countries could be regarded as the ideal of development.

While the President and US officials cloaked the pressure on Western Europe and especially on the EEC in florid language, business circles expressed their intentions without beating about the bush. The US Chamber of Commerce, for example, in a special bulletin issued under a characteristic title *The Impact of the Common Market on the American Economy*, stated: "In its action and reaction to the Common Market, the United States must consider its world-wide interests and commitments, including Japan and the less-developed countries not associated with the growing European Economic Community."[2] The concept of "world-wide interests" included the striving of the United States to preserve the postwar monetary system and expand American exports in world trade.

The purpose of Kennedy's entire external economic policy consisted in stopping the process of fencing off the European Economic Community from the world market by a common external tariff because this also led to monetary and finan-

---

[1] *The Department of State Bulletin*, No. 1181, February 12, 1962, p. 232.

[2] *The Impact of the Common Market on the American Economy*, The Chamber of Commerce of the United States, Washington, 1962, p. 4.

cial isolation, to undermining the dollar in the postwar monetary system. Dean Rusk, the then Secretary of State, trying
to prove the need for close economic contact between the
EEC and the United States in a speech made on February 21,
1962, referred to the fact that "two immense trading areas,
two common markets, so to speak: the common market of
the United States and the common market of Europe" exist
"on the two sides of the Atlantic".[1] What remained to be
done was to unite them on the basis of reciprocal tariff
concessions so as to gain a mutually greater advantage.
Judging by the fact that not only Rusk and Under-Secretary
Ball but also many other officials spoke on the need for
integrating the "free world", that is, of uniting capitalism
in defence of the dollar in order to repulse the oncoming
monetary crisis, such unification was lacking and it was not
achieved.

Objective factors weakened the dollar and the monetary
system of capitalism as a whole. The ruling circles of the
United States and other countries were faced with the need
to make decisions and they decided to preserve the postwar
monetary financial system at all costs. This was the purpose
of Kennedy's foreign and internal policy which amounted to
defence of the dollar.

In addition to applying the Trade Expansion Act designed
to increase American exports, President Kennedy sought to
restore confidence in the dollar by purely financial measures.
He tried to stop the exchange of dollars for American gold
by foreign dollar holders. This could not be achieved without
the help of the governments of other countries. That is why
as early as 1961 understanding was reached, via diplomatic
channels and through personal contacts of officials, on collective efforts to maintain the price of gold at the established
official level. The so-called Gold Pool was formalised.
Through it the central banks of the Pool member countries
began to coordinate their efforts to maintain the price of
gold at the fixed level. The Bank of England, empowered to
act as the chief agent of the Gold Pool, had to regulate the
demand for gold and, in case of a big demand, to satisfy
it without allowing a panic. The inevitable losses of gold

---

[1] *The Department of State Bulletin*, No. 1185, March 12, 1962, p. 404.

were compensated by the United States to the extent of 50
per cent and the other half was distributed between other
members of the Gold Pool—Britain, France, the Federal
Republic of Germany, Italy, Belgium, the Netherlands and
Switzerland, although the latter was not affiliated with the
International Monetary Fund. Thus, through the Gold Pool
the United States undoubtedly eased the pressure of foreign
dollar holders on the American gold reserves. During the
next few years the American policy of defending the dollar
largely rested on the Gold Pool. This meant that its members spent a part of their gold reserves on supporting the
American dollar.

Under the influence of the monetary and financial crisis
the Organisation for Economic Co-operation and Development (OECD) was set up. It came to be known as the "Mas-
ters' club". Formally, the OECD, as it were, was a successor
to the Organisation of European Economic Co-operation
(OEEC), which was set up during the Marshall Plan period.
But in its aims the OECD was a different organisation, although it included the selfsame West European countries.
Besides West European countries, it was joined by the
United States, Canada, Australia and Japan (since 1964),
which had not belonged to the OEEC. Thus, the OECD became an intercontinental organisation formally set up on
December 14, 1960, as a result of a convention signed by its
participants in Paris.

The main aims of the OECD were "to achieve the highest sustainable economic growth and employment and a
rising standard of living in member countries, while maintaining financial stability, and thus to contribute to the
development of the world economy".[1] The subsequent development of this organisation has shown that "financial
stability" and ensuring the "liberalisation" of the international movement of capital and monetary questions hold
the central place in its activity. Through it the US ruling
circles are trying to pool the efforts of the principal capitalist countries in combating the monetary crisis and to
preserve freedom of action for American capital.

[1] *The Flow of Financial Resources to Countries in the Course of Economic Development in 1960*, Paris, 1962, p. 4.

Among the measures of international significance mention should be made of the Group of Ten (United States, Britain, France, FRG, Italy, Japan, Canada, Netherlands, Belgium and Sweden), set up on Washington's initiative; these ten big capitalist countries have reached an understanding, through the International Monetary Fund, in case of emergencies when the stability of the monetary system is upset, to furnish credit to those who are in a difficult position owing to a balance-of-payments deficit. The total sum of such credits could be brought up to $ 6,000 million. What was envisaged was the exchange by the central banks of national currencies at parity, with the commitment, upon the expiration of a definite period, to perform a reverse operation.

This is really a loan to a country in need of foreign exchange, which offers the creditors its national currency as security. If upon the expiration of a definite period there is no improvement in the balance of payments, as was the case with Britain in 1964-1965, the operation has to be repeated. All these manipulations with reciprocal loans merely attested to the mounting financial difficulties of capitalism.

The Group of Ten thus, as it were, assumed patronage over the IMF. Actually, it was this group, as we shall see later on, that was tackling the most important problems as they arose during the development of the crisis in capitalism's monetary system in subsequent years.

A number of measures taken in 1961 somewhat improved the US balance of payments, and the Government hastened to utilise this result for pacifying public opinion.

On September 20, 1962, President Kennedy, speaking in Washington before participants in the joint session of the Boards of Governors of the International Bank for Reconstruction and Development and the International Monetary Fund, stated: "We in the United States feel no need to be self-conscious in discussing the dollar. It is not only our national currency—it is an international currency. It plays a key role in the day-to-day functioning of the free world's financial framework. It is the most effective substitute for gold in the international payments system[1]."

---

[1] *Vital Speeches of the Day*, October 15, 1962, p. 7.

Thus, President Kennedy, addressing a forum of international financiers, came out in open support of the postwar monetary system of capitalism based on the dollar. This was also in line with his practical policy of defending the dollar. The President reported that in 1962 a decrease in the balance-of-payments deficit was expected, namely, $ 1,500 million, as compared with $ 2,500 million in the preceding year, and hastened to assure the audience that the dollar itself was strong. In conclusion, he voiced the opinion that the United States could remove the balance-of-payments deficit overnight if this were its aim. For this, in his opinion, it would only be necessary to recall the troops from abroad, reduce aid and raise custom tariffs on imports. "But," he drew the conclusion, "the basic strength of the dollar makes such actions as unnecessary as they are unwise."[1] The President alluded to the danger of a "shortage of dollars" for the capitalist world.

We are far from suspecting the late President of not believing himself in what he was saying. No, apparently, such a notion of the strength of the dollar and the possibility of swiftly coping with the situation was widespread in the United States at that time. But public opinion at large did not take into account the serious economic changes, not in favour of the United States, which occurred at the beginning of the 1960s.

What alarmed American economists most was the obvious lag of the annual growth rate of industrial output and the increment of the gross national product: both were less than half that in the EEC countries and did not even reach those of Britain.

A considerable part of American capital in various forms was invested abroad but not within the country. Moreover, a substantial part of the profits on US capital abroad was not repatriated but was added to the investments. In other words, the investment of American capital abroad on the whole had a slowing-down effect on economic growth rates of the United States itself in the 1950s.

As for the US balance of payments, the deficit caused by big military spending abroad was mounting further because

----

[1] *Vital Speeches of the Day*, p. 7.

of the so-called portfolio investments of American capital
in foreign loans, securities and deposits in foreign banks.
Such portfolio investments of American capital not only
increased the balance-of-payments deficit but, together
with deposits in dollars on the accounts of foreign holders,
were the cause of general inflation and high prices. Thus,
there were weighty reasons for changing the investment
policy of the United States.

It was this path that President Kennedy took after two
years in office had convinced him that more radical measures than the mere stimulation of exports were required to
eliminate the country's balance-of-payments deficit and
defend the dollar. That is why, without relaxing his efforts
to expand exports and even intensify them through collective negotiations with US trading partners (known as the
Kennedy Round), the President put forward in 1963 another programme for normalising finances and economic
growth.

Outwardly this programme seemed to affect only the
United States but in fact it concerned the entire monetary
and financial system of capitalism. In his presidential message of July 18, 1963, Kennedy asked Congress to introduce
a tax (called the Interest Equalisation Tax) on the profits
of American capital outflowing abroad in the form of portfolio investments. The introduction of this tax was linked
with a substantial reduction of the federal income tax on
private persons and corporations. The Interest Equalisation
Tax on capital going abroad was of great importance to the
country's monetary and financial policy. Its main purpose
was to stop the outflow of American capital in undesirable
forms of portfolio investments (the question of direct investments in foreign industry was not raised), to achieve a
balance-of-payments equilibrium and thereby strengthen
the position of the dollar in international payments. President Kennedy, just like his advisers, believed in the effi-
cacy of these measures. He believed that the US dollar, as
hitherto, would play the principal role in the capitalist
monetary system.

Shortly before his tragic death, speaking at the joint
meeting of the Directors of the International Bank for
Reconstruction and Development and the International

Monetary Fund in Washington on September 30, 1963, he
assured international financiers: "We are determined—and
I believe in your interest as well as our own—to maintain
the firm relationship of gold and the dollar at the present
price of $ 35 an ounce, and I can assure you we will do just
that."[1]

On November 22, 1963, President Kennedy was assassinat-
ed, but his policy of defending the dollar and maintaining
the postwar monetary system of capitalism remained. It was
continued, at least for two years, by his successor Lyndon
Johnson. A bitter struggle between different groups of US
finance capital was fought around this policy and particularly during the passage of the bill on the Interest Equalisation
Tax for which there were special reasons.

Table 12

**Selected Economic Data: United States
and Western Europe**

	United States	EEC	Great Britain
Population — mid-year 1960 (millions)	181	169	52
GNP at current prices in 1961 ('000 million dollars)	505	179	65
National income per capita, 1961 (dollars)	2,310	771	1,080
Gold and foreign exchange reserves, end 1961 ('000 million dollars)	17	16.0	3.3
Growth of production, 1950-1960 (per cent)	38	70	(36)
Annual growth rate in GNP, 1951-1960 (per cent)	2.6	5.3	2.7
Annual growth rate in industrial production, 1951-1960 (per cent) . .	3.0	7.4	3.2

S o u r c e: *The Impact of the Common Market on the American
Economy*, p. 23.

---

[1] *The Department of State Bulletin,* October 24, 1963, p. 612.

«DEFENCE OF THE DOLLAR» AT THE EXPENSE OF OTHER CAPITALIST CURRENCIES

The policy of "defending the dollar", which was the hub of President Kennedy's home and foreign policy, was also pursued by Lyndon Johnson. At the Presidential elections in the autumn of 1964 Johnson advocated the continuation of Kennedy's measures. Moreover, it was necessary to approve the bills drawn up under Kennedy, the Interest Equalisation Tax bill, which meant a tax on capital invested abroad, and the bill on reducing the federal personal and corporate income tax. Both bills had a bearing on the defence of the dollar and the capitalist monetary system and were designed to improve the balance of payments and to liven up the economy within the country since its growth rate was lagging behind those of other countries.

The question was not whether the Interest Equalisation Tax would stop the outflow of capital or not but whether the measure was at all necessary since the country received from its foreign investments a net difference of $ 2.700 million.[1] The groups of American capitalists which had already invested or intended to invest free capital abroad were hostile towards any restriction of investment. This striving for "freedom" in utilising capital was spurred on by the fact that the rate of return and the level of interest on capital abroad were higher than in the United States with its low industrial growth rates in those years.

---

[1] *Economic Report of the President Transmitted to the Congress, January 1962*, Washington, 1962, p. 149,

But these private group interests stood in opposition to the general class interests of US finance capital, to the desire to preserve the dominant position of the dollar in the world monetary system and the advantages following therefrom.

The breakdown of this system threatened to bring about the complete outflow of the American gold reserves, an increase in the dollar price of gold, i.e., the actual devaluation of the US currency and chaos in credit relations of the capitalist world. The latter was all the more dangerous because the United States was the chief creditor country. In addition to these arguments in favour of restricting the outflow of capital in the undesirable forms of portfolio investments the following point was raised: faced with a tax on foreign portfolio investments, American investors would try to find a use for their capital within the country, including industry, which could provide an additional stimulus to economic growth. From this point supporters of the Interest Equalisation Tax—among whom were the most prominent advisers of President Kennedy and influential circles of the Democratic Party—built a bridge to other measures. In their opinion, the Trade Expansion Act and the law reducing income tax were to open new spheres for the application of the capital flowing out abroad in the form of loans, and so on. A reduction of the federal personal and corporate income tax (according to estimates, by $ 11,000 million in the course of the fiscal year) was to extend the consumer demand and enable corporations to increase output in the country.

Thus, behind the apparently separate tax questions lay a whole economic programme. It was a programme for a massive economic offensive by US finance capital against foreign competitors, in defence of its shaken position in the world economy. The expansion of exports and the Interest Equalisation Tax were to serve as the weapons in this offensive.

While the expansion of American exports could directly strike at the interests of foreign competitors, the operation of the Interest Equalisation Tax could no less sensitively affect those who were accustomed to utilise the relatively cheaper American credits abroad.

The point is that every tax on capital, as a rule, is shifted by its owner on to the users of capital. Accordingly, when introducing an equalisation tax on incomes from portfolio investments, the US Government expected that American creditors would immediately raise the interest rate on loan capital for foreign borrowers. Thus, the interest rate on American credits would rise to the level of rates in other countries and would be "equalised" with them. Hence the name "Equalisation" Tax.

Such an influence on American creditors with the help of the tax would bring pressure to bear on international credit, narrowing its base and causing a world-wide rise of the interest rate on capital.

Foreseeing that, while the Equalisation Tax was going through the legislative machine, American capital might flee to other countries, the authors of the bill provided for its retroactive operation. That is why, although the law was passed and came into force on September 2, 1964, after more than a year of discussion and struggle between different capitalist groups, its operation to some extent had made itself felt even prior to the adoption of the Act, immediately after the bill was made public.

The Equalisation Tax Act provided for tax on profit yielded by capital invested abroad depending on the period for which it was invested, up to 15 per cent and on the whole raised the cost of credit by 1 per cent per annum on the average. This caused a general tendency to raise the credit rate in the world capital market. So it was not surprising that Washington was showered by reproaches and protests from the foreign recipients of American credits. There were even formal government protests, for example, by Japan. The reason for the protest was that the Act made an exception for Canada. The Japanese Government laid claim to a similar privilege. Actually, the Japanese Government was dissatisfied not only because Japan had to pay more for the American capital received to cover the deficit in the US balance of payments, but also because the tax brought about a general rise in interest rates.

In the so-called Ten Points of his Presidential programme, made public in January 1964, Lyndon Johnson directly associated the sixth point on the Interest Equalisation Tax with the defence of the gold content of the dollar and the balancing of international payments. "We must continue," he stated, "through such measures as the Interest Equalisation Tax, as well as the co-operation of other nations, our recent progress toward balancing our international accounts. This Administration must and will preserve the present gold value of the dollar."[1]

The determination of the United States to preserve the foundations of the capitalist monetary system and its backbone, the dollar equated to gold at an unchanging ratio, was once again reaffirmed.

In this context it is necessary to quote one more point of the Presidential programme, namely, the fifth, concerning the tasks of US foreign trade. "We must expand world trade. Having recognised in the Trade Expansion Act of 1962 that we must buy as well as sell, we now expect our trading partners to recognise that we must sell as well as buy. We are willing to give competitive access to our market, asking only that they do the same for us."[2]

It is difficult to give an adequate definition to this point of the programme because it is impossible to precisely determine the fundamental difference between the demand for liberalising international trade and the open declaration of a competitive struggle.

As for the Interest Equalisation Tax on foreign portfolio investments, ways of evading it were found before long (specifically, through Canada, investments in which were exempted from the operation of this law). It should be noted that Canada is not only the main sphere of investment for American capital. It has at the same time, as it were, become a kind of transfer junction for it. It is safe to assume that a considerable part of the US investments officially listed in Canada have in one way or another been reinvested, particularly in the British Commonwealth. Canada has become a loophole utilised by US investors for circumventing the Interest Equalisation Tax. As a matter of fact, this is not a new trick.

[1] *The Department of State Bulletin. Foreign Policy Briefs*, No. 14, January 20, 1964, The President 10 Points Program.
[2] Ibid.

US capital flowed to other countries via Canada not directly but indirectly. Instead of being repatriated to the United States, the big profits on capital in Canada were reinvested not only in Canada but also in other countries.

A picture of the distribution of US private investments abroad was presented in October 1962 by Secretary of State Dean Rusk at a meeting of businessmen in Hot Springs. Canada held first place. According to Rusk, of the $34,700 million of direct private investments abroad the biggest part was in industrially developed countries. Of them $11,800 million were in Canada and $7,700 million in Europe, of which $3,500 million in Britain and $3,000 million in Common Market countries. A large sum, about $8,200 million, was invested in Latin America, $2,500 million in Asia and approximately $1,000 million in Africa.[1]

As pointed out earlier, the Interest Equalisation Tax did not apply to direct investments. But even after it was introduced on portfolio investments, not only direct investments but also all other increased, as was reflected in the balance of payments.

Table 13 shows that, notwithstanding the tax designed to curb the outflow of American capital, no noticeable changes for the better occurred. On the contrary, the net investments of private capital abroad in 1964 rose steeply. Direct investments which were not restricted also continued to rise. In 1964 there was, on the whole, a definite growth in long-term and short-term investments (deposits and others) through banks. Apparently, the private interests of finance capital prompted investors to disregard the state interests which the federal legislative and executive bodies sought to protect. Anxiety on this score was quite often voiced in the press and in official statements. Similar anxiety was also displayed in other capitalist countries. It was aroused not so much by the failure of Washington's measures to protect the dollar as by the very fact of legislatively restricting foreign investments of US capital. This measure taken by a country rightly regarded as the world creditor was unusual from the viewpoint of capitalist practices. It affected the

---

[1] *The Department of State Bulletin*, November 5, 1962, p. 686.

Table 13

US Balance of Payments
(million dollars)

	1963	1964	1965
Balance of goods, services, remittances and pensions	5,030	7,611	5,963
US Govt. grants and capital flow, net	—3,581	—3,560	—3,375
Grants, loans and net change in foreign currency holdings, and short-term claims	—4,551	—4,263	—4,277
Scheduled repayments on US Govt. loans	644	580	681
Non-scheduled repayments and selloffs	326	123	221
US private capital flow, net	—4,456	—6,523	—3,690
Direct investments	—1,976	—2,416	—3,371
Foreign securities	—1,104	—677	—758
Other long-term claims: Reported by banks	—754	—941	—231
Short-term claims: Reported by banks	—781	—1,523	325

(Source: *Federal Reserve Bulletin*, November 1966, p. 1726.)

interests of other countries, restricting the possibilities of credit, and raising the interest on loan capital. This, however, was the practical and not the main aspect of the matter.

The fundamental aspect was that the regulation of the interest rate by taxing profits on investments abroad was introduced into world practice by the creditor country itself. This in effect was an attempt to somehow compel private capital to forego its selfish interests in favour of the general state interests, which in a capitalist country are the general class interests of the bourgeoisie.

It was an attempt to somehow mitigate the basic contradiction of the capitalist mode of production—between the social nature of production and the private capitalist form of appropriating the results of production. In the given case some groups of US finance capital preferred foreign port-

folio investments as the best form of appropriating interest, a part of the profit, while this, through currency circulation, adversely affected the US economy and the entire
world monetary system favouring the United States.

It is not surprising that the state as represented by President Johnson and his Administration tried somehow to
combine in new forms private capitalist and state interests.
The relevant measures once again demonstrated that the
state machine in the USA, as in other capitalist countries,
protects the general interests of the capitalist monopolies.
In all questions of principle the voice of the monopolies is
decisive.

The Johnson Administration in particular sought to
somehow reconcile the group interests of monopoly capital
in the United States itself and to coordinate them with the
interests of other capitalist countries within the framework
of the monetary system functioning under the aegis of the
IMF. But Washington's efforts did not produce the expected
results both because of differences within the US ruling
circles and also because the International Monetary Fund
itself had begun to totter. The latter was specifically linked
with the weakening of Britain, one of the pillars of the IMF.

Britain was a principal organiser of the IMF because
during the war it tried to ensure the normal functioning
of the international credit system, of which the United
States was the centre (when the war ended Britain, after
a period of vacillation between inflation and deflation, nevertheless decided to normalise its currency). It was this
question that was settled by the devaluation of the pound
in 1949, after which Britain utilised the IMF for imparting
firm convertibility to her currency, and in this respect
competed to some extent with the United States.

The pound, just as before the war, gradually assumed a
prominent place in international payments, alongside the
US dollar, and became a reserve currency for other countries. Britain's quota in the IMF, as noted earlier, was the
largest after the United States. She succeeded also in increasing her gold and exchange reserves, which, incidentally,
was facilitated by the fact that British capital held strong
positions in gold-producing countries, especially in Africa.
The reinforcement of British positions in the monetary

system was also facilitated by her ties with the dominions and countries of the sterling area, which kept resident accounts in London. "The major distinctions which characterised the sterling area are: a) a system of monetary control extended to currency circulation between the area and the rest of the world modelled after the British pattern and based on an unchanging rate of currencies to sterling and in effect single for the entire area; b) participation of the area's countries in the 'dollar pool', that is, the obligatory handing over to the central reserves in London, at the stable fixed rate, the entire or part of the receipts in dollars and other scarce foreign currencies and also of gold; c) the keeping of the biggest part of the foreign exchange reserves of the area members in the form of sterling balances in British banks."[1]

This definition of the essence of the sterling area and the role of Britain in it shows that in the capitalist monetary system this area represented, as it were, a state within a state. The form of this coexistence was the "dollar pool", which enabled London to concentrate the gold and foreign exchange reserves of the sterling area and, on this basis, to impart to the pound the necessary stability of an international currency on a par with the dollar. For British finance capital it was important that this system should operate smoothly and that Britain should play a leading role in the foreign trade of the sterling area countries, while they strictly adhered to monetary discipline: they concentrated their foreign exchange reserves in the form of sterling balances in London banks. Lenin drew attention to the specific features of Britain's financial position. It is not by chance that he quoted the following excerpt from an article by Alfred Lansburgh: "The continual holding of a large portfolio of British bills of exchange means, in practice, that the country in question puts considerable resources at London's disposal, which for its part London can, and does, use to further finance the foreign trade of other countries and in this way strengthen its own sterling currency and its own clearing function.

---

[1] S. M. Borisov, *Sterlingovaya zona v valyutnoi sisteme kapitalizma* (The Sterling Area in Capitalism's Monetary System), Moscow, 1957, p. 41.

Thus, owing to the gold value of the pound sterling, Great Britain is always able to put at the service of her credit system, besides her own large capital assets, also several thousand million marks of foreign money."[1]

Such was the traditional role of Britain and she tried to play it after the Second World War too.

In the 1950s, thanks to the system of trade preferences, the role of Britain in the commerce of the sterling area countries was quite substantial. This helped her maintain at a high level the role of London as one of the biggest financial centres of the capitalist world. In 1958 Britain had a gold stock of $ 2,807 million, bigger than any other West European country. At that time it was equal approximately to the gold reserves of France, Italy and the Netherlands combined.

The British pound, as the second international currency after the dollar, resting on the financial relations which arose in the sterling area, played an important part in international payments. The ruling element of Britain to a certain extent adhered to the same financial policy as the US ruling circles. It widely introduced its currency into other countries unperturbed by the mounting sum of Britain's liquid liabilities abroad. Britain was the second creditor country after the United States, but the long-term investments of British capital, although they contributed considerable sums in the form of profit on capital to the balance of payments, could not compensate for the adverse trade balance. Britain's foreign trade clearly lagged behind other countries owing to a slow economic growth rate, while the latter was, to a considerable extent, explained by the technological lag of industry. The investment policy of British monopoly capital greatly leaned towards foreign investment to the detriment of home investment. The result of all this was that the second biggest creditor country constantly had a strained balance of payments, which in 1964 endangered the position of the pound.

Britain's gold and foreign exchange reserves were substantially reduced, while the presentation of its liabilities for payment in gold or hard currency was mounting.

---

[1] V. I. Lenin, *Collected Works*, Vol. 39, p. 79.

Finding herself in a difficult financial position, Britain resorted to what seemed to be a normal way out—a loan from the International Monetary Fund amounting to $1,000 million. But this failed to normalise the country's finances and strengthen the pound.

It should be borne in mind that IMF loans differ from ordinary ones in that the recipient country, in accordance with its quota and the existing rules, pays into the fund a sum in its own currency equivalent to the loan. This sum, upon the expiration of a definite period (not more than four years) has to be exchanged or, as it were, redeemed, for hard currency or gold. In this case the currency of the borrowing country, as it were, replaces a promissory note or bill. In essence, there is no difference in principle between a bill of exchange and bank notes. Bank notes, in Marx's definition, are a liability of the bank issued to the holder. The parallel between a bill of exchange and the national currency deposited in the IMF to cover the loan received in foreign exchange can also be supplemented by the point that, just like the discounting of a bill, the IMF may sell the national currency if there is a demand for it from other Fund members. Consequently, it may happen that other IMF members will fully or in part buy the deposited national currency for their needs. This does not mean, however, that the borrowing country will be freed from repaying the loan. It will pay for its currency by exports and international services when, in case of a favourable trade and payments balances, it will receive, in final settlement, its own currency held by other countries.

But all this, as a Russian saying has it, looked easy on paper, but there were many hurdles in real life. And it was these obstacles that proved too much for Britain's foreign payments. The main one was the deficit of the balance of payments, while Britain's liquid liabilities in pound sterling were at the disposal of other countries in excessive amounts. That is why the £ 1,000 million deposited with the IMF was the additional issue which filled the cup to overflowing. These financial operations, far from improving Britain's financial position and reinforcing the pound, on the contrary, worsened it. This was conclusively demonstrated by the fact that the following year Britain had to resort to another international loan for an even bigger sum, $ 1,500 million.

Britain's big loans upset the financial position of the IMF which found itself burdened with too many pounds for which there was no demand. More than that, foreigners began to withdraw their sterling balances from British banks in order to transfer them to other countries and exchange for gold. This led to the outflow of Britain's gold and exchange reserves. The situation in the entire monetary system became more tense than before the onset of the sterling difficulties. But the position of the dollar still seemed to be stable. This is partly explained by the fact that speculators, unable to exchange sterling for gold and in anticipation of its devaluation, exchanged pounds for dollars. Greater dangers for the American dollar and the entire capitalist monetary system were already discernible behind all these feverish activities in the world money markets.

The specificity of the situation was that both the leading world creditors, the United States and Britain, had landed in a tight spot. Moreover, the reason was one and the same— the excessive piling up of long-term credits, the gap between long-term foreign investments and short-term liquid liabilities of these countries which exceeded their national gold and foreign exchange reserves and other assets. The private capital of these countries continued to extract high profits on foreign investments and frequently acted contrary to the national interests. All this was a manifestation of capitalism's general crisis. But one of the main attributes of capitalism in the period of imperialism, the export of capital, remained.

If we compare the revenue of the leading capitalist countries from external economic ties in relation to their national product, the United States and Britain stood out for the high incomes (100 per cent) on the invested capital. Particularly big was the share of these incomes in the United States. Let us recall that in the case of a creditor country income on investments exceeds its payments of profits and interest on capital. From this viewpoint, the United States and Britain likewise stood out among the main capitalist countries.

Table 14 shows that of all the countries only in the United States and Britain did income on capital abroad substan-

Table 14

External Receipts and Payments of Some Countries as Compared with Their National Product (per cent of GNP)

Countries	Trade		Transport		Tourist travel		Profit on capital		Other services	
	receipts	pay-ments	receipts	pay-ments	receipts	pay-ments	receipts	pay-ments	receipts	pay-ments
United States	3.8	2.8	3.3	3.8	1.9	3.4	9.1	2.2	2.0	0.8
Britain	14.2	14.4	2.7	2.8	0.7	0.8	3.1	1.7	1.6	1.0
Canada	15.7	15.4	1.2	1.5	1.4	1.5	0.5	1.9	0.8	0.6
FRG	14.9	12.9	1.2	1.4	0.6	1.3	0.3	0.7	0.5	1.4
France	12.1	11.3	0.6	0.7	1.2	0.8	0.5	0.4	1.4	1.2
Italy	11.6	13.9	1.5	1.8	2.4	0.3	0.3	0.5	1.9	1.1
Benelux	28.6	28.6	1.7	1.7	1.1	1.4	1.4	1.2	3.2	2.1
Sweden	20.1	21.4	3.9	1.7	0.5	0.9	0.4	0.1	0.8	1.5
Japan	9.2	8.5	0.8	1.6	0.1	0.1	0.2	0.4	0.3	0.8

S o u r c e: *Economic White Paper for 1964*, Tokyo, 1964, p. 44. (In Japanese.)

tially exceed payments under this item in percentage of their gross product.

This characteristic feature of a creditor country was less strikingly pronounced in countries like Belgium, the Netherlands and Luxemburg, and also in France where the ratio of receipts from foreign investments to the national product exceeded payments under this item by a fraction of a percent. It is even more pronounced in Sweden where receipts on capital in percentages were four times higher than payments, although they amounted to 0.4 per cent of the gross national product. But since the magnitudes by countries depend on the absolute value of the gross national product, the actual sums of external income and expenditure on capital differ considerably.

Mention should also be made of one more circumstance usually emphasised by US ruling circles at all kinds of international trade and tariff negotiations—this is the low ratio of foreign trade, particularly exports, to the GNP. This was the reason given for the need to increase exports by President Kennedy in his speech at the conference on exports held in the White House on September 17-18, 1963. He explained the need and possibility of extending exports as a major item of the balance of payments by the fact that the United States exported 4 per cent of its national product, while, according to him, the respective percentage in other countries was in the Federal Republic of Germany 16, Italy 10, Japan 9, and Sweden and the Netherlands 19 and 35 per cent respectively.[1] The President did not try to analyse the reasons for the high ratio of exports in West European countries. This follows from their greater trade interdependence expressed in similarly big imports. But notwithstanding the low ratio of exports to the gross national product, the United States had regularly a favourable balance of trade. Thus, in 1961 the excess of exports over imports by only 1 per cent of the GNP amounted to $ 5,500 million.

The crux of the matter is not a shortage of receipts from the export of goods and capital, but the spending on military ventures abroad. Secretary of State Rusk pointed out at the meeting in Hot Springs that the military expenditure

---

[1] *The Department of State Bulletin*, October 14, 1963, p. 596.

abroad amounted annually to about $ 3,000 million and
in general military appropriations in the budget amounted
to 10 per cent of the GNP.[1] Under these circumstances the
export of US capital could not but lead to a balance-of-
payments deficit. Johnson appealed to the patriotic sense
of American businessmen, urging them voluntarily to limit
investments abroad, above all, portfolio investments.

The Treasury Department, on instructions from the President, also tried to influence various corporations so as to
make them spend less money abroad in the form of portfolio
investments and to draw more from overseas, repatriating
a much bigger share of the profits than usually. But this
did not produce a notable result either. Not only direct
investments continued to rise.

In 1964 short-term investment by American banks abroad
almost doubled. US banks exploited the flight from the
pound for currency speculation. The demand for Eurodollars
increased in Western Europe and this to a certain extent
restrained the presentation of American liquid liabilities
in exchange for gold.

There were also other reasons which restrained the outflow
of American gold in 1964. Foreign states obviously adopted
a wait-and-see attitude as regards the legislative measures
designed to normalise the financial settlements of the United
States with other countries: the Interest Equalisation Tax,
the reduction of the Federal personal and corporate income
tax which Johnson succeeded in pushing through Congress
before the Presidential elections. They also waited for the
outcome of the elections, since the future foreign economic
policy of the United States depended on them.

Lastly, mention should be made of the purely financial
measures for protecting the dollar adopted in that period.
Washington, for example, reached an agreement with the
International Monetary Fund to the effect that the latter
would place at the disposal of the United States, in exchange
for dollars, part of its assets in convertible national currencies. If a demand were made for American gold in repayment of US liabilities, the American Treasury could place
into circulation the respective national currency instead of

---

[1] *The Department of State Bulletin*, November 5, 1962, p. 684.

gold. For this reason from 1961 onwards the United States, which formerly had no foreign currencies in the liquid form, began to accumulate a reserve of foreign exchange. In the first quarter of 1964 it was brought up to $ 440 million.

In addition, US financial agencies, together with a leading group of West European banks participating in the Bank for International Settlements in Basel, began energetically to regulate the price of gold in the London market by influencing the demand through the massive sale of gold which satisfied for a time the speculative demand.

A part in these operations was taken by the Federal Reserve Bank of New York (it usually represented abroad the entire Federal Reserve System), the central banks of Britain, France, the Federal Republic of Germany, Italy, Belgium, the Netherlands and Switzerland, in other words, countries possessing the biggest stock of gold. They formed the so-called Gold Pool for regulating the price of gold and set up a gold fund for this purpose. Half of this fund was provided by the United States, and the remaining half in fixed proportions by the central banks of the other countries. They, in turn, resorted to "gold intervention" in the market, whenever necessary, through the Bank of England, i.e., they would unexpectedly create an excess of the gold supply over the demand, and lowered its price. But naturally this operation led to a loss of part of the gold reserves of every country that was a member of the Gold Pool. It is not surprising that the United States regarded these collective actions with satisfaction.[1] But naturally this "help" to the United States in maintaining the price of gold in dollars or defending the dollar hardly aroused enthusiasm among the ruling circles of the countries, whose central banks undertook to bolster up the shaky dollar with their gold reserves. Sooner or later these props had to collapse.

---

[1] See *Federal Reserve Bulletin*, March 1964, p. 305.

DIFFERENCES OVER CHANGING
THE CAPITALIST MONETARY SYSTEM

After the big $ 1,000-million loan which Britain received in 1964 the pound sterling remained at risk. It noticeably lost its role as the second world currency, after the American dollar. International financial circles were pondering over the question of how the further weakening of the pound would affect the position of the dollar. The fall of sterling could seriously complicate the monetary system, which was already unstable.

First, countries whose central banks participated in the Gold Pool were faced with a considerable outflow of their gold stock for supporting the fixed price of gold in dollars, in effect, for supporting the dollar.

Second, the glutting of the world monetary system with dollars made the task of maintaining the stability of the US currency more difficult because the American ruling circles were obviously not inclined to abide by the agreed rules in their international payments. They only spoke about the need for eliminating the US balance-of-payments deficit, but actually tolerated it because of the extensive investments of capital and big military spending abroad. As before, they covered the deficit with dollar liabilities, with their national currency, which had become an international medium of circulation.

While other countries having a balance-of-payments deficit were forced either to spend gold on covering it or to reduce their imports of goods and services and to restrict the export of capital, and, consequently, to restrain business activity, the United States could afford to neglect all these measures. The dollars were turning the deficit into a means which stimulated, rather than restrained, business activity. A balance-of-payments deficit turned into a weapon of US aggressive foreign policy and an instrument for the expansion of American capital in other countries.

True enough, after the adoption of the Interest Equalisation Tax Act the impression was created that an obstacle had been set to the expansion of American capital. The facts, however, showed that even after its enforcement, the outflow of capital in different forms was kept up, the balance-of-payments deficit remained and US liquid liabilities abroad continued to rise.

On the other hand, direct long-term investments of capital abroad also grew swiftly. The deficit in the balance of payments and the rise in investments, as it were, represented two sides of the coin, which could not but draw the close attention of economists in capitalist countries.

The ruling circles of the other capitalist countries, especially those whose central banks co-operated with the Federal Reserve System in supporting a stable price for gold, could not remain indifferent observers. They understood that they were facilitating US expansion in the monetary and financial sphere to their own detriment. They waited for the outcome of the elections, but after Johnson was elected they insistently raised the question of measures to end the US balance-of-payments deficit.

At that time such a possibility seemed feasible. This delusion was intensified by the fact that in February 1964 Johnson succeeded in pushing through the House and the Senate a bill reducing the personal and corporate income tax. Utilising this, Johnson's supporters and he himself during the election campaign emphasised that this measure would provide additional possibilities for economic growth because the tax reduction would save the taxpayers $ 25 million daily. This was to stimulate a demand for goods. In turn, the additional demand for goods was to provide an added stimulus to production. If we also point out that, in accordance with the 1962 Trade Expansion Act, the US Government was engaged in intensive talks (the Kennedy

Round), seeking to increase its exports, the picture of the general trade and economic expansion becomes clear.

The situation in the international monetary system was becoming a pressing question, and it was discussed by statesmen of the capitalist countries and in the press, and debates flared up everywhere.

Two main opposing viewpoints could be singled out in these discussions. Both of them became publicly known, in one way or another, since the beginning of the 1960s because of the troubles in the monetary system, but their wide-scope discussion started in 1965.

One of these concepts is associated with the name of Professor Triffin, the American economist. His view in brief is that all the shortcomings of the world monetary system stem from the abnormal situation created when the principal role of the international medium of circulation is played by a national currency. Up to a definite time this shortcoming was tolerable, but in the long run the monetary system ran up against the dollar crisis. To prevent further complications, as some bourgeois economists assume, it is necessary to create a genuinely international currency. In their opinion, the conditions for the creation of such a currency are available. Specifically, this could be facilitated by the existing international monetary and financial organisations. The operation of the international currency was conceived on the same principles as those governing the functioning of bank notes, i.e., credit money in general.

As for gold, once under international control, it would lose its function as the main means of international settlements. It would preserve value like every commodity, but would lose the money fetishism which was inherent in it for centuries.

It is easy to see that the plan for creating an artificial international currency proceeds from an agreement among the capitalist countries, or at least the most important of them, and presupposes the restriction of the sovereign rights of states in the sphere of money circulation. Moreover, this plan stems from the assumption that such an understanding would be of a permanent, and not of a temporary, nature.

It was assumed that capitalism would develop in the direction of "organised capitalism". This utopian tinge was also emphasised by the point that the foreign press named such an international currency "paper gold".

Prior to the exacerbation of the monetary crisis in the second half of the 1960s financial circles attached no serious significance to such plans.

Another concept is associated with the name of Jacques Rueff. Its author is not inclined to idealise capitalist realities.

He understands that the capitalist countries base their relations on real values and that gold has played, and will play, the cardinal role in these calculations.

Rueff explains the shortcomings of the present monetary system by saying that for a number of reasons, mainly owing to the improperly conceived measures of governments and international organisations, the role of gold as an automatic regulator of international circulation has been restricted. The price of gold has been artificially reduced as compared with the price of other commodities. Therefore, in his opinion, to bring back stability to the capitalist system, it is necessary to return to the gold standard, taking gold as the basis of international settlements and more or less doubling its price as compared with the one fixed in 1934 ($ 35 per troy ounce of gold). Then it will be possible for the United States to redeem its liquid liabilities with the gold stock it has. (The question was put in these terms at the beginning of the 1960s when the US gold reserves amounted approximately to $ 17,000 million or about 40 per cent of the world stock).

It is easy to see that such an objectively realistic approach to the problem at that time seemed far-fetched to international financial circles: the crisis had not yet undermined the world monetary system to such an extent that international, especially American, financial circles should seriously ponder over questions of radically changing it. On the contrary, it still seemed to them possible, as before, to arrange world currency circulation on the basis of the dollar within the framework of the Bretton Woods system.

Academic disputes about the merits and demerits of the two concepts turned in February 1965 into a keen political discussion in which literally the entire world press took part. It was triggered off by a speech made by President de Gaulle.

President de Gaulle criticised the monetary system because the dominance of the dollar in it gave unjustified advantages to the transatlantic partner of the West European countries. These advantages in the economic sphere were being exploited for introducing American hegemony in the international policy of the capitalist world. President de Gaulle called for a return to the gold standard, expressing the official opinion which reflected the policy of the French state.

Small wonder that the entire world press reacted to General de Gaulle's statement. The tone was at once set by the American and British press, which rejected the proposal for a return to the gold standard. It was followed by the press of other countries, particularly newspapers and journals connected with banking and business circles afraid of a radical change in the existing monetary system.

Commenting on the statement of President de Gaulle, *The Economic Times*, an influential Indian newspaper, for example, wrote: "Although official circles refrain from commenting on President de Gaulle's proposal for a return to a gold standard for international exchange and for a new world monetary system founded on something more than the dollar and the pound sterling, there is little doubt that the Union government would take a dim view of such a proposal, should it be pressed before the International Monetary Fund."[1]

In general the negative attitude to changes in the monetary system on the basis of the gold standard conformed to the official views of Washington and London. Business and government circles of these two world financial centres hastened to voice objections to de Gaulle's proposal and offered assurances that the monetary system required no radical change and that it was not anticipated.

It is in this vein of pacifying world opinion that President Johnson's message to Congress was coached. The connection between this message, made public on February 10, and de Gaulle's statement in France a week earlier is per-

---

[1] *The Economic Times*, February 6, 1965.

fectly obvious. The dispute of the two presidents across the Atlantic became a new landmark in the development of the crisis. To muffle the crisis by all possible measures without emerging beyond the bounds of the existing system—such was the opinion of US finance capital. This was also the purpose of Johnson's programme which incorporated ten points; in submitting it to Congress the President claimed that it was fully adequate for eliminating the monetary and financial difficulties. Normalisation of the balance of payments was regarded as the chief means. "On the basis of searching study of the major causes of our continued imbalance of payments," the President wrote in his message to Congress, "I therefore propose the following program[1]:

"First, to maintain and strengthen our checkrein on foreign use of U.S. capital markets. I ask Congress to extend the interest equalization tax for 2 years beyond December 31, 1965; to broaden its coverage to nonbank credit of 1 to 3 year maturity.

"Second, to stem and reverse the swelling tide of U.S. bank loans abroad, I have used the authority available to me under the Gore amendment to the act to apply the interest equalization tax to bank loans, of 1 year or more.

"Third, to stop any excessive flow of funds to Canada under its special exemption from the equalization tax, I have sought and received firm assurance that the policies of the Canadian government are and will be directed toward limiting such outflows to the maintenance of a stable level, of Canada's foreign exchange reserves.

"Fourth, to limit further the outflow of bank loans, I am asking the Chairman of the Board of Governors of the Federal Reserve System in co-operation with the Secretary of Treasury to enroll the Banking Community in a major effort to limit their lending abroad.

"Fifth, to ensure the effective co-operation of the banking community, I am requesting legislation to make voluntary co-operation by American bankers in support of our balance-of-payments efforts, under the government's auspices, exempt from the antitrust laws wherever such co-operation is essential to the national interest.

---

[1] *The Department of State Bulletin*, March 1, 1965, p. 283.

"Sixth, to reduce the outflow of business capital, I am directing the Secretary of Commerce and the Secretary of the Treasury to enlist the leaders of American business in a national campaign to limit their direct investment abroad, their deposits in foreign banks, and their holding of foreign financial assets until their efforts—and those of all Americans—have restored balance in the country's international accounts.

"Seventh, to minimize the foreign exchange costs of our defense and aid programs, I am directing the Secretary of Defense, the Administrator of AID (Agency for International Development) and other officials immediately to step up their efforts to cut overseas dollar cost to the bone.

Eighth, to narrow our tourist gap, I encourage our friends from abroad as well as our own citizens, to 'see the U.S.A.', and I request legislation further to limit the duty-free exemption of American tourists returning to the United States.

"Ninth, to earn more trade dollars, I am calling for a redoubling of our efforts to promote exports.

"Finally, to draw more investment from abroad. I am requesting new tax legislation to increase the incentives for foreigners to invest in U.S. corporate securities."

It is indicative that, when putting forward the programme of efforts for regulating the balance of payments and defending the dollar, the President did not miss the chance to offer comforting assurances. According to his message, there was no reason for fears about the future of the dollar. Those who hoped to weaken the dollar, hoped in vain. "The world willingly uses our dollars as a safe and convenient medium of international exchange," President Johnson wrote. He added right there and then: "But we cannot—and do not—assume that the world's willingness to hold dollars is unlimited."[1]

In an attempt to demonstrate the strong side of the US financial position, President Johnson, like other officials, emphasised that the United States as a creditor country had public and private liabilities of foreigners totalling $ 88,000 million or $ 37,000 million more than foreigners had in the United States. This wholesale lumping together of long-

---

[1] *The Department of State Bulletin*, March 1, 1965, p. 283.

term investments with short-term liabilities and the undiffe-
rentiated comparison of both was done chiefly for propaganda
purposes: indeed, to make private capital act in conformity
with national, and not personal, interests is not an easy
task, to say the least. If in his programme the President all
the time laid emphasis on the desirability of co-operation
from bankers and industrialists with the government, he
did so for the very reason that such co-operation was absent.

The President's programme paid much attention to all
kinds of restrictions on the outflow of capital abroad. The
question was even raised of limiting direct investments,
though this followed from an understanding with business
community leaders. Thus, the expediency of introducing
American capital into foreign industry where the profit on
capital was higher was challenged. And all this was done
because of the dollar crisis which shook the mainstays of the
world dominance of US finance capital.

Private capital was faced with the necessity, contrary
to its nature, to renounce a higher profit abroad. It is difficult to conceive of better proof of capitalism's general crisis.
The export of capital for the first time after the advent of
imperialism ran up against not external but internal difficulties and contradictions of the capitalist system. The
social system of production and distribution came into
conflict with the private nature of appropriating profit—the
result of an entire society's labour. Continuation of the old
policy of absolutely unrestricted foreign investment threatened to completely undermine confidence in the dollar abroad
and to stimulate a flight from the dollar towards gold. This
intensified the tendency of exchanging dollars for American
gold. Here is the source of President Johnson's intention to
pool the efforts of the government with voluntary measures
of the US financial and industrial tycoons in order to curb
the outflow of capital from the country.

It cannot be said that the American bankers and industrialists were so naive as not to realise the danger of upsetting the capitalist monetary and financial system. They were
well aware that this would disorganise the credit relations
which bind the capitalist system into a single whole.

A touching scene of the unity between the financial
magnates with their government was enacted at the meeting

in the White House on February 18, 1965, a week after the President sent his message to Congress. The meeting was devoted to the questions raised in the President's programme. The official bulletin of the Department of State featured Johnson's speech at this conference under the heading "Government-Business Partnership on Balance-of-Payments Problems". This speech made by the President to the real rulers of the United States is characteristic in many respects.

"I asked you here to-day," the President said, "because you are America's leader in the world of international business and banking."[1] This was the truth: the men assembled in the White House personified US finance capital.

In his speech Johnson stated that in 1964 the outflow of private American capital ran to more than $ 2,000 million over 1963 and to more than $ 2,500 million over 1960.[2] The President thus noted the none-too-gratifying results of the measures the Government had employed since 1960 to curb the outflow of capital so as to regulate the balance of payments. He admitted that the measures being taken could result in private capital missing a chance to receive an additional profit but he expressed confidence that the country, industry and stockholders would have better opportunities for obtaining profit. "So I am asking you today to join hands with your Government in a voluntary partnership," Johnson said. "I am asking you to show the World that an aroused and a responsible business community in America can close ranks and make a voluntary program work."[3]

In conclusion Johnson drew attention to the need not only to curb the outflow of capital abroad but also to speed up the return of profits from abroad, which was one of the tasks most difficult to achieve since profit on capital in other countries was higher than in the USA. In such cases there is always the desire to reinvest profit in expanding production, to leave it on deposit in local banks, and so on.

While the "business community in America" represented in the White House was demonstrating to the world its

[1] *The Department of State Bulletin*, March 1, 1965, p. 283.
[2] Ibid., p. 336.
[3] Ibid.

"solidarity" and readiness to eliminate the difficulties facing it, the no less business-minded community united in the Federal Reserve System of US banks was preparing a bill which laid bare the country's worsened monetary and financial position.

This was a bill abolishing the gold security on deposits in the Federal Reserve System. It was swiftly railroaded through all the legislative links and acquired the force of law on March 3, 1965. The bill abolished the Act of 1945 under which the Federal Reserve System had to have gold security amounting to 25 per cent not only for its notes in circulation, but also for deposits of member banks.

The need for such security aroused no doubt because deposits are a source of the constantly functioning circulation media, bank money. With the help of their deposit accounts banks, often without the knowledge and consent of the Government, could create an inflational upswing of business activity that might lead to a derangement of circulation and credit. It was to avoid such a contingency that gold security of deposits, alongside security of Federal Reserve notes in circulation, was stipulated in the 1945 Act. Why was it necessary to abolish the gold backing of deposits early in 1965 when the clouds of crisis thickened over the American dollar and the world monetary system? The chief reason was that, owing to the outflow of US gold reserves in the previous few years, the gold stock drew close to the level where it might actually be less than that demanded by law for backing bank deposits with the Federal Reserve system and its notes in circulation combined.

Thus, on September 21, 1949, when the United States had a gold stock of about $ 23,400 million, the deposits of the Federal Reserve system and its notes in circulation amounted to $ 40,700 million, i.e., were secured by gold to the extent of 57.5 per cent. On December 31, 1964 the gold reserves dropped to $ 15,000 million, while the deposits and notes in circulation rose to $ 54,800 million, i.e., the gold security was 27.5 per cent. If the gold reserves were reduced by some $ 1,500 million, the law would actually be violated and the gold backing would drop below 25 per cent.

The US ruling circles acted quite simply: if the law does not conform to the emerging circumstances, all the worse

for the law. They simply annulled the law on gold security
of the deposits and thereby opened a loophole to inflation.
But these seemingly internal events in money circulation
were by no means isolated from a world monetary system
that was intimately linked with the US dollar.

The point is that one and the same gold stock served as
security for both deposits and notes of the Federal Reserve
System circulating within the country, and its liquid liabilities, notes and bills, circulating outside. If matters reached
a point when the internal circulation of bank notes lost
its gold security, all the more so was this the case as regards
external circulation. The free surplus of gold for external
operations connected with covering the balance-of-payments
deficit and maintaining the stability of the dollar was steadily shrinking.

Table 15 shows that after the security of deposits and notes
in circulation required by law, of the entire American gold
stock of $ 15,075 million at the end of 1964 only $ 1,376 million could be used for external operations linked with US
liquid liabilities. But the liquid dollar liabilities abroad
exceed this free surplus many times over.

In other countries which at the end of 1963 had $ 25,000
million in the form of reserves of foreign circulation media,
chiefly dollars and pounds, half consisted of dollars. Moreover, about $ 15,000 million foreign liquid assets were in
private hands, half of them in dollars[1]. As compared with all
this the free gold (above the gold backing of deposits and
notes in internal circulation) was insignificant.

These figures are from a statement by US Under-Secretary
of the Treasury on Monetary Affairs F. Deming made at
the University of Ohio in Columbus on April 29, 1965.
It may be assumed that he did not try to be very exact in
estimating the liquid liabilities of the United States abroad
because this could dampen the mood of his audience. He
spoke about American circulation media abroad which could
be presented and actually were presented for payment or
exchange for American gold.

Thus, by abolishing the gold backing of bank deposits
in the Federal Reserve System early in March 1965, US

---

[1] *The Department of State Bulletin*, June 14, 1965, p. 957.

Table 15

Consolidated Reserve Position of the Federal Reserve Banks
(million dollars)

	As of 21 September 1949	As of 31 December 1963	As of 31 December 1964
F. R. Bank deposits	17,523	18,392	19,454
F. R. notes	23,248	32,878	35,342
Liabilities requiring reserves	40,771	51,270	54,796
Required reserves:			
Against deposits	4,381	4,598	4,864
Against notes	5,812	8,220	8,835
Total required reserves . .	10,193	12,818	13,699
Free gold certificate holdings	13,247	2,419	1,376
Gold certificate reserves . .	23,440	15,237	15,075
Ratio of gold certificate reserves to deposit and net liabilities (per cent) . . .	57.5	29.7	27.5

S o u r c e: *Federal Reserve Bulletin*, February 1965, p. 230.

legislators wanted to release more than $ 4,800 million in gold, which is shown in Table 15 as reserves against deposits, and to bring up the amount of free gold to $ 6,000 million. In this way, they sought to demonstrate the readiness of the United States to continue to utilise its gold for maintaining the convertibility of the dollar in world circulation, but all they actually showed was that the gold basis of the dollar had shrunk.

Mr. Deming assured his listeners that "the reserve currency status of the dollar is greatly buttressed by the fact that the United States is the only country which stands ready to deliver gold at the fixed price of $ 35 an ounce to foreign monetary authorities upon request".[1] From this it followed

---

[1] Ibid., p. 956.

that the ruling circles of the United States still hoped to
preserve the monetary system unchanged, but this required
a great exertion of effort, up to changing internal legislation
related to money circulation.

In view of the increased difficulties in preserving the
mainstays of the world monetary system, the problem of
liquid assets in world circulation arose. Official US circles
tried to utilise it for proving the need to preserve dollars
in world circulation as the main component in world liquid
resources. Transition to the gold standard, in their opinion,
might produce world deflation. When the question was
broached of raising the price of gold in dollars, they emphasised
that the USSR as a country having a substantial gold-producing industry would be the winner. Wittingly or unwittingly, this led to the necessity of preserving the dollar as a
means for the penetration of American capital into other
countries. "The dollar in this capacity," Under-Secretary of
the Treasury Joseph W. Barr stated on September 21, 1968,
"is held by private banks, business and individuals throughout the world as a medium of exchange for their international transactions."[1] He saw in the fact that the dollar as
a national currency has international circulation only a
blessing for the rest of the capitalist world. Referring to
the authority of another financier Robert Roose, Barr saw
the positive role of the dollar in that national resources
could easily be invested in a liquid form on similar terms
of return. Offering a definition of liquidity, Barr stated:
"For the world as a whole, you would probably define liquidity as the amounts of acceptable international resources
(gold, convertible currencies and automatic credit at the
IMF) available for trade, finance and reserves."[2] This shows
that the American official viewpoint on liquidity was confined
to purely quantitative bounds of international circulation
media. Consequently, there could be only a question of
quantitative characteristics: whether there was a large or
small quantity of a particular circulation medium, gold
or dollars.

---

[1] *Vital Speeches of the Day*, No. 1, 1968, p. 18.
[2] Ibid., p. 20.

Such a formulation of the question makes it clear that in the capitalist monetary system dollars as liquid resources in international circulation ensure trade and other payments. But these liquid assets themselves are a liability of the United States issued by the Federal Reserve System. As such, they are in effect a liability of this system payable to the holder. Under the economic law of the circulation of bank notes, they must return to the bank that issued them when a definite cycle of circulation is completed (e.g., redemption of a discounted bill) or if the bank notes are in surplus in circulation and are presented to be exchanged for gold. The whole point, however, is that this law of circulation of bank notes was violated. The United States, as shown above, in the first quarter of 1965 was already unable to exchange the dollars in world circulation for gold. It was this that increased the strain in the international capitalist monetary system.

It goes without saying that the United States could ease this tension were it not for the balance-of-payments deficit and were the favourable balance of trade preserved. This would mean that other countries would cover their deficit in trade with the United States with the US dollars they hold. On the other hand, this would mean that the United States would pay for its liquid liabilities with its exports.

The same problem could be solved by restraining the export of capital, by stepping up the influx of profits on US capital invested earlier in other countries. But although under the item of profits on capital there were considerable net receipts in the US balance of payments, they could not eliminate its deficit. It is not surprising that a new massive outflow of gold began in 1965 and the law on the gold cover of deposits of the Federal Reserve System had to be abolished in order to satisfy the demand for American gold in exchange for dollars.

On the whole, the monetary system of capitalism entered the second half of the 1960s in no better shape than in the first half.

The main reason was rooted in the weakening of the international financial positions of the United States and Britain, the two countries whose currencies form the foundation of the capitalist monetary system. Thus, the gold stock of the

United States dropped from $ 17,800 million at the end
of 1960 to $ 16,000 million in 1962 and to $ 14,000 million
at the end of 1965. On the other hand, US liquid liabilities
to other countries at the end of 1965 exceeded $ 29,000 mil-
lion as compared with $ 24,000 million at the end of 1962. [1]
Thus, the gold reserves decreased by $ 2,000 million between
1962 and 1965, while liquid liabilities grew by $ 5,000 mil-
lion.

In the first half of the 1960s the gold stock of Britain
reduced slightly: at the end of 1960 it amounted to $ 2,800
million; in 1962 to $ 2,600 million and at the end of 1965
to $ 2,300 million; on the other hand, her external liquid
liabilities in foreign currency at the end of 1965 exceeded
$ 5,900 million as against $ 2,900 million at the end of 1962.
To this we have to add Britain's external liabilities in sterling which, in terms of dollars, reached $ 12,700 million at
the end of 1965 as compared with $ 10,700 million at the
end of 1962. Most of the sterling liabilities were in North
America ($ 7,100 million) and countries of the sterling area
($ 5,300 million).[2]

The swift growth of the external liquid liabilities of
countries whose money represented the key currencies in
the monetary system of the capitalist world, threatened
to develop the crisis further, the more so because the balance
of payments of both the United States and Britain was
unfavourable. In the mid-1960s the weakest link in the entire
system was Britain, whose financial and commercial positions in the sterling area were weakened by competition
from other advanced capitalist countries.

Hence it is not by accident that Britain, which resorted
to an international loan of $ 1,000 million dollars in 1964
had again to request an even bigger loan ($ 1,400 million)
in 1965. As the weakest link in the world monetary system,
Britain became the epicentre of the crisis in the next two
years.

---

[1] *International Financial Statistics*, No. 6, 1969, p. 322.
[2] Ibid., pp. 316-317.

THE ESSENCE OF THE MONETARY CRISIS
AND ITS MANIFESTATIONS.
DEVALUATION OF THE POUND

While in internal circulation, as pointed out earlier, gold can be replaced by paper money of mandatory circulation and by credit money, in world circulation paper money of mandatory circulation is out of the question. In world circulation gold can be replaced only by credit or bank money. The latter assume different forms—from bank notes or bills of central state banks and commercial drafts to the so-called current accounts in international banks. This clarifies Marx's statement that one of the principal costs of circulation is money itself (meaning gold) because it itself has value. Circulation of credit money presupposes that the unfavourable balance which arises in a particular period will be paid in gold by the country which has a balance-of-payments deficit. Marx, speaking of gold as world money, emphasised that "its function as a means of payment in the settling of international balances is its chief one".[1]

From this it follows that capitalist countries, as before, must have a reserve of real world money—gold. After the Second World War many capitalist countries were without the necessary reserves of gold. About three-quarters of the world stock of monetary gold was concentrated in the United States, and a large quantity of it was in private hands. This enhanced the role of credit or bank money. Thus, American dollars, as a form of bank money, began to play a big part in world circulation. But their role was not independent of

---

[1] Karl Marx, *Capital*, Vol. I, p. 143.

gold. The relationship between dollars and gold lay in the fact that the United States always expressed readiness to exchange its dollars for gold at the fixed price, and actually did so. The need for world media of circulation after the war frequently compelled other countries to use dollars in mutual settlements and this ensured them a place in the channels of world circulation and the reserves of other countries.

After the Second World War the British pound, like the American dollar, regained its role as a world currency. This was facilitated by the fact that London was the financial centre of the British Commonwealth. The Commonwealth countries used the British pound as a convenient substitute for gold in their mutual settlements. Concentrating their foreign exchange holdings in London banks, these countries created a basis for sterling acting as an international currency, although the gold reserves of Britain were actually much smaller than those of the United States.

Thus, the monetary system of capitalism consisted of three main components—gold, US dollars and British pounds.

Moreover, in the first two decades after the war countries like France, the Federal Republic of Germany, Italy, Belgium and Holland which restored their economy and money circulation, accumulated considerable reserves of gold as well as dollars and pounds. It is natural that the currencies of France, the FRG and some other countries often began to play the role of international circulation media.

In accordance with the rules of the IMF, the currencies of these countries acquired the status of convertible currencies. On the basis of the same rules, these states were obliged to exchange their currency at the official rate during international settlements either for gold directly, or for the convertible currency of the USA and Britain. In this case too we have a connection of national convertible currencies with gold. It was reinforced by the fact that the exchange rates of the convertible national currencies of the above countries, according to the IMF rules, must not fluctuate from gold parity (the gold content) and also in relation to the dollar by more than 1 per cent either way, and for Common Market countries by 0.75 per cent.

This gave rise to the multinational nature of the international currency circulation on the basis of national currencies, which sooner or later had to come into contradiction with the world hegemony of the USA and Britain.

It was this contradiction that made itself felt in the 1960s, when it became clear that in world circulation the US dollar and the British pound had become severed from the gold basis and as credit money were not adequately secured either by liquid international liabilities of other countries or gold. This became obvious when the United States and the Gold Pool which supported it faced big difficulties in maintaining the price of gold at $ 35 per ounce.

The multinational nature of international money circulation on the basis of various currencies, whether wanted or not by international financial circles, tended to weaken the international monetary hegemony of Britain and the United States, and to restore the direct functioning of gold as world money, which was expressed in the exceedingly big redistribution of gold between capitalist countries.

Today it is beyond doubt that the gold standard is possible only in the form of a restoration of the role of gold in intergovernmental circulation. Attempts to return to a gold standard in national money circulation of capitalist countries apparently can no longer rest on a solid foundation. But in internal circulation of capitalist countries too the interests of private capital dictate a certain liberalisation of the market circulation of gold, as evidenced by the existence of a number of world gold markets.

One of the most important of them is located in London. In keeping with tradition, it was via London that newly mined gold of different countries entered the reserves of Britain herself and also of other capitalist states. That is why many financial operations linked with regulating the rates of currencies not only of Britain herself and the United States but also of other countries were effected in London, the more so, since the Bank of England acted as the chief agent of the Gold Pool.

But the situation in the mid-1960s was such that the Bank of England had to concentrate efforts on defending its own currency—the pound. The large sums accumulated in the reserves of other capitalist countries in the form of liquid liabilities of Britain in sterling and foreign exchange were becoming superfluous as the convertibility of other currencies was consolidated. The need for pounds among the countries of the sterling area also declined to the extent to which Britain yielded her place in their foreign trade to other capitalist states. The growing strength of the West European Common Market, to which British capital sought admission, was particularly unfavourable for Britain.

The external economic position of Britain and consequently also of her currency was complicated by the fact that her balance of payments remained adverse despite all the exertions of the government to eliminate it. This further increased the pressure of the external liquid liabilities of Britain on her finances.

To protect the pound, Britain had to utilise her gold and foreign exchange reserves and the big international loans received in 1964 and 1965. She was the first among the principal capitalist countries to raise the Bank Rate which fluctuated at 6-7 per cent, in other words, was 2-3 per cent higher than in other West European countries and the United States.

But an increase of the Bank Rate as a measure of attracting loan capital (foreign and its own) has meaning and produces a positive result only during an upswing of economic activity in the country, and this was not the case in Britain. Without it a high interest on loan capital misses the mark. It may produce undesirable consequences, restraining internal credit and money circulation, and adversely affecting business activity. Such was actually the situation of Britain's economy when it entered the second half of the 1960s.

International financial circles were extremely worried by the emerging situation, which was reflected in the activity of international financial organisations, conferences, meetings and other forums. The danger of the oncoming crisis of the monetary system kept the international circles on edge and impelled them to look for ways to prevent the catastrophe. It was in this situation that the idea of a reform of the international monetary system originated. It cannot be claimed that it was universally welcomed.

The substance of the reform idea amounted to a decision to create a special fund within the IMF framework for furnishing emergency loans to members of the organisation when difficulties arise owing to a balance-of-payments deficit and currency rate fluctuations. For these loans to act swiftly and automatically, the system of Special Drawing Rights (SDR) was introduced. Hence the name of the reform—the creation of SDRs.

Having such rights in accordance with its quota in the Fund, the needy country is able to receive through the IMF the sum needed for covering the deficit in the balance of payments. Accordingly, the sum of the SDRs of the given country will be reduced, while the SDRs of the country to which these drawing rights were transferred during settlements on the balance of payments, will be increased.

It is easy to see that the volume of credit is expanded in the given case. Such a situation is unjustified and even dangerous because it compels countries which already have a balance-of-payments deficit to aggravate the situation by putting off the final redemption of the credits with real values for an indefinite period. Either exported goods or gold can serve as these real values. But such conditions may not materialise.

In a word, there were a number of weighty considerations against introducing SDRs at a time when not all the efforts to preserve the monetary system in its previous form had been exhausted.

Serious differences on a reform of the monetary system arose at the 21st IMF annual session (Washington, September 1966) and the 22nd session (Rio de Janeiro, September 1967). They were attended by representatives of IMF member states who reflected the official views of their governments.

At both sessions the US delegate, Secretary of the Treasury G. Fowler, spoke up in favour of creating the SDR system in the IMF or of additional means of international payments.

Opposing the view of the US delegate, the French representative, the then Minister of the Economy and Finances Michel Debré, also favoured a reform of the monetary system, but on the basis of returning to a gold standard not subordinated to the dollar. The arguments of both were highly indicative of the monetary and financial policy of the USA and France.

While Washington's policy, despite the expressed desire for a reform of the monetary system (which previously it had in effect rejected), proceeded from the desire to preserve the mainstays of the system based on the domination of the dollar, France's policy aimed at advancing gold to the fore, in particular, at raising its price considerably. The latter measure was to increase the value of the stock of world monetary gold in terms of currencies and thereby ensure the selfsame international "liquidity", whose scarcity, according to American official spokesmen, already faced capitalist countries. The further continuation of the policy of introducing dollars into world circulation by using dollars for covering the deficit of the US balance of payments was regarded in French financial circles as the cause of the "world tendency toward inflation". From this followed France's request that US ruling circles stop covering the balance-of-payments deficit in a way that promotes its financial and economic expansion at the expense of other countries.

US representatives at international forums and in the press kept harping on the same note: the increase in the price of gold would supposedly give unjustified advantages to the countries which had already accumulated a substantial stock of gold, or to gold-producing countries. Moreover, they missed no opportunity of reproaching France for accumulating gold.

These rather strange arguments failed to consider the fact that the countries which succeeded in accumulating gold reserves (France, FRG, Italy, Belgium, Netherlands, Switzerland and others) had done so, as the United States did previously, because of a favourable balance of payments. Consequently, these reserves embodied national labour which was undervalued owing to the low price of gold in dollars.

An increase in the price of gold could only remove this injustice. If it were a question of "benefit" the United States itself would gain to the same extent from the higher price of gold. But the whole point was that such a measure would be in effect a devaluation of the dollar. It would undermine the role of the dollar in the international monetary system and deprive US finance capital of a powerful instrument of foreign expansion and easy covering of the country's balance-of-payments deficit.

As for the price of gold in the context of a reform of the monetary system, a convincing argument was presented in articles by J. Rueff published in *Le Monde* and in *The Wall*

Street Journal on June 5-7, 1969. "The gold price," he wrote, "was fixed at the present level in 1934 by President Roosevelt. Since then, all prices in the United States have more than doubled."[1]

While international financial circles engaged in debates over a reform of the financial system, the objective economic laws were impelling the capitalist monetary system towards a radical change.

In 1966 the balance of payments of the USA and Britain, as in preceding years, was unfavourable, whereas France's balance of payments was favourable. In view of this, the American and, especially, the British press frequently carried articles voicing anxiety over the financial policy of Paris. It is no departure from the truth to say that as early as 1966 the American and British press expressed opinions directed against France's policy of freeing the country from dollar monetary dependence. At the same time the possibility of playing on French-West German contradictions in the Common Market were probed. Indicative in this respect was the article the British *Economist* printed in August 1966 under the title "French Reserves: Whose Burden?". The article unambiguously revealed the British and US opposition to the policy of France and her demands for restoring the gold standard. The British journal stated that "when General de Gaulle stepped up his gold offensive eighteen months ago, some international financial officials in America and Europe (meaning, of course, primarily Britain.—*A.S.*) played down the likely damage by suggesting that France itself might be reaching the end of its surplus, and therefore its capacity for financial trouble-making".[2]

But, the journal noted further, these circles "were wrong". This is followed by proof: in 1965 France had a favourable balance of payments of about $ 1,000 million.

While the world reserves of monetary gold increased by $ 250 million, France increased her reserves by $ 1,000 million. Moreover, *The Economist* noted anxiously, in the first seven months of 1966 French gold reserves had risen by almost another $ 500 million to reach $ 5,160 million.

---

[1] *The Wall Street Journal*, June 9, 1969.
[2] *The Economist*, August 13, 1966, p. 668.

The journal then compared the gold reserves of France with the reserves of gold and foreign exchange in the FRG. The conclusion was that the French gold stock was already $ 800 million greater than in the FRG, while France was behind in its foreign exchange reserves. A comparative table of the gold and foreign exchange reserves of France and the FRG is given as of June 30, 1966—the French gold stock was $ 5,026 million and the FRG's $ 4,310 million. The foreign exchange reserves of France amounted to $ 795 million, and of the FRG to $ 1,884 million.[1]

The London *Times* also came out against the French monetary and financial policy. It complained that France was utilising her favourable balance of payments and her "surplus dollars have been steadily converted into gold".[2]

Arguments about the supposed inadequacy of the monetary reserves in capitalist countries were put forward. While, in ten years (1958-1968) international trade had doubled and invisible exports had risen by 40 per cent, the monetary reserves of capitalist countries amounted only to five months of world imports. By the way, this point does not prove anything, since no one has studied to what extent clearing and other settlements increased.

Besides attacks on the monetary and financial policy of France in the US and British press, attempts were made to impede French exports, infringe France's balance of payments and bring about an outflow of capital. This was facilitated by the fact that during the first half of the 1960s, France was a country of cheap credit. If we compare the discount rates of the central banks of different countries over a number of years, we find that Britain and the United States, more than other countries, resorted to measures of governmental credit regulations to influence private capital in the interests of their financial policy.

Table 16 shows that at the end of 1965 Britain had the highest Bank Rate. She outstripped in this respect Japan, despite the high cost of Japanese credit. In Japan this was explained by the increased demand for loan capital owing to the swift industrial growth rate and the high business

---

[1] *The Economist*, August 13, 1966, p. 668.
[2] *The Times*, September 1, 1966.

Table 16

Discount Rate of Central Banks
(end of year, in per cent per annum)

	1958	1960	1963	1965
United States	2.50	3.00	3.50	4.50
Britain	4.00	5.00	4.00	6.00
France	4.50	3.50	4.00	3.50
FRG	3.00	4.00	3.50	4.00
Italy	3.50	3.50	3.50	3.50
Switzerland . .	2.50	2.00	2.00	2.50
Canada	3.74	3.50	4.00	4.75
Japan	7.30	6.94	5.84	5.48

S o u r c e. *International Financial Statistics*, No 2, 1966, p. 21.

profits. In Britain the high Bank Rate was explained by a financial policy designed to attract foreign money capital and encourage the repatriation of British capital, and also profits on formerly invested capital abroad.

For creditor countries like the USA and Britain the item of profit on capital abroad is of great importance in the balance of payments. Suffice it to say that between 1963 and 1965 annual profits on capital abroad in the balance of payments of the United States amounted on average to $ 5,050 million and of Britain, to $ 1,157 million. But this revenue could not compensate for the external expenditures on other items. As a result, under the current balance, exclusive of the movement of capital (IMF Statistics includes profit on capital in the current balance), the United States had during this period an average annual payments deficit of $ 2,875 million and Britain a deficit of $ 506 million. Here was the root cause of US and British financial troubles.

It is characteristic that foreign investment income of the USA (profit on capital invested abroad, exclusive of undistributed profit) in the 1966 balance amounted to $ 6,200 million, or only $ 300 million more than in 1965. Yet private American assets abroad rose by $ 5,000 million. Consequently, the growth of investment receipts from the outside in the balance of payments did not correspond to the increase of American assets abroad, specifically new investments of private American capital. In 1966 the latter amounted to $ 3,900 million.[1]

While new private capital investments abroad totalled $ 3,900 million in 1966 and private American assets rose by $ 5,000 million, or by more than $ 1,000 million, where could this sum come from if not from the profit on capital left abroad despite the government's appeals to repatriate more profits.

According to the Economic Report of the President submitted to Congress in January 1967, profit on American capital in the manufacturing industry of West European countries amounted to 12-14 per cent between 1962 and 1965.[2] But they were far from being fully repatriated. This once again demonstrates that profit on long-term and, even more so, on direct investments of private American as well as British capital abroad no longer acted as the mainstay of the balance of payments when the monetary crisis of the 1960s developed. Motivated by their private interests, investors abroad refrained from repatriating a considerable part of the profit, especially in expectation of a further aggravation of the monetary crisis and the devaluation of the dollar and the pound.

The United States and Britain, although creditor countries, continued to export capital, notwithstanding the obvious symptoms of a monetary derangement and the huge sums of their liquid liabilities accumulated abroad. The dollar and the pound, as it were, remained vehicles for the movement of long-term private capital abroad. Discharging this function, dollars and pounds remained in international circulation and in the reserves of other countries as liquid liabilities subject to payment in gold or commodity exports.

The external liquid liabilities of the United States, which amounted to $ 29,800 million in 1966, reached $ 33,100 million in 1967. Respectively the liabilities of Britain in pounds and foreign exchange rose respectively from $ 21,700 million to $ 22,800 million.[3]

---

[1] *Federal Reserve Bulletin*, April 1967, p. 505.
[2] *The Department of State Bulletin*, February 27, 1967.
[3] *International Financial Statistics*, No. 6, 1969, pp. 316, 322.

But a circumstance pointing to the extremely precarious position of the pound was revealed in the movement of the external liquidity of Britain in 1967. Britain's liquid external liabilities in pounds unexpectedly decreased from $13,300 million to $ 12,300 million or by $ 1,000 million. At the same time its liabilities, or to put it more simply, debts, in foreign currencies rose from $ 8,400 million to $ 10,500 million, or by $ 2,000 million.[1] Thus what would seem to be a positive development, a decrease in pound liabilities, was explained by the fact that Britain supported the pound with the help of foreign loans. For a private debtor a reduction of his old debt with the help of new borrowing offers no way out of the situation; nor was it for Britain. Her difficulties piled up in 1967.

The cardinal issue facing international financial circles in 1967 in its full magnitude could be briefly defined as the problem of the price of gold. The capitalist world was swiftly losing faith in the stability of the dollar and the pound and pinning its hopes on gold. The exchange of US and British currency for gold, the unceasing demand for monetary gold gave rise to the tendency towards a rise in the price of gold in international markets, primarily, in London. To stem these tendencies the machinery of the Gold Pool had to operate at full capacity. But this merely increased the outflow of gold from the reserves of the USA and other Pool members. It is not surprising that the word "gold" began to figure more and more often in the capitalist press.

Early in January the drive against an increase in the price of gold was opened by the influential London *Times* with an article entitled "Powerful Voice Against Gold-Price Rise". The newspaper ascribed this powerful voice to Milton Gilbert, economic advisor to the Bank for International Settlements, and undertook to examine the problem of gold because the French economist Rueff, the well known proponent of raising the price of gold, was scheduled to speak in London on the following day, and in the same month the Group of Ten was to hold its next meeting together with IMF top officials on the problem of gold. Thus, the newspaper hastened to condition the mind of its readers accordingly.

---

[1] Ibid.

It is difficult to say to what extent it succeeded, but it did cite some essential facts. Referring to the annual gold review of the First National City Bank of New York, it reported that in 1966 "all of the newly mined gold went into private hand". According to estimates, it amounted to about 1,500 tons.[1] Yet the official world gold stock even declined somewhat. According to *The Times*, in 1965 of the 2,000 tons of newly mined gold only 250 tons found their way into official monetary reserves.

But those who bought gold paid for it not in gold but in currency, chiefly in dollars and pounds. It is easy to understand the newspaper's alarm: all this pointed to a desire to get rid of American and British currency, to convert it into gold, which threatened to deepen the monetary crisis.

The central banks of the leading capitalist countries, for their part, succeeded in considerably increasing the share of gold in their monetary reserves.

The newspaper pointed out that as of September 1966 the share of gold in total monetary reserves of countries was as follows (percentage): Switzerland over 90; France, the Republic of South Africa and the Netherlands 80-90; Belgium and Spain 70-80; the FRG, Italy, Venezuela, Britain and Portugal 60-70; Australia and Canada 40-60; India, Mexico, Sweden and Denmark 20-40; Japan, Austria and Norway 10-20 per cent.

Thus the striving to accumulate gold was displayed not only by private persons but also by central banks, which tried to have more gold, rather than convertible currencies, in their reserves. More than half of the 20 countries listed had over 60 per cent of their reserves in gold.

In view of this, the British and US press assigned a special place to French financial policy. In January 1967 *The Economist* reported France's intention to liberalise her gold market and withdraw from the Gold Pool. Indeed, at the end of January France did liberalise her gold market and her monetary and financial relations with other countries up to the free import and export of gold, foreign exchange and securities. In the summer the Bank of France withdrew from

---

[1] *The Times*, January 3, 1967.

the Gold Pool, not wishing to spend French gold on supporting the US dollar.

France's liberalisation of her monetary and financial
operations with other countries early in 1967 was premature.
The monetary system based on the dollar and the pound
was not yet sufficiently undermined. Washington's financial policy was still supported by international financial
circles.

The essence of liberalising the financial relations of France
with other countries, under the law of December 28, 1966,
which came into force on January 31, 1967, was the unlimited convertibility of the franc, abolition of all foreign-ex-
change restrictions, including those on free money transfers,
imports and exports of gold, money and securities; liberalisation of the issue of foreign securities and investments
(except direct, on which some restrictions were preserved),
and so on. France thereby demonstrated her readiness to
support a change in the monetary system on the basis of
the gold standard.

On February 8, 1967 Georges Pompidou, who at that time
was the Prime Minister, speaking at a luncheon in the Association of Economic and Financial Correspondents, stated,
not without grounds, that the "international monetary system was functioning poorly because it gave advantages to
countries with a reserve currency: these countries can afford
inflation without paying for it". He reaffirmed what had been
said by General de Gaulle two years earlier, stressing that
France regarded gold as the only solid basis for an international monetary system because it did not yield to manipulations. He admitted that for this reason France had
converted a considerable part of her exchange reserves into
gold.

We showed earlier that other countries too did not lag
behind France in this respect. As a result, the exchange rate
of the pound began to decline and the price of gold to rise.
To maintain the rate of the pound, it was necessary to use
a considerable part of the gold and foreign exchange reserves
of Britain and of the Gold Pool. The demand for gold mounted; at the end of 1967 only in five days 80 tons of gold were
sold on the London market. On some days 20 tons were sold,
which was several times greater than normal operations in

12*

London. The efforts to restrain its price made it necessary
for Gold Pool members to sell part of their gold reserves
on the market. All this spread uncertainty in internationas
financial circles.

Apprehensions arose that the chain of monetary relations,
strained to the extreme, would break at its weakest link,
namely the British pound. These apprehensions were inten-

Table 17

**Britain's External Liabilities
and Claims in Sterling**
(million pounds)

	1963	1964	1965	1966	September 1967
Liabilities					
Total	4,859	5,409	6,016	6,397	6,204
Overseas sterling countries . .	2,942	3,048	3,061	3,074	2,991
International organisations	627	991	1,481	1,656	1,439
Claims					
Total	667	1,110	1,151	1,236	1,292
Overseas sterling countries . .	350	457	466	483	493
Net Liabilities . .	3,892	4,299	4,865	5,161	4,912
Overseas sterling countries . .	2,592	2,591	2,595	2,591	2,498
International organisations	627	991	1,481	1,656	1,439

sified by the continued deterioration of Britain's balance
of trade.

It can be seem from Table 17 that the sum of liabilities
of both Britain and sterling area countries decreased in 1967.
This was linked with the commencing outflow of foreign
sterling deposits from British banks, the forced redemption
of some liabilities in view of the increased centrifugal forces
in the sterling area, and so on. The decrease in Britain's
sterling liabilities concealed not a strengthening but a

weakening of the country's financial position in general and in the sterling area in particular. The latter was especially dangerous for the pound.

Investments of private British capital abroad continued during the first half of 1967; in the first quarter £ 84 million were invested and in the second quarter £ 78 million. But at the same time foreign, chiefly American, capital was invested in Britain and, moreover, a long-term credit was received from the US Export-Import Bank for the purchase by Britain of the latest American aircraft for £ 19 million in the first quarter and £ 23 million in the second quarter, and as a result the balance of capital movements proved to be "favourable" on the whole.

During the first half of 1967 Britain's balance of payments deteriorated.

Table 18 shows that in the first half of 1967 the balance of current account in visible and invisible trade was unfavourable. The unfavourable balance in the first half reached £ 103 million. This was almost twice as high as the unfavourable balance of current account on visible and invisible trade in 1966.

Nor is it difficult to see the main cause of the unfavourable balance on visible and invisible trade. It consisted of the excessively burdensome so-called governmental invisible payments, chiefly the military expenditure abroad, connected with Britain's participation in NATO and her support of aggressive US policy. It is also characteristic that in the second quarter of 1967, when Britain was faced with extremely serious monetary and financial difficulties threatening a devaluation of the pound, the government spent £ 30 million ($ 84 million) on the purchase of US aircraft and missiles.

Britain thus entered the third quarter of 1967 with a clearly worsened condition of external accounts. At the end of June her gold and foreign exchange reserves amounted to £ 1,012 million (about $ 2,834 million) as compared with £ 1,118 million (about $ 3,130 million) in January. Gold amounted to £ 610 million in her monetary reserves ($ 1,708 million).[1] Under the normal course of foreign pay-

---

[1] *Bank of England Quarterly Bulletin*, No. 4, 1967, December, p. 424.

Table 18

Britain's Balance of Payments
(million pounds)

	1964	1965	1966	1967	
				first quarter	second quarter
Imports (f.o.b.)	5,014	5,053	5,221	1,426	1,428
Exports (f.o.b.)	4,471	4,784	5,110	1,344	1,339
Visible trade balance	—543	—269	—111	—82	—89
Payments by Britain to the United States, for aircraft and missiles	—2	—12	—41	—23	—30
Visible balance	—545	—281	—152	—105	—119
Government invisible payments	—432	—446	—460	—118	—117
Other invisible receipts and payments	+575	+617	+553	+205	+151
Current balance	—402	—110	—59	—18	—85

Source: *Bank of England Quarterly Bulletin*, No. 4, 1967, December, p. 416.

ments, when sterling countries kept their sterling balances in London and made through them a considerable part of their mutual settlements, no special complications arose. But the whole point is that the further accumulation of Britain's sterling liabilities became impossible. The desire to convert these liabilities into something more tangible raised the demand for gold in exchange for pounds. The desire to convert sterling into other currencies, gold and reliable securities exerted pressure on the rate of the pound. It

dropped to the lowest limit permissible by the IMF Rules—
$ 2,78 per pound (at the parity rate of $ 2.80). To avoid
a drop in the rate, Britain's financial agencies were compelled
to buy sterling and to spend either gold or convertible
foreign currency on maintaining its rate. A considerable
part of Britain's foreign loans were thus utilised for bolster-
ing up the shaky pound. But this did not eliminate the
danger.

Unable to convert pounds directly into gold, capitalists
playing at the stock exchanges first converted pounds into
dollars and other currencies and then rushed to buy gold in
all accessible markets—from Frankfurt-on-Main to Pretoria,
from Paris to London. Thus, the first result of the pound
crisis was a steep rise in the price of gold in the world
markets as compared with the official price fixed by the
IMF. This created a big threat to the American dollar,
because the official price of gold was fixed in dollars and was
guaranteed by the US Government. Thus, the difficulties
facing the pound seriously affected the US dollar, raised the
problem of the price of gold and cast doubt on the stability
of the entire capitalist monetary system. The crisis of the
pound was one of the striking forms in which the crisis of
the monetary system of capitalism and its general crisis
were displayed.

That is why international financial circles eagerly sought
a way out. Frequent meetings and conferences of financiers
and bankers were convened. Most of these forums were
marked by the exploration of a reform of the monetary system
and, on the whole, produced no results. They merely attested
to the inability of international financial circles to stem
the spread of the crisis, which reduced British finances to
a lamentable state at the end of 1967. But the raising of the
question at these assemblies is of interest from the viewpoint of the problems brought on by the crisis. That is why
we shall examine some of these meetings.

A meeting of financial experts to discuss aspects of the
world monetary system was held on January 16, 1967 in
Bologna, Italy. It was attended by exponents of two fundamentally opposed views: Professors Triffin and Bernstein,
on the one hand, and Jacques Rueff, on the other. The former
advocated the concept of liquidity and the latter upheld his

views on the need to go over to a gold standard and raise the price of gold. Naturally, this conference could not arrive at a common platform. It is known from press reports that Lord Robbins, the representative of the British business world, "called for the creation of an Atlantic monetary system controlled by the Atlantic community".[1] This, however, contained hardly anything new, since the postwar monetary system of capitalism was in effect controlled by the USA and Britain.

A meeting of American bankers was held in Pebble Beach, California, at the end of January and it was addressed by the then US Secretary of the Treasury Fowler. As could be judged from press reports, the bankers concentrated attention on practical matters. They particularly discussed the possibility of transition by the USA to limited convertibility of the dollar into gold. Thus, US bankers had already thought of refusing to exchange dollars for gold. Apparently, at that time they did not consider it advantageous to themselves, since not all the possibilities of the dollar as a means of financial and economic expansion of American monopoly capital had been exhausted.

The Foreign Ministers of Britain, the United States, France, the Federal Republic of Germany and Italy met at Chequers, the country residence of the British Prime Minister, on January 23 to discuss chiefly a reduction of central banks' discount rates. The need for this arose because an increase in discount rates as an instrument of credit policy began to restrain and derange national and international credit.

During 1967 Finance Ministers and bank governors of the Group of Ten countries met on a number of occasions. All these meetings invariably had to face the question of a reform of the monetary system, and the question was constantly shifted from one meeting to another (March 6 and June 19 in Paris, July 17 and August 26 in London, and others).

Lastly, the very same questions of a monetary reform were on the agenda of the 22nd annual session of the IMF, held in Rio de Janeiro between September 24 and 29, 1967.

---

[1] *The Times*, January 16, 1967

The session decided to set up, within the framework of the IMF, a special fund and the SDR system as a kind of prototype of an international currency.

We recall all these collective actions of capitalist countries, and especially the busy round of meetings by the Group of Ten which undertook to act as a fire-fighting brigade, to demonstrate that all these measures were incapable of preventing the imminent collapse of the British pound, the second world currency after the dollar.

The final act of the drama which ended in the devaluation of the pound was enacted between September and the first half of November. In fact, everything boiled down to one more attempt, with the help of international loans, to prevent the shaky pound from collapsing. In October agreement was reached with the Swiss Bank corporation, Swiss Credit Bank and the Union Bank of Switzerland on furnishing a loan of 450 million Swiss francs ($ 104 million) at an annual interest rate of 5.5 per cent to Britain. It is noteworthy that the Swiss bankers explained this step by the supposed desire to compensate, at least in part, the outflow of capital caused by the military events in the Middle East.

In November British financial agencies conducted negotiations with Swiss banks about a much bigger international loan—ranging from $1,000 to $3,000 million. The press even reported a supposed understanding on this point but the devaluation of the pound on November 18, 1967 spiked these reports.

The question arises of whether the Wilson Labour Government acted too hastily? Did it not miss the opportunity to receive one more international loan and thereby emerge from the difficult financial situation without resorting to devaluation? In our opinion, the devaluation of the pound became inevitable and the British Government, by taking its decision, acted in full conformity with the IMF rules, which do not allow a prolonged and considerable fluctuation of exchange rates from parity.

The rate of the pound as a convertible currency at parity of $ 2.80 per pound could not fluctuate more than $ 2.78-$ 2.82. In October-November the rate of the pound stood for a long time at the lowest boundary — $ 2.78. According to a statement by the Conservative Opposition, during the parliamentary debate after devaluation, the Government had spent up to $1,000 million from its reserves on maintaining the rate of the pound but had been unable to achieve any positive result.

Let us assume that on receiving a further big international loan the British Government had resumed its attempts to maintain the rate of the pound. It would be hardly possible to expect that the big sum of the loan would have stabilised the pound. The crux of the matter is that the mechanism for regulating a rate when it declines requires the creation of a shortage in the money market of the given currency and other liquid liabilities, bills of exchange and short-term treasury bills in the given national currency. Then those who need it for immediate payments will pay more for the given currency and its rate will naturally rise. But as regards the pound, this method failed for a number of reasons.

First, Britain had an unfavourable balance of payments and, consequently, she herself had to cover the deficit, and could not expect receipts of foreign exchange from other countries.

Second, her liquid liabilities to other countries were big, and therefore the former were able to demand the exchange of sterling liabilities for gold and foreign currency in amounts larger than Britain's reserves.

Third, by buying pounds and other British liabilities for foreign exchange received in the form of a loan (e.g., dollars), Britain's financial agencies increased the supply of dollars in the world market, which would inevitably reduce their rate. Lastly, the owners of dollars, on receiving them in exchange for pounds, could well claim to exchange them for gold. Thus, the cycle closed on gold, the demand for which actually rose sharply and the price of which was climbing. The devaluation of the pound was a logical consequence of the development of the monetary crisis and one of its manifestations.

But what is devaluation? It is the law-sanctioned reduction of the gold content of a national monetary unit, its depreciation, as it were. This means that all the balances in the given currency, no matter who owns them, are simultaneously depreciated. And since a huge part of the media of circulation is represented by liabilities of the central state bank, such a depreciation is simultaneously an admission of the fact that the bank is unable to redeem these liabilities at their former value. Devaluation is partial bankruptcy, enabling financial agencies to untie their hands at the expense of others. Hence it is not surprising that Engels once wrote: "Wealthy England secured relief by bankruptcies in its obligations toward the continent and America."[1] In 1967 devaluation was designed, if not in full then in part, to untie Britain's hands in relation to all holders of her liabilities within and outside the country.

Therefore, the degree of devaluation was of considerable significance. It infringed the interests of creditors, domestic and foreign, and also of all persons who had a fixed income in pounds, in favour of debtors and the biggest of them, the state itself. That is why the question of the degree of devaluation of the pound was the subject of discussion in international financial circles and was coordinated with the IMF.

It will be recalled that on November 18, 1967 the pound was devaluated by 14.3 per cent and its parity to the dollar became 1 : 2.40 ($ 2.40 per pound). This is a comparatively modest devaluation. It is smaller than the devaluation of the pound on September 18, 1949. At that time the parity of the pound to the dollar was reduced from 4.03 to 2.80 or by 30.5 per cent.

It is not surprising that, the day after the devaluation of the pound, devaluations began in sterling area countries and in countries which had very close financial and economic ties with Britain. The currencies of more than 20 countries were devalued to varying degrees. This was explained by the fact that the countries which had not only sterling balances in Britain but also liabilities in their own currency, sought to avoid one-sided harm.

It is also necessary to bear in mind the export advantages associated with devaluation. And in this respect countries which devalued their currencies did not want to lag behind Britain.

Stimulation of British exports was one of the practical tasks in devaluating the pound. It was the more urgent

---

[1] Karl Marx, *Capital*, Vol. III, Moscow, p. 493.

because the growth of British exports, keeping pace with the country's comparatively slow industrial development, lagged behind other advanced capitalist countries. Between 1959 and 1966 British exports increased by 47 per cent, while those of the United States rose by 72.5 per cent, France 94 per cent, FRG more than 100 per cent, Italy almost 180 per cent and Japan by over 100 per cent.

But the further development of the world monetary crisis showed that, in contrast to the devaluation of national currencies which are not convertible, the devaluation of currencies which have such a status in accordance with IMF rules does not exert a big stimulating effect on exports. The reason for this is that convertible currencies like the pound sterling are preserved in international circulation channels, even after devaluation, in quantities sufficient for interested countries to pay for imports after devaluation. Hence British exporters were deprived of the possibility of receiving the difference in the rate during the exchange of the currency obtained for their goods.

THE GOLD PROBLEM
AND THE FURTHER UNDERMINING
OF THE MONETARY SYSTEM

Devaluation can produce different results: in some cases it leads to a more or less prolonged financial equilibrium (the effect expected from the measure); in other cases it becomes merely a temporary interruption of the inflation process and a new stage in the development of the monetary crisis.

The devaluation of the pound in 1967 did not bring about a change for the better in Britain's financial situation. The crisis of the monetary system had become so deep that an individual country or group of countries could not break out of it through devaluation.

For Britain devaluation became a factor which somewhat eased the pressure of the internal debt and stimulated exports. But at the same time the centrifugal forces in sterling area countries were intensified, creating prerequisites for the further weakening of Britain's external economic position.

As for foreign trade, British exports rose from $13,869 million in 1967 to $14,812 million in 1968, or by 6.8 per cent. At the same time imports rose from $17,186 million to $18,520 million, or approximately by 7.7 per cent. In 1968 foreign trade improved as compared with 1967 in the sense that exports did not decline, as was the case in 1967 prior to devaluation. While in 1967 exports dropped from $14,132 million to $13,869 million, or by 1.8 per cent, the 6.8 per cent increase in 1968 may be regarded as a positive feature. But all this cannot be credited solely to devaluation. In any case, in a number of other countries the growth in exports was more substantial. Even in the United States, despite the slower growth of exports as a result of the war in Vietnam, they increased by 7.9 per cent. As for Japan, it registered a 24-per cent rise in exports in 1968. This shows that even without devaluation other countries continued to outstrip Britain in export growth rates.

Why was Britain unable to fully exploit all the advantages which could be expected from devaluation? Because at the moment of devaluation her liquid liabilities to other countries were very big. Let us assume that devaluation reduced the liabilities by about 14.3 per cent. They nevertheless remained too burdensome. From this angle moderate devaluation was clearly inadequate.

On the other hand, receipts from bigger exports became a source for redeeming a certain part of the liquid liabilities and consequently could not be utilised for developing the export-oriented industries so as to utilise the favourable export situation.

That is why, as soon as British foreign trade encountered the need to increase imports of raw material for accelerating industrial production, including output for export, difficulties in maintaining the current export-import balance began to make themselves felt. Instances of a dangerous reduction in the rate of the devalued pound began to recur.

But the financial difficulties of Britain in the post-devaluation period were no longer the main channel of the continued monetary crisis. Manifestations of the crisis appeared in the sphere where gold and the American dollar are interconnected. The tendencies to exchange dollars for gold or to buy gold for dollars mounted. This led to a steep rise in the price of gold. Only one means remained to restrain the price of gold—to satisfy the bigger demand by dumping new lots of gold on to the markets and exchanging the dollars directly presented to US financial agencies for American gold.

The task of maintaining the price of gold became the more difficult because after France's withdrawal from the Gold Pool in the summer of 1967 the efficiency of this organisation clearly diminished. Gold Pool members reluctantly sacrificed part of their reserves on maintaining the American dollar. In the meantime the gold stock of the United States shrank noticeably. At the end of 1967 it amounted to $ 12,065 million as compared with $ 13,235 million at the end of 1966, a decrease of about $ 1,200 million in one year.

In December 1967 the demand for gold remained at a high level. In the London market sales on some days reached up to 100 tons, many times the usual figure.

The rush for gold showed that this time mistrust of the dollar grew over into a panicky fear of devaluation, i.e., an official raising of the price of gold in dollars, as demanded by J. Rueff and other advocates of restoring the former role of gold in the world monetary system. Only this can explain the search for gold which was already under way at the end of 1967 and at the first stage was consummated in the huge "gold rush" in March 1968.

It arose from the desire of capitalists to have in their operational reserves of currency a guaranteed stock of gold and not the desire of hoarders of precious metals to acquire gold in order to satisfy their craving for it. Gold by no means disappeared from world circulation, as could be judged from the cessation of the growth of official world gold stocks at the disposal of financial agencies of capitalist states. We must not forget that the private capitalist sector is itself in need of gold. It is held by capitalists. That is why world gold smuggling is thriving. Therefore all the more unconvincing is the theory that gold is supposedly losing its role as world money and is being demonetised. As for the increase in its price by 15-20 per cent, this was said to result from the operations of hoarders and speculators.

It is important to note that such views originated in the Anglo-Saxon countries which have always worshipped the golden calf more than other countries. Matters went to such extremes that the London *Economist* with a serious air began to contrast Rueff's views about the need to enhance the role of gold and raise its price with Lenin's well-known statement that after the victory of the proletariat or of the socialist revolution on a worldwide scale gold could be used for building public lavatories. "Did Lenin know better than Rueff?"[1] was the title given by *The Economist* to the article. In it, apparently for the obvious purpose of frightening

---

[1] *The Economist*, December 2, 1967, p. 976.

Rueff's supporters, the journal pointed out that the USSR
was mining gold valued at between $150 and $400 million
annually and it had a gold stock estimated at between
$2,000 million and $7,000 million. As for the data about
gold in the USSR, their extremely doubtful precision should
be left on the conscience of the editors of *The Economist*.
But as regards the views of Lenin about gold simple decency
demanded that the journal should have not limited itself
to the ironic remark about public lavatories made of gold,[1]
but should have pointed out right there and then that Lenin
advised, until the victory over capitalism on a worldwide
scale, to save gold, sell it at the highest price and buy goods
with it at the lowest price. From this it follows that Lenin
did not mean that gold would be demonetised under capitalism and would cease to discharge its function as world money and as a medium of world circulation. It is easy to
understand why Lenin spoke so scornfully about gold during
the complete victory over capitalism. As for Lenin's approach
to gold from the purely economic viewpoint, he did not regard it with contempt.

At the beginning of the 1920s Lenin expected to use the
gold fund as a means of production. He considered this
theoretically and practically correct, and it was only because
of the extreme necessity of easing the food difficulties of the
working class that he arrived at the conclusion: "Contrary
to our old Programme the gold reserve must be used for
consumer goods."[2]

In this context we consider unjustified the allegation that,
in view of the crisis, the role of gold is being fundamentally
altered: a supposed "degeneration of the private monetary
reserve into a hoarded treasure", as it were, is taking place;
that this is a "new phenomenon" determined by the deepening of state-monopoly tendencies in the currency and monetary relations of capitalism.[3]

Nor must we consider that "the demonetised gold, exclud-
ed from the capitalist money mechanism which, at least

[1] V. I. Lenin, *Collected Works*, Vol. 33, p. 113.
[2] V. I. Lenin, *Collected Works*, Vol. 32, p. 224.
[3] S. M. Borisov, *Zoloto v ekonomike sovremennogo kapitalisma* (Gold
in the Economy of Contemporary Capitalism), Moscow, 1968, p. 33.

within national economies, is fully served by unconvertible paper money, can now already receive, and is actually receiving, the market price in this paper money, just as is done by the rest of the entire commodity world".[1]

The following example is cited as proof: in Paris a gold bar in the gold market and a car cost (or could cost) 5,560 paper francs. Can this serve as proof of the demonetisation of gold? In our opinion, it cannot.

First, that internal circulation can be fully served by paper money of mandatory circulation was established by Marx. He also demonstrated the predominant function of gold as world money of full value.

Second, the sale of gold for paper money, like the sale of a car or any other commodity, by no means attests to the demonetisation of gold. To sell gold for gold would be an absurdity. In the past too gold was sold or exchanged for paper or credit money. It was the meaning and purpose of the gold monetary standard to exchange paper money for the precious metal. But when coins were exchanged for paper money (in essence the same thing as "bought" for paper money) of a definite nominal value, as, for example, Russian paper money in the last century, this exchange was made with a definite difference for full-value specie or without it— it was unimportant. But when gold bullion of definite weight is sold (exchanged) for a definite sum of paper money there can be no difference. Simply a bigger or smaller amount of paper money has to be given for the bullion as compared with its parity (gold content). It is this that is known as the rate of exchange of a currency. The parity of the US dollar was 0.888671 g of gold.

It is a different matter that in the free market one could not buy such a quantity of gold for one dollar. This simply shows that it is not gold that is determined by paper money but vice versa, paper credit money (the mandatory circulation of paper money in international settlements is ruled out because there is no, and there cannot be, any supranational authority) circulates with a definite disagio as compared with its gold parity.

---

[1] Ibid., pp. 36, 37.

The monetary crisis at the end of the 1960s was caused by the reluctance of US financial circles to recognise the depreciation of the dollar. They continued to impose on world circulation elements of mandatory paper money circulation which are alien to it. But it is impossible to divorce world circulation of credit money from the gold basis and even less so to demonetise gold under capitalism. All this has been proved by the present monetary crisis.

The existence of gold markets clearly demonstrates that the so-called "degeneration of the private monetary reserve into a hoarded treasure" is far-fetched. These gold markets for all the former attempts to control them and even more so now, with the existence of what is customarily called the free market price of gold, are, as it were, money exchanges or offices. Strictly speaking, what takes place in the gold markets is not the purchase of gold for paper money but the exchange of paper money for gold or vice versa. It is these markets that show whether paper money corresponds to its parity or gold content, and if not, what the real exchange rate is. To picture the situation differently means to turn the problem upside down. An automobile purchased for paper money is, above all, an article of consumption. Gold received in exchange for dollars is an immutable embodiment of exchange value, which is not intrinsic in dollars. Owing to this all the measures taken by the US ruling circles to ease the crisis remain futile. In the first quarter of 1968 it became clear that all talk about gold as a "barbaric relic" which must be eliminated were groundless under the conditions of capitalism. The elimination of gold is tantamount to the elimination of exchange value, which runs counter to the capitalist commodity economy. Life is refuting any far-fetched ideas about the "demonetisation" of gold. The gold rush on the eve of 1968 dampened the New Year mood of many financiers, bankers and politicians in capitalist countries, including US President Johnson.

The desire to exchange US dollars for gold was so great that Lyndon Johnson instead of merrymaking within his family circle had to tackle currency and balance-of-payments problems. This gave rise to the well-known programme for combating the monetary crisis advanced by Johnson at a press conference held at his Texan ranch which

ushered the United States in 1968, a stormy year for its
finances.

This programme dealt mainly with the balance of payments, the elimination of deficit and the prevention of the
outflow of the gold reserves. The balance of payments also
became a key issue because the elimination of deficit was
demanded not only by France, but also by other US partners
from the Group of Ten. Elimination of the balance-of-payments deficit was rightly regarded as essential to stopping
the financial and economic expansion of US capital. It is
not surprising that some financial circles in the United
States and abroad, in one form or another, expressed their
dissatisfaction with the measures proposed by Johnson.
These were the circles which invest American capital abroad
and the users of American capital in other countries.

The first measure suggested by Johnson was aimed at a
more rigid restriction of loans to foreign states by taxation,
relying at the same time on the voluntary co-operation of
banking corporations.

Nor was the second measure, a more rigid reduction of
government spending abroad, new in any way. But this
measure remained merely a pious wish in view of the war
in Vietnam and the aggressive policy of the Pentagon in
other regions of the world.

Johnson called for restricting American investments
abroad. But for private capital the decisive factor was not
patriotic motives but the actual rate of return on the capital
invested abroad and at home. When the rate of return is at
stake, finance capital is fully cosmopolitan. Therefore,
while Johnson urged American investors to refrain from the
excessive export of capital, foreign capitalists withdrew
their deposits from US banks in order to place them in more
profitable spheres in other countries. That is why, Johnson's
programme called, at least until an equilibrium in the balance of payments was achieved, for attracting foreign capital into the United States in the form of bank deposits and
medium-term loans. For these purposes emissaries of US
financial agencies, Nicholas Katzenbach and Walt Rostow,
were sent to Western Europe and Asia.

Before long the US Treasury made the sale abroad of the
so-called medium-term Rusa bonds (so named after the Assist-

ant of the Treasury who advanced this idea) one of the main points of the Administration's financial programme.

The effort to stabilise the country's finances was complicated by the unbearable military spending and the huge budget deficit which demanded a 10-per cent surcharge on the Federal individual and corporate income tax (a corresponding bill had been introduced in 1967 but was kept back in Congressional committees). Lastly, the increased internal public debt, which, by the decision of the Congress, the Administration intended to raise to $ 358,000 million, also pressed on the government's finances and hindered their normalisation. Little wonder that inflation in the country spread further.

Johnson's press conference designed to pacify world opinion missed its mark. Mistrust of the dollar continued to mount and the money exchanges in all countries were in a feverish state. Gold rose in price and disarray prevailed in international financial circles. It was in this situation that the gold rush reached an unparalleled scale in March 1968. In its scale and intensity it could be more aptly described as a panic.

A conference of the Gold Pool, consisting of governors of the central banks of the United States, Britain, the Federal Republic of Germany, Italy, Switzerland, Belgium and the Netherlands, was hastily summoned in Basle on March 12. It adopted one more decision: to preserve the former constant price of gold in dollars — $ 35 per troy ounce—or to preserve the gold parity of the dollar and the former rates of the currencies of IMF countries to the dollar. To pacify public opinion, a corresponding statement was issued, but it had no effect. The panic, far from waning, was intensified and it became impossible to satisfy the demand for gold. That is why, at the request of President Johnson, banks in West European financial centres stopped foreign exchange operations or were temporarily closed.

The governors of the central banks met again on March 15, this time in Washington. It was here that the decision on introducing a system of dual gold prices was adopted. The participants decided to preserve the former price of gold at $ 35 per ounce for operations between states performed by central banks, and to allow the free fluctuation of the market price of gold under the influence of supply and demand. By this forced decision the governors of the central banks, on behalf of their governments, admitted that they were powerless to further regulate the price of gold by economic methods, as was formerly the case.

The decision to preserve the old price of gold in interstate operations applied to the sphere of administrative regulation and, therefore, the further existence of the Gold Pool on the former principles became meaningless.

According to the foreign press, the Washington decision of the central banks, introduced a system of dual prices, or a dual gold market—official and free. This decision was presented in an epically calm tone.

The conference of the governors of the central banks in Washington sanctioned dualist principles in the capitalist monetary system and created definite contradictions between the private capitalist sector of the economy and the official sector of interstate monetary relations.

The March decisions made by the governors of the central banks of the leading financial countries in fact showed that the International Monetary Fund, which allowed a group of highly developed capitalist countries to decide on the questions facing it, was undergoing a serious crisis. These decisions endangered the entire system of regulating exchange rates around one hub—the dollar and its unchanged relation to gold. In view of the separation of the official and the private gold market by these decisions, the gold reserves became frozen and the connection between them and private capitalist circulation of gold was severed. This all the more bolstered up the decision not to buy newly-mined gold for centralised state reserves at the market price.

After the March decision concerning the dual system of gold prices, the United States began even more insistently to place its medium-term loans in other countries, to accumulate reserves in foreign exchange, to withdraw free dollars from world circulation, and thus reduce the possibility of presenting dollars to be exchanged for gold through interstate channels and, therefore, at the unchanged ratio between the dollar and gold.

In their turn, governments of countries supporting the dual price system began to some extent to keep a certain amount of American currency in their reserves, thereby creating a sham stability for the US gold reserves after the Washington decisions made in March 1968.

The "solidarity" of the central banks of the leading capitalist countries achieved in March 1968 in supporting the system of dual prices that they had adopted resembled the solidarity of seamen on an old schooner caught in a heavy storm. To avoid sinking, the seamen in such cases work hard to lash the sails, but at each creaking of the boat, everyone is ready to grab a lifebelt and jump overboard, abandoning the others to their fate.

In the first quarter of 1968 the monetary crisis which had assumed the form of an unprecedented gold rush was resolved in the market circulation of gold at freely fluctuating prices, which proved to be 15-20 per cent higher than the official price. The central banks of the major imperialist countries, at least in words, refrained from controlling these prices. But the fact that they did not buy gold to replenish their reserves speaks of the opposite. This measure was designed to prevent an additional demand for gold and thereby give the prices of the free market a chance to become stabilised.

Simultaneously an offensive on all fronts was launched on the economic position of France so that her policy should not hinder the contemplated introduction of the SDR system by the IMF which, it was assumed, could offer a way out of the difficult situation for countries with a balance-of-payments deficit and, particularly, for Britain and the United States.

Since March 1968 was a turning point in the international monetary policy of capitalism, it is of interest to trace the changes in the world stock of gold and its reserves in the principal capitalist countries in the subsequent period. These figures reveal new tendencies in the distribution of the world gold and foreign exchange reserves of capitalist countries.

The ten countries whose gold reserves exceed $1,000 million are given in the table. It is these countries that are in the epicentre of the present monetary crisis. These are, first, the United States, Britain and partly Canada; second, the other members of the Common Market. A somewhat

Table 19

International Liquidity[1] 1966-1971
(end of period, million of US dollars)

	1966	1967	1968	1969	1970	1971 June
World gold holdings[2] . .	43,185	41,605	40,910	44,010	41,285	41,265
of which IMF[3] . .	2,279	2,100	1,969	1,882	4,102	4,783
International liquidity	72,635	74,270	77,330	78,195	92,510	104,835
gold	40,910	39,505	38,940	39,125	37,185	36,480
Foreign exchange . .	25,395	29,010	31,900	32,345	44,485	55,550
Developed countries[4] . .	60,520	61,280	63,245	62,640	74,325	84,485
gold	38,345	36,610	35,510	35,675	33,895	33,200
Foreign exchange . .	16,330	19,425	21,845	20,860	31,080	40,585
Developing countries . .	12,115	12,990	14,085	15,550	18,185	20,355
gold	2,565	2,895	3,430	3,455	3,290	3,280
Foreign exchange . .	9,065	9,585	10,065	11,485	13,405	14,970
Selected countries						
United States: gold . .	13,235	12,065	10,892	11,859	11,070	11,081
Foreign exchange . .	1,321	2,345	3,528	2,781	630	280
Britain: gold	1,940	1,291	1,474	1,471	1,349	(13,422)[5]
Foreign exchange . .	1,159	1,404	948	1,054	1,212	(1,212)
France: gold	5,238	5,234	3,877	3,547	3,532	3,825
Foreign exchange . .	507	874	323	286	1,257	(3,203)

Continuation

	1966	1967	1968	1969	1970	1971 June
FRG: gold	4,292	4,228	4,539	4,079	3,980	4,426
Foreign exchange	2,480	2,873	3,894	2,748	8,455	12,292
Italy: gold	2,414	2,400	2,923	2,956	2,887	3,131
Foreign exchange	1,621	2,221	1,524	1,194	2,059	3,030
Belgium: gold . .	1,525	1,480	1,524	1,520	1,470	1,676
Foreign exchange	458	782	362	712	780	706
Netherlands: gold .	2,448	2,619	2,463	2,529	3,234	3,797
Foreign exchange	305	556	269	370	764	406
Switzerland: gold .	2,841	3,089	2,624	2,642	2,732	3,158
Foreign exchange	704	607	1,669	1,783	2,401	3,734
Japan: gold	329	338	356	413	532	738
Foreign exchange	1,469	1,453	2,261	2,614	3,188	13,783

[1] Gold + Reserve position in IMF + Foreign exchange + Special Drawing Rights (1970-71).
[2] Excluding Persian Gulf States, China, Eastern Europe, the USSR and Cuba.
[3] IMF, EPU/EF and BIS.
[4] Australia, Canada, Japan, New Zealand, South Africa, United States and Western Europe.
[5] In May 1971.

S o u r c e: *Monthly Bulletin of Statistics*, March 1972, pp. 212-218.

special position is held by Switzerland and the Republic of South Africa. Switzerland is not a member of the IMF but plays an important part in the monetary and financial affairs of the capitalist world. Substantial reserves of monetary gold are concentrated in that country which, moreover, is the traditional haven for the capital of deposed kings, dictators and others thrown out of the saddle by socio-economic upheavals. Swiss bankers also engage in substantial pawning operations with gold which are kept secret.

The Republic of South Africa is the main gold-producing country in the capitalist world (70-75 per cent of the total). It is the main supplier of gold for the capitalist countries, and for a number of years for the Gold Pool. Prior to the aggravation of the monetary crisis South African gold entered international circulation chiefly via London; moreover, the Bank of England played, not without benefit to itself, the role of a transfer junction.

What tendencies in the movement of the gold and exchange reserves of capitalist countries were displayed at the end of 1960s?

To begin with, the world stock of monetary gold noticeably decreased, including that in the national reserves of capitalist countries. The latter dropped from $ 40,900 million at the end of 1966 to $ 38,900 million at the end of 1968, or by $2,000 million.

This gold no doubt migrated from the system of state monetary and financial agencies of capitalist countries to the private sector. The newly-mined gold in 1967 and 1968 (about $ 2,800-3,000 million) also went into the same sector. We must not assume, however, that this gold turned into inert capital. In the safes of capitalists and their associations it claims the role of security, giving rise to credit and credit media of exchange. It is not precluded that the total sum of the increased world liquid resources, which at the end of 1968 amounted to $ 76,300 million as compared with $ 71,800 million at the end of 1966, was partly based on hidden gold resources. Incidentally, at the end of 1969 the world monetary reserves of gold again exceeded $ 39,000 million.

The shocks which Britain felt and continued to feel as a result of the monetary crisis upset the system of replenishing the reserves of monetary gold in capitalist countries. The gold-producing countries, in the first place, the Republic of South Africa, refused to sell or exchange the newly-mined gold at the lower price for pounds and dollars.

The central banks in the leading capitalist countries, in turn, acted in a united front against South Africa, refusing to satisfy its demand for an increase in the price of gold because this would imply the devaluation of the dollar and a revision of the entire system of exchange parities between the IMF countries.

In boycotting the purchase of South African gold, the central banks of the principal capitalist countries expected that South Africa would be forced to dump big lots of gold on to the free market in order to cover the deficit in its balance of payments, and thereby bring down the price of gold. This was done for the same purpose of preserving the existing system of interstate settlements on the basis of the unchanged parity of the dollar.

But these exertions obviously did not produce the expected results. Contrary to expectations, they did not succeed in forcing South Africa to capitulate on the question of the gold price even several months after the March 1968 gold rush. At the end of 1968 on account of newly-mined gold South Africa brought up its gold stock to $1,243 million as compared with $637 million at the end of 1966, and $742 million in March 1968 during the gold panic.[1] In other words, its gold stock more than doubled. In three months of 1969 alone its reserves rose further and reached $1,367 million at the end of March 1969. Additional proof that the boycott of South African gold was ineffective was the increase in the reserves of convertible currency to $244 million at the end of March 1969 as against $98 million at the end of 1966 and $120 million in March 1967.

Lastly, mention should be made of the changes in the distribution of the gold reserves in other capitalist countries.

The United States had difficulty in keeping its gold stock at a level somewhat exceeding $10,000 million and

---

[1] *Monthly Bulletin of Statistics*, May 1969, p. 218.

had to resort to the forcible replenishment of its reserves from Canada, the IMF and other sources.

The gold stock of France decreased from $ 5,200 million in 1967 to $ 3,800 million at the end of 1968. This drop was a result of special reasons which stemmed from the further deepening of the monetary crisis and the drawing into its orbit of West European countries which formerly had not felt the crisis to the same extent as the USA and Britain, whose currencies played a vital part in the monetary system of capitalism.

SPREAD OF THE MONETARY CRISIS
TO EEC COUNTRIES. THE CURRENCY
WAR AND DEVALUATION
OF THE FRENCH FRANC

The world monetary crisis affected the economies of all capitalist countries, but to a differing extent. Prior to 1968 the crisis hit first of all the USA and Britain, whose currencies played a special part in international circulation. After the devaluation of the British pound in 1967 and particularly after the gold rush and the forced introduction of a system of dual gold prices in March 1968, new phenomena appeared in the development of the crisis.

US ruling circles opened a new round of the battle for preserving the existing monetary system and began to act according to the principle that attack is the best form of defence. France, the main proponent of the idea of recreating the mechanism of the world monetary system on the gold basis, was chosen as the chief target. Since the March gold rush had compelled the US ruling circles to retreat from their former position on the question of gold prices and to allow free price formation on the gold markets, they decided to take revenge. To discredit the idea of recreating the monetary system on the gold basis, US financial circles considered it necessary first of all to undermine the monetary and financial position of France. That is why Washington's anti-French policy, pursued even earlier, developed into open hostilities in 1968, and became a real currency war.

It goes without saying that the hostile actions towards France employed by the US ruling circles with the help of their West German counterparts were not openly advertised. More than that, they were pursued as much as possible by methods regarded fully legitimate in international financial relations. These included restriction of French exports, reduction of tourist travel by US citizens to France and other sources of foreign exchange receipts in France's balance of payments. At the same time measures were taken to increase the outflow of capital from France, above all American, and of profits on long-term investments. This was also facilitated by the political situation in France resulting from the May-June strikes in 1968. Although the deliberate removal of capital would have been effected under any political circumstances, the events of 1968 were widely exploited for stimulating the outflow of capital, not only foreign but also French capital. Various means were artfully employed, including the deliberate spread of rumours about the forthcoming revaluation of the West German mark.

The question of revaluing the West German mark was not new. There had been talk of it even earlier, since the exchange rate of the West German mark in previous years had been invariably higher than its parity or its relation to the American dollar: 4 marks = $ 1. Thus at the end of 1962 it was 3.998 marks; in 1963, 3.975; in 1964, 3.977; in 1965, 4.006; in 1966, 3.977 and in 1967, 3.999 marks. Thus, the rate of the mark quite frequently drew close to the limit allowed by the IMF rules for a rise in the exchange rate (among EEC countries 0.75 per cent) above parity or 3.97 marks to the dollar.

As for the French franc, at a parity of 4.93706 francs to the dollar, its rate in 1962 was 4.900; in 1963 4.902; in 1964 4.900; in 1965 4.902 ; in 1966 4.952 and in 1967 4.908. From this it follows that the rate of the franc at least up to 1966 was high and firm, which was explained by the general stable economic situation and the country's favourable balance of payments.

Aware of this, the ruling circles of the USA and the FRG launched no head-on attacks on the franc, but waited for a convenient moment. It came in 1968. By that time France's balance of payments had become unfavourable but the deficit was of a by no means chronic nature. Without a big outflow of capital in 1968 and 1969 the monetary and financial position of France could not have led to the devaluation of the franc on August 11, 1969.

This is demonstrated by the fact that from the end of 1966 to March 1968, when the gold rush shook the monetary system of capitalism, the gold stock of France remained stable, exceeding $5,200 million. France did not resort to IMF loans, as was repeatedly done by Britain when she found herself in the vortex of the monetary crisis. France also had in her reserves considerable sums of convertible currency sufficient for maintaining international payments. It might rather have been expected that after the January statement of President Johnson on the US balance of payments the monetary crisis would still more affect the economic situation in the USA.

Indeed, early in 1968 there was greater nervousness than before among US ruling circles. The war in Vietnam and the Pentagon's aggressive plans dictated military spending in the following fiscal year of up to $79,800 million, and the usual revenue could not cover the tremendous military expenditure. The budget deficit reached the astronomical figure of about $30,000 million and so President Johnson demanded of Congress a 10-per cent surcharge on the Federal personal and corporate income tax.

The shrinkage of the gold reserves continued. They dropped below $12,000 million, and a further decline could invalidate the law on the 25-per cent gold cover for Federal Reserve notes in circulation. In view of this and also trying to release gold for international operations, W. Martin, President of the Board of Governors of the Federal Reserve System, raised the question of annulling the law on the gold security of bank notes in circulation. This was a method paving the way for further inflation and a symptom of the grave financial situation and the fear of the further weakening of the dollar in the world monetary system. Washington abolished the gold cover of bank notes within the country on the pretext of releasing the gold reserves for backing dollars in international circulation.

Dismay in ruling circles close to the White House was also displayed in the replacement of high officials. Robert McNamara resigned from the post of Defence Secretary, Charles Zwick was appointed Director of the Budget instead of Charles Shultze, and Arthur Okun headed the Council of Economic Advisers instead of Gardner Ackley. US financial and economic circles openly discussed questions of inflation and possible deflation; Martin himself regarded inflation as a real necessity. There is no doubt that disarray in US ruling circles over further financial and economic policy only accelerated the stormy onset of the crisis in March 1968 which raised the problem of gold on its full scale.

The difficult position of US financial circles early in 1968, however, did not prevent them from applying a policy designed to weaken France's financial position. Matters reached a point of the direct boycott of French goods, not to mention other financial means of pressure.

The organised reduction of the imports of French goods to the United States on the pretext that the public did not buy them, withdrawal of American deposits from French banks, reduction of commercial and other credits, and intensive export of profits on American capital invested in France worsened the country's balance of payments.

Last but not least, the most effective method was employed—rumours were spread about the revaluation of the West German mark and devaluation of the franc. The scheme was simple: to catch the speculative elements among the French bourgeoisie on a double hook of greed. If the franc were to be devaluated or its gold parity reduced, this would mean a decrease in the purchasing power of the franc, especially in international payments. If the West German mark were revalued this would mean a rise in its purchasing power as compared with the existing parity.

From this it followed that by converting their free capital in francs into marks and depositing them in German banks one could wait for the revaluation of the mark and then gain a double benefit equal to the difference in the exchange rate of the devalued franc and revalued mark.

The temptation of a double gain was so great that francs were exchanged for marks and capital transferred to the Federal Republic of Germany, disregarding the swiftly dropping rate of the franc set by the West German banks at their own discretion. An organised outflow of Eurodollars from France was also organised as well as the massive demand for payments on French liabilities, and so on.

France's financial agencies apparently underestimated the oncoming danger to the country's balance of payments and its financial position. Otherwise it is difficult to explain why up to July 1968 the discount rate of the Bank of France was 3.5 per cent, while in Britain it was 8 per cent and in the United States it was raised from 5 to 5.5 per cent in April 1968. Only on July 3 was the discount rate of the Bank of France raised to 5 per cent. Although the discount rate of the central bank of the FRG at that time was low, only 3 per cent, this did not prevent the outflow of capital from France to the FRG under the influence of rumours about the revaluation of the mark and the political situation in France. The pressure on the franc reached its peak in November 1968, when the question of devaluing the franc was seriously raised for the first time. The government took a number of restrictive measures as regards the export of capital, and the discount rate of the bank of France was raised to 6 per cent as of November 12, 1968. But at the same time it was learned that no revaluation of the mark was contemplated, although this was demanded by Paris and London.

The latter is explained by the fact that the speculative fever had spread across the English Channel and the pound was faced with the same threat as the franc. For British currency the speculative fever over the revaluation of the mark was all the more dangerous because the pound had no such gold backing as the franc. In this connection it is of interest to present comparative data on the gold and foreign exchange reserves of the four principal countries which had a bearing on undermining the franc in 1968.

Table 20 shows that prior to March 1968, when under the influence of the gold rush and the monetary panic the system of dual gold prices was introduced, France's gold and exchange reserves remained stable. But in the following months the situation changed drastically and by the end of 1968 the gold reserves of France had dropped from $5,235 million to $3,877 million, or by $1,358 million. Moreover, France exhausted its automatically granted credits in the IMF. French foreign exchange reserves decreased between March 1968 and March 1969 to $159 million, or almost by 80 per cent.

The gold stock of the United States underwent no essential changes during this period judging by the table. But the data given in it are largely a result of artificially reducing the balance-of-payments deficit with the help of loans, foreign deposits in American banks and so on. The FRG gave substantial loans to US financial agencies. From 1968 onwards both government and private American loans were placed abroad intensively. As early as July 2, 1968 the London *Times* noted that new issues of American loans in Western Europe had reached $ 1,278 million and amounted to 75 per cent of all the new loans. The newspaper quite anxiously noted that the crisis was continuing and incidentally was expressed in steep ups and downs of discount rates and big migration of capital from country to country. In August 1968 the *International Herald Tribune* pointed out that from January to June only one American company engaged in placing foreign loans, the Morgan Guarantee Trust, marketed loans for $ 1,480 million as compared with $ 260 million during the whole of 1967.[1]

At the end of 1968, when it was nevertheless established that the balance of payments would end in a deficit, big short-term loans were made to create a semblance of a favourable situation. To support President Johnson's call to draw up the balance of payments without a deficit, American corporations hastily repatriated from abroad about $ 1,000 million. Apparently, a considerable part of the repatriated capital came from France against which the monetary and financial policy of US ruling circles was directed.

Viewing the measures to improve the US balance of payments in 1968 as a deliberate embellishment of reality, the London *Times* wrote on February 17, 1969: "The true deficit last year was over $ 3,000 m." The newspaper mentions as an adverse fact the steep decline of the favourable trade balance by $ 3,400 million (the favourable trade balance dropped from $ 3,500 million in 1967 to under $ 100 million in 1968). This decrease was not compensated by the somewhat increased favourable balance of invisible trade. Specifically, the investment income rose by $ 600 million. It is this item that is utilised by American corporations in order, if necessary, at the most unexpected moment

---

[1] *International Herald Tribune*, August 20, 1968.

Table 20

**International Liquidity of the United States,
Britain, France and the FRG Before and After 1968**
(millions of dollars)

	1966	1967		1968		1969
		March	December	March	December	March
UNITED STATES:						
total liquidity	14,881	13,854	14,830	13,927	15,710	15,758
gold	13,235	13,184	12,065	10,703	10,892	10,836
position in IMF . . .	326	357	420	478	1,290	1,321
foreign ex- change . .	1,321	314	2,345	2,746	3,528	3,601
BRITAIN:						
total liquidity	3,100	3,259	2,695	2,722	2,422	2,470
gold	1,940	1,677	1,291	1,493	—	—
position in IMF . . .	—	—	—	—	—	—
foreign ex- change . .	1,159	1,582	1,404	1,229	—	—
FRANCE:						
total liquidity	6,733	6,720	6,994	6,906	4,201	3,987
gold	5,238	5,240	5,234	5,235	3,877	3,827
position in IMF . . .	988	1,015	886	883	1	1
foreign ex- change . .	507	465	874	788	323	159
FRG:						
total liquidity	8,028	8,019	8,152	8,539	9,937	8,209
gold	4,292	4,294	4,228	3,972	4,539	4,541
position in IMF . . .	1,257	1,260	1,052	1,134	1,515	1,354
foreign ex- change . .	2,479	2,465	2,872	3,433	3,883	2,314

S o u r c e: *Monthly Bulletin of Statistics*, May 1969, pp. 212, 218.

to severely weaken the balance of payments of the country from which profit on capital is exported and to somewhat remedy their own balance.

The situation was different as regards France. Her capital in other countries was small. She had no such broad opportunities for manoeuvring and had to rely only on her gold and foreign exchange reserves. With their help she defended the franc twice, in November 1968 and May 1969.

The speculative movement of capital assumed such proportions that it is estimated that in two days (May 8 and 9, 1969) the Federal Republic of Germany received $ 4,000 million or 20,000 million francs. To avoid a further outflow of private capital and the melting away of the gold stock, France devalued her currency by 12.5 per cent on August 11, 1969, i.e., to a somewhat smaller extent than the British pound was devalued in 1967 (14.3 per cent).

The devaluation of the franc conclusively demonstrated that the crisis had spread to Common Market countries. It engendered new trade and economic difficulties among them, weakening the trade integration of the European Economic Community.

At the special session of the Agriculture and Finance Ministers of EEC countries convened in Brussels after the devaluation of the franc, serious differences flared up over the agricultural exports of France, which as a result of devaluation began to rise. French exporters received a stimulus to sell their agricultural commodities in other Common Market countries, while the exporters of farm produce of these countries to France lost during the exchange of the French currency received for their national currency the entire difference between the old and the new parity of the franc. This example of trade inequality engendered by devaluation is so typical that we shall discuss it in somewhat greater detail.

Usually, exporters in a country with a devalued currency sell their goods at the world market prices or those existing in the importing country. Since French agricultural commodities are sold within the bounds of the EEC at common prices expressed in American dollars at parity, by exchanging the sums received for the exported goods in devalued francs, the French exporters naturally receive more francs than

14*

exporters of agricultural produce from the FRG and other Common Market countries. This could impel French firms to step up the export of farm produce to the West German market to the detriment of similar local produce.

Now let us examine the question from the other side. A certain part of West German produce is exported to France. Let us assume that at the old exchange rate of the franc the price was sufficiently equalised and such export was profitable. As soon as the franc had been devalued, the equilibrium was upset. West German exporters for their goods sold in France receive the same sum in francs as before, but in exchanging the francs for marks receive fewer marks. For them it becomes disadvantageous to export their goods to France and their output has to be sold in the home market or exported not to France but to other Common Market countries.

The devaluation of the franc thus introduced big shifts in trade among EEC countries. It separated the market of every country in the Common Market and at the same time stimulated French exports. It was for this reason that the very first session of the Agriculture and Finance Ministers of EEC countries in Brussels was marked by heated debates over the changes introduced by the devaluation of the franc in mutual trade, above all in agricultural commodities, and also in other goods.

To paralyse this effect on mutual exports, various plans were put forward at the conference for limiting France's export advantages. Among the restrictive measures was a suggested tax on French agricultural exports to other EEC countries. Whatever concrete forms this tax assumed, its essence was the same: to remove the advantages which French exporters of agricultural commodities could gain from the devaluation of the franc. This tax was also to be somehow used for compensating the losses of firms in EEC countries which traded in farm produce.

It should be borne in mind that all these measures could be carried out only at the expense of the direct producers of agricultural commodities, the farmers of France and other countries.

It goes without saying that the devaluation of the franc, apart from shifting the entire commodity mass of the country with the devalued currency towards exports, inevitably led to higher prices in the home market. Given the unchanged nominal wages of workers and other employees and also of all persons with fixed incomes, this inevitably depressed their standard of living. It is from this source under any devaluation and also the inflational drop in the purchasing power of the population that the export reserves are created, with the help of which exports are expanded and a country's balance of payments is improved. But these theoretical expectations are not always realised. Britain is a case in point.

Table 20 shows that 18 months after the devaluation of the pound Britain's monetary and financial position had not improved appreciably. Through devaluation the Government succeeded in somewhat easing the pressure exerted by the public debt on the country's finances but it did not radically improve the external balance. Britain's foreign exchange reserves stood at an exceedingly low level.

It is not surprising that the least change in the economic situation, and especially an event as important as the devaluation of the franc, unfavourably affected the pound and the entire system of Britain's external payments. The pound, whose rate was already low, was placed on the brink of a new devaluation by France's action.

Without examining Britain's financial position after devaluation in detail, it should be emphasised that the pound still lacked stability owing to the weakened financial and economic position of Britain in the sterling area, her slow industrial development compared with other economically developed countries and the high production costs of her manufactured goods.

Britain could not realise in full measure the export advantages following from the devaluation of the pound because her short-term liquid sterling liabilities and her external debts in foreign exchange were too high. The military spending of Britain to meet the wishes of her transatlantic friends was too burdensome. It was becoming clear that the devaluation of the pound in November 1967 was insufficient and the possibility of its recurrence was not ruled out.

The monetary crisis continued to spread through Western Europe, not missing EEC countries either.

The question arises, did it bypass the Federal Republic of Germany? It did not. The facts show that prior to the devaluation of the franc the FRG succeeded in gaining certain benefits from the crisis of the capitalist monetary system. This was reflected by an increase in its gold and foreign exchange reserves.

But the initial results of the devaluation of the franc showed that the monetary crisis encompassed in its orbit all EEC countries, not excluding the FRG. The problem of agricultural exports concerned above all the FRG, its home market of farm produce.

The favourable financial position of the FRG, set against the financial difficulties of France and particularly Britain, made its convertible currency a fully acceptable medium of circulation and accumulation of reserves by other countries alongside the dollar and the pound widely used for these purposes.

All conditions were thus created for maintaining a stable high exchange rate for the West German mark. But in this way the export position of the FRG, alongside the less stable and devalued currencies, became vulnerable. Foreign goods, especially of countries with a devalued currency, gained additional advantages in the West German market in competition with local goods.

A further problem arose—the expedient use of surplus money capital. In a situation in which the "industrial miracle" in the FRG had subsided the internal market was subjected to inflational pressure from outside and foreign investments became inevitable. They were dictated not only by the attribute of every capital to be a self-growing value, to bring a profit, but also by the fear of the ruling circles of placing the economy of the FRG in a disadvantageous position, surrounded by an inflational stream of goods from other countries.

But the foreign investment of West German capital in the industries of other countries was inevitably linked with the sharpening of the competitive struggle with foreign financial monopolies, especially American.

The monetary crisis placed American investors in quite a tight spot. But there position was sufficiently strong and they manoeuvred in every possible way to cushion the jolts and blows of the crisis, to preserve the postwar monetary system of capitalism and the special position of the American dollar in it.

As a means of reducing the country's balance-of-payments deficit Washington, as shown earlier, itself widely resorted to obtaining foreign loans. It was not against utilising West German money capital on a wider scale. In effect, every such loan helped the American monopolies themselves to invest capital in profitable spheres of production abroad.

Such a role of West German capital would fully have suited the transatlantic friends of the FRG. They expected to ease the blows of the monetary crisis with the help of West Germany. But these hopes were unjustified. West German finance capital itself wanted to exploit the emerging situation for consolidating its position in the international capital market in general and within the bounds of the EEC in particular.

In this context mention should be made of the revaluation of the West German mark in October 1969. This step conformed to the demands of the IMF charter and could formally be regarded as a loyal act designed to strengthen this organisation and the capitalist monetary system. In itself the rise in the parity of the mark as a result of its revaluation by 8.5 per cent did not essentially change currency circulation between the FRG and its trading partners because at that time the actual rate of the West German mark was considerably above parity (DM4=$1). Thus, the new parity set as a result of revaluation (DM3.66=$ 1) did not affect current payments.

The revaluation of the West German mark pursued other aims. To begin with, the new Federal Government emphasised by this action that it did not intend to preserve the shaky monetary and financial position which had arisen during the election campaign and alarmed the people. The main thing was that revaluation demonstrated the strength of the mark, which was of great significance from the viewpoint of consolidating the position of West German finance capital in the economy of Western Europe.

In contrast to the devaluation of currencies designed to stimulate exports, revaluation has no such effect on exports; rather the reverse, it can restrain them and stimulate imports. But since the size of the revaluation of the mark was insignificant, its impact on the foreign trade of the Federal Republic could not be substantial either. The main effect of revaluation was felt in the international movement of capital. It created the necessary prerequisites for the further penetration of West German capital into other EEC countries. To a certain extent, the West German mark began to assume in the European capital market the role of the Eurodollars whose outflow from Europe for a number of reasons increased in 1969.

At the same time the stability of the West German mark, emphasised by its revaluation, facilitated an increase of deposits of free capital in West German banks, which enabled the latter to extend their operations within and outside the country.

The change in the parities of the currencies of two leading EEC countries—France and the FRG—in the second half of 1969 in opposite directions by no means eliminated the acute monetary, financial and trade contradictions in Western Europe. Quite the reverse, it intensified them. This applied above all to the EEC countries and Britain.

INITIAL ATTEMPTS TO SOLVE
THE MONETARY PROBLEMS OF CAPITALISM

The entire history of the present monetary crisis of capitalism shows that the world monetary system has outlived its usefulness and began to function poorly towards the end of the 1960s. Naturally, international financial circles tried to conceal this by talk about minor shortcomings, mishaps which, supposedly, could be eliminated by partial improvement measures without touching the mainstays of the system.

The Wall Street Journal, the mouthpiece of US Big Business, for example, wrote on the day when the devaluation of the franc came into effect that if the existing system allowed a somewhat freer change of currency rates, France could probably have achieved a transition to a realistic rate gradually. The newspaper of American bankers and stock exchange brokers referred to the rigid IMF rule stipulating that currencies which have a convertible status or are convertible into gold and currencies of other countries cannot deviate from their parity upwards or downwards by more than 1 per cent and in EEC countries, according to their agreement, by not more than 0.75 per cent. Otherwise a change in parity must be followed by devaluation during a prolonged decline in the rate or revaluation in the case of an increase.

However, while advocating freer and more flexible fluctuations of the rate of exchange, the newspaper was compelled to remark that flexibility of exchange rates was also no cure-all for the monetary system. It voiced the thought that disorder in monetary markets would exist so long as large countries obstinately applied an internal inflation policy.

So, to judge from the statements of *The Wall Street Journal*, US banking circles admitted the imperfection of the system and the adverse effect of an internal inflation policy (especially that of the United States) and the need for some changes. But why did they begin their arguments with the system of regulating exchange rates, for what purpose was it introduced?

During any changes of exchange rates upwards or downwards in international payments on credit transactions the payer will be the winner and the receiver the loser or vice versa. In the past, when there was a free gold standard, as soon as the fluctuation of the rate went too far, payments in gold were employed in order not to bear losses on a big difference in exchange rates. This happened as soon as the difference in rates went beyond the cost of transporting gold (including freight and insurance, expenses for packing the gold and guarding it en route). A kind of automatically operating system existed for settlements in gold. Let us assume that between the two places of residence of trading partners the cost of transporting gold, including all the enumerated expenses, was 0.75 per cent of its value. As long as the difference in exchange rates did not exceed this figure, partners paid (directly or through foreign exchange banks) in the respective currencies. Wide use was made in international payments of drafts (hence the exchange rate was often called the bill rate), cheques, payment orders, bank notes paid into the bank in one national currency credited to the account of the receiver in another national currency. In all these transactions, naturally, account was taken of the difference in the exchange rates.

But as soon as the difference in the rates went beyond the cost of transporting gold, which came to be known as the gold point, the person for whom the difference in the rate was disadvantageous resorted to payment in gold. He sent bank notes to the central Bank or gave respective instructions to the bank serving him to exchange bank notes for gold at parity (and under the gold standard such an exchange was made without hindrance) and settled with his foreign partner in gold.

Such a mechanism of going over to international payments in gold operated automatically, and even before the deficit of a country's balance of payments was revealed in full measure and led to its redemption in gold.

The situation became different when gold was no longer available for private settlements, as happened after the Second World War. Here, wittingly or unwittingly, payments had to be made in foreign exchange, most often in some convertible currency — dollars or pounds. The exchange rates of all national currencies were tied to the dollar, whose relation to gold remained unchanged. Payments in gold in settlement of an unfavourable balance of payments were made through central banks. In such a case, without a rigid regulation of rates a real orgy could occur in the fluctuation of exchange rates. It was to avoid such a situation that a control system was introduced in the form of the IMF Rules. Moreover, the limit of the permissible fluctuations was close to the former "gold points".

It has been demonstrated in practice that such a system is linked with "sharp jolts" in monetary circulation. International circles have not yet devised, and will not be able to devise, a shock absorber of these "jolts", although they have been trying to adopt for this purpose the so-called SDRs of the International Monetary Fund.

Another thing was also ascertained. Under such a system, which enabled dollars to oust gold from private international payments, inflation in the United States developed into international inflation, which enabled American capital to dominate world currency circulation and the international movement of capital. This abnormal situation caused the natural regulator of spontaneous capitalist circulation, artificially severed from price formation in the huge quantity of commodities circulating between countries, to stop functioning. This resulted in huge balance-of-payments deficits and the loss by the United States of a considerable part of its gold reserves, the forced introduction of a system of dual gold prices and the devaluation of two major currencies in the capitalist world with a subsequent chain of devaluations in other countries.

The deepening of the monetary crisis, however, was not averted. It continued, just as the pressure of internal infla-

tion in the United States on international circulation continued. But although it had a chronic balance-of-payments
deficit, the United States did not feel any financial necessity
to eliminate it and to curtail its financial, economic and
military expansion. The US Federal Reserve System utilised
the dollar as an instrument of inflation affecting the entire
world. This brought about a general rise of prices and un-
sound economic development fraught with big upheavals
and difficulties which face some countries today and may
face others tomorrow.

Aware of these effects, international financial circles,
under the aegis of the United States, for a number of years
now have been trying unsuccessfully to normalise the monetary system. To put it more concretely, the matter is tackled
chiefly by financial agencies of the Group of Ten.

This group, which decides all the main questions of the
monetary system outside the IMF, rejected the plan for
restoring the role of gold in the international monetary
system by raising its price and, to avoid still bigger crisis
upheavals, facilitated the introduction of Special Drawing
Rights of the IMF, which we shall discuss later in greater
detail.

At one time the role of a shock absorber during sharp
jolts in mutual monetary settlements between IMF countries
was played by so-called "Swop" loans or the exchange of
national currencies with the obligation to change them
back after a specified period. But the monetary crisis
in Britain revealed the inability of this form of international
loan to prevent the spread of the crisis and the devaluation
of the British pound with all the consequences following
therefrom.

Towards the end of the 1960s too many dollars had
accumulated in bank accounts and their owners lost confidence in their ability to convert them into real values.
They felt that inflation, originating in the United States,
was slowly but surely depreciating these accounts and
therefore every time they were used as credit the interest
rate rose. An interest of 7-8 per cent and even more on
reliable first-class bills in the most important banks, up to
the central banks, became the rule rather than the exception
(an example is the Bank of England). We can imagine what

the cost of credit in ordinary commercial banks was like. At the beginning of our century such a rate of interest would have been regarded as usurious. Against the background of inflationary economic activity, however, it looks like a normal phenomenon.

The inflationary overheating of the economy in the principal capitalist countries inevitably intensified the competitive struggle in the world market. This rivalry, in view of the devaluation in countries of the sterling and franc areas, entered into a phase of bitter struggle with the help of monetary dumping. The traditional methods of protecting home markets through tariff barriers, the establishment of import quotas, and the like were revived. To circumvent these obstacles, private capital intensified its efforts to entrench itself in the industries of other countries through direct investment or mixed enterprises. This tendency, in turn, only increased the deficit of the balance of payments which undermined the currency of the respective countries.

But while a balance-of-payments deficit was becoming for some countries the cause of certain monetary and financial complications, including the devaluation of the national currency, the United States tried to divert this threat by covering its balance-of-payments deficit with its national currency. Jasques Rueff wrote that "the accumulation of dollar credits had increased dollar balances abroad from $ 15,000 million in 1958 to around $ 35,000 million at the end of 1968".[1] The liquid liabilities of the United States, accumulated on dollar accounts in other countries, continued to mount because of the country's balance-of-payments deficit. Under different circumstances the United States would have had to pay for these liabilities with its gold (and it partly did so, losing from the end of 1961 to the end of 1968 more than $ 6,000 million of its gold stock). But after it had succeeded, with the help of the central banks of the Gold Pool countries, in blocking the monetary stock of gold in March 1968, the foreign dollar liabilities of the United States turned into a millstone suspended on a rotten rope and hanging over the world monetary system. Under what circumstances this rope would snap

---

[1] *The Wall Street Journal*, June 5, 1969.

and how destructive the blow of the millstone would be
no one was able to predict exactly, but all were aware
of the danger.

The US ruling circles did not close their eyes to this
menace either. They realised that it was no longer possible to
repay the dollar liabilities accumulated abroad on banking
accounts and in the official reserves of other countries in
the usual manner. This could be done only through the
devaluation of the dollar. But if this happened, did it make
any difference what sum of liabilities would be liquidated
in this way? That is why the ruling circles of the USA
were willing to drag out the show-down endlessly, while
at the same time, behind cover of talk about reducing the
balance-of-payments deficit and controlling inflation, conti-
nuing the former policy of inflation and dollar expansion.

It was against this background of general monetary instability that the panicky shifting of capital from one country
to another became possible, just like the continuous search
for gold and hard liquid assets. A case in point is the panicky
flight of capital from France to the FRG and Switzerland
in November 1968 and May 1969.

These big shifts of capital were a logical consequence of
the policy of the financial and economic restrictions employed
by the United States and the FRG against France. But
they once again thoroughly shook the entire monetary
system and spread even greater fear of its inability to
continue functioning in the existing way. This especially
affected the position of the British pound up to a point
where there was talk in international financial circles about
another devaluation.

Mention must be made, however, of the fact that, fearing
the devaluation of the franc, the owners of free capital in
1969 converted it not into pounds or dollars but into marks
and deposited them in West German banks, although the
interest rates in the FRG at that time were lower than
in Britain and the United States. This was explained to
a certain extent, by the speculative expectation of a revaluation of the mark. A big part, however, was also played by
the fact that the deposits in West German banks in marks
were regarded by the owners of foreign capital as a quiet

haven which could protect their capital from the destructive force of a monetary crisis.

It goes without saying that the FRG was thus becoming a financial centre not only of the Common Market but of the whole of Western Europe. The West German mark began to play the important part of a stable currency competing with the American dollar, if not on a world scale, at least on the scale of Western Europe.

In 1968, for example, of all the loans issued in the West European financial markets 31 per cent were loans in West German marks. In the first half of 1969 their share amounted to 45 per cent and reached $ 953 million. The preference given to marks offered ground for the assumption that sooner or later American dollars would have to make room in the West European capital market. But for this the West German mark had to preserve its stability. The parity in relation to the American dollar, 4 : 1 (DM4=$ 1) which existed up to October 1969 was most convenient for replacing the dollar, if need be, in definite spheres of international payments. The question was not, as in the sterling or franc areas, that of creating a West German mark area but of extending the participation of West German finance capital and its instrument, the mark, in the world circulation of capital in general.

In this connection food for thought is afforded by statements which appeared in *The New York Times* three days after the devaluation of the franc that the time had come for introducing official changes in the exchange rates. In countries with a favourable balance, like the FRG, this change should be towards raising parity. In countries suffering from a balance-of-payments deficit, towards reducing parity. This had to be done without the threat of restricting trade, the level of employment and reducing capital investments. These considerations voiced by a leading US newspaper in 1969, as it were, anticipated the measures taken by President Nixon in August 1971.

It is easy to notice that these arguments contained advice to the FRG to revalue its currency, just as to other countries with an unfavourable balance to change parity downwards in good time and "properly". On October 24, 1969 the revaluation of the West German mark became an accomplished fact. What was to be done with the dollar itself? If the dollar were measured with the yardstick recommended by *The New York Times* it had already lost its former relation to gold and, consequently, it would be necessary to change this ratio by reducing the gold content of the dollar or devaluing it. But Washington preferred not to talk about it so as not to disturb public opinion.

This, however, was a constant subject of discussion in Western Europe. Apparently, though, certain American banking circles were inclined to heed suggestions about changing the ratio between the dollar and gold, since an article by such an eminent votary of gold as Jacques Rueff was published in *The Wall Street Journal*. It seems to us of interest once again to refer to the views voiced by its author a few days prior to the devaluation of the franc.

He resolutely rejected the idea that it was possible to avoid a monetary crisis in any other way except by raising the role of gold in international payments and expounded a number of correct ideas. He thought it necessary to create a situation in which the owners of unpaid money accounts should gain confidence that they would be able to exchange their accounts for real assets with a stable average purchasing power. This attribute can be possessed by gold which, in contrast to paper money, has real production value.

But Rueff lapsed into a one-sided exaggeration of the possibilities of organised capitalism and he proposed that an international gold convention be concluded under which member states could buy and sell gold directly or through the medium of the dollar. But such a convention already existed, namely, the Bretton Woods Agreement. And the price of gold was fixed at $ 35 per ounce. But this system had obviously outlived its usefulness. And the crux of the matter was not only that the price of gold was undervalued but that it was artificially regulated. Even if the price of gold were raised but were to remain regulated in a similarly artificial way to one extent or another, the crisis in the monetary system would continue.

As long as capitalism exists, any artificial regulation of the price of gold in international circulation inevitably turns into a violation of the law of value and leads to phenomena of a muffled monetary crisis which nonetheless makes itself constantly felt.

Speaking about the need to conclude an international gold convention, Rueff held that this would correspond to the procedure of co-operation established between banks of issue. But the experience of the Gold Pool and other conventions, on the basis of which organisations like the IMF exist, proves that international forms of regulating currency circulation through control over the price of gold lead to the one-sided prevalence of interests and to a deepening of crisis phenomena.

Capitalism is undergoing a general crisis and, on this basis, a crisis in the sphere of international circulation, too, is inevitable. But the crisis phenomena engendered by American imperialism through its monetary and financial policy of economic and military aggression are by no means unavoidable.

For many years after the Second World War the monetary system of capitalism, it seemed, was inseparable from the American dollar. It was regarded not only "as good as gold", but actually stood above gold, controlling the price of the monetary metal. And since the purchasing power of the dollar declined, this to the same extent led to the depreciation of gold. This circumstance by itself sooner or later had to aggravate the contradiction between gold and the dollar as a medium of international circulation. At the same time it was steadily supplemented by the wide use of the dollar by US finance capital for its economic expansion and the penetration of the industries of other countries and also its use by Washington to cover the US balance-of-payments deficit resulting from the Pentagon's military ventures. Thus, the American dollar was widely introduced into the channels of international currency circulation and dollars were accumulated in the monetary reserves of other countries.

Since the monetary system of contemporary capitalism seemed inconceivable without the dominant role of the dollar, some people in the West, especially in the United States, came to think that capitalism could get along without the "barbaric metal", gold. The realities refuted this view and at the same time took vengeance on the dollar for belittling, over many years, the role of gold as a measure of value and as world money. It may be said without fear of exaggeration that the 1960s were years of the gradual decline in the role of the dollar and the mounting of the crisis which is now racking the entire world capitalist system.

At the end of the 1960s the world monetary crisis substantially undermined the capitalist monetary system. At the same time it should be noted that this marked the beginning of a functional disorder of the organisational foundations of the entire system headed by the International Monetary Fund. There are sufficient grounds for such a conclusion.

The corner stone of the postwar monetary system was undoubtedly the little-changing ratio of national currencies to the American dollar or gold content parities when the US dollar with a gold content of 1/35th of a troy ounce was invariably taken as a unit. The parities of national currencies, expressed in relation to the dollar, were agreed upon with the IMF.

On the whole the central banks of capitalist countries loyally observed the rules of the IMF and did not allow deviations of the current exchange rate of national currencies by more than 1 per cent from parity upwards or downwards, although for this purpose the central banks often had to exert considerable effort and at the time spend a considerable part of their gold and exchange reserves, as was the case with the Bank of England in 1967 and the Bank of France in 1968-1969. In both cases the devaluation first of the pound and then of the franc was not avoided. Such a change in parities, dictated by the circumstances, corresponded to the charter of the IMF.

Experience has shown that the devaluation of the national currency of a big capitalist country during a monetary crisis does not lead to a mechanical restoration of the equilibrium of monetary and financial relations on the basis of the new parity or the relation to the dollar as a stable unit. Devaluation of the national currency of a big capitalist country creates for a certain period the preconditions for monetary dumping, the stimulation of the export of goods to foreign markets to the detriment of the home market on account of the difference in prices in the home market resulting from devaluation and in world prices expressed in stable currencies not subject to the devaluation. Thus, favourable opportunities are created to step up exports from countries with a devalued currency (to the detriment of the home market). At the same time countries with stable currencies and even more so having currencies with a high rate, are deprived of such conditions. For them, on the contrary, additional stimuli for the import of goods are created. All this ultimately deranges the previously existing structure of trade and payments balances of capitalist countries and often causes painful disturbances in their mutual settlements.

Let us recall that both the decrease in the parity of the franc (devaluation) by 12.5 per cent, like the increase in the parity of the West German mark (revaluation) by 8.5 per cent, occurred after a shifting of free capital to the FRG. This circumstance alone led to considerable disproportionality in the movement of international capital.

It is, however, exceedingly difficult to prevent such extremely adverse shifting of capital from one country to another, as demonstrated by the futile attempts to do so by raising the discount rates and by restrictive administrative measures.

MONETARY CONTRADICTIONS BETWEEN
THE EEC AND THE USA
IN THE EARLY 1970s. BREAKDOWN
OF THE BRETTON WOODS SYSTEM

The devaluation of the French franc and the revaluation of the West German mark in the second half of 1969 intensified contradictions both within the European Economic Community and between the Six and the United States. The sharp divergence of currency rates within the EEC endangered the common agricultural market based on single prices. It became more difficult to maintain a stable correlation of the currencies of the Common Market countries to the US dollar.

At the threshold of the 1970s an economic recession began in the United States, its financial difficulties mounted and the balance of payments deteriorated, increasing the influx of dollars into world currency circulation.

Inflation spread further in the United States as in other capitalist countries. Inflation processes in individual countries merged into general inflation in the capitalist world. A considerable part in this development was played by the mounting influx of dollars into world circulation.

While prior to the second half of the 1960s the introduction of dollars in world circulation was justified on the grounds that growing world trade needed liquid assets, the financial shocks at the end of the 1960s demonstrated that the point was not the shortage of liquidity. Exchange rates fluctuated widely, and in order to maintain their currencies in a definite relation to the dollar, countries had to buy dollars for their national currency and accumulate them in their exchange reserves on an increasing scale, correspondingly

expanding money circulation in the United States, Japan
and other countries. This raised the rate of the dollar and
reduced the rates of national currencies but not for long.
This is how the United States, together with dollars, exported
inflation to other capitalist countries. In view of this situation
a number of countries increasingly pressed the United
States to put an end to its balance-of-payments deficit
and to the method of covering it by introducing dollars
into world circulation and the exchange reserves of other
countries.

To eliminate the unfavourable balance of payments, the
United States would have to do away with its main causes:
the excessive expenditure of foreign currency abroad along
Pentagon channels and the wide outflow of American capital
abroad. This required a radical change of the country's
monetary and financial system.

In view of the economic recession the United States could
not consistently implement anti-inflation measures, although
at the end of the 1960s the spread of inflation assumed a
threatening scale. The steps to restrain inflation by credit
restrictions taken in 1969 and the first half of 1970, proved
to be abortive. More then that, some of the measures supposedly designed to "normalise" the monetary system facilitated the spread of inflation. This applies specifically to the
so-called Special Drawing Rights (SDR). The SDR system
was set up within the framework of the International Monetary Fund early in 1970, at first in an amount exceeding
$ 3,400 million. In the next two years this sum went up
to $ 9,500 million. SDRs, also called "paper gold", were
widely published as a prototype of an artificial international
currency. But they began to play the part of additional
liquid assets, which promoted inflation. Like book-keeping
entries in respective accounts, SDRs arise out of the real
international circulation process. Real trade and other
settlements between countries are made in convertible
currencies by private corporations and banks. Their foreign
exchange receipts land in central banks through conversion
in national currencies of the respective countries. Thus,
the money stock in circulation of a country increases on
account of the issue of notes by the central banks. The central
banks make settlements among themselves in SDRs, which

remain in their accounts for a long time. The use of SDRs is inevitably accompanied by the appearance of additional bank notes in national currencies. And since the sum of SDRs is steadily mounting, the money stock grows respectively. From this it follows that the accumulation of SDRs, like dollars, promotes inflation. Such in general outline is how the operation of the SDR system stimulates inflation.

As for the concrete procedure of SDR circulation, it is simply the voluntary mutual crediting of IMF member countries which have joined the Special Drawing Right account (not all member countries have done so).

Depending on a country's quota in the IMF and its economic potential, it is allocated a sum of SDRs which can be disposed of by the given country or its central bank. This is the limit of mutual crediting. The new international medium of payment cannot be utilised as ordinary money on current accounts or/and trade transactions of private corporations or persons. The biggest sums of SDRs naturally are allocated to highly developed countries which have the largest quotas in the IMF.

When some countries use SDRs for settlements of their adverse balance of payments, the original SDRs sum on their accounts is reduced; at the same time the accounts of other countries accepting the SDRs are correspondingly increased. The percentage of decrease of the SDR sum is an indicator of the intensity of the system's operation. The four-year experience of the system shows that the use of SDRs is of a limited, artificial nature. Nevertheless, since the beginning of the 1970s US financial circles have been the chief SDR votaries.

It is not by chance that the SDR unit, which has no special name, was made equal in gold content to the dollar. It was to serve as a symbol of the dollar's stability. When the system was introduced, Washington sharply changed its tight money policy.

In the last quarter of 1970 and the first quarter of 1971 this was clearly displayed in a number of reductions of the discount rate by the Federal Reserve System, which extended bank credit and lowered its cost. From November 13, 1970 to January 18, 1971 the discount rate was lowered four times and brought down from 6 to 5 per cent, while in other

West European countries and Japan it was higher and, consequently, the return on capital was greater. Because of this the influx of American capital to these countries in the form of dollars continued on a growing scale.

Difficulties in the sphere of monetary relations in 1971 were accompanied by greater crisis phenomena in the capitalist world and stiffer competition. In the report of the CPSU Central Committee to the 24th Party Congress (March 1971) Leonid Brezhnev stated: "Even the most developed capitalist states are not free from grave economic upheavals. The USA, for instance, has been floundering in one of its economic crises for almost two years now. The last few years have also been marked by a grave crisis in the capitalist monetary and financial system. The simultaneous growth of inflation and unemployment has become a permanent feature. There are now almost eight million unemployed in the developed capitalist countries."[1] It was further noted in the Report that "...the main centres of imperialist rivalry have become clearly visible: these are the USA, Western Europe (especially the Six Common Market countries) and Japan. The economic and political competitive struggle between them has been growing ever more acute."[2]

In May 1971 a panic swept through many money markets in the capitalist countries. It assumed the form of a flight from the US dollar which literally flooded the markets. Many central and big private banks temporarily refused to accept dollars and to engage in operations with them. Some banks temporarily closed down, waiting for the situation to clear up. As the crisis grew deeper the demand for, and the price of, gold rose. Dollar holders, especially private banks, were anxious to convert their dollars, if not into gold, at least into more stable currencies, specifically West German marks and Japanese yen. The usual speculative mainsprings came into action. They were based on the expectation that sooner or later the currencies of the FRG and Japan would be revalued, while the dollar would be devalued.

The calculations of speculators fitted into the following approximate scheme. If one were to keep dollars up to

---

[1] *24th Congress of the CPSU*, Moscow, 1971, p. 20.
[2] Ibid.

their devaluation, say, by 10 per cent, this would mean a loss of $ 10,000 per $ 1,000,000. If, on the other hand, the dollars were to be converted into stabler currencies one would not only prevent a loss of $ 10,000 but even gain $ 10,000 from the expected revaluation.

In this connection the central banks of the FRG and Japan became the main centres of concentration of US dollars. The influx of dollars also increased to one extent or another in the exchange reserves of other capitalist countries. Thus, the total official sum of foreign exchange in the reserves of capitalist countries, which amounted to $ 32,200 million at the end of the first quarter of 1970, climbed to $ 44,500 million at the end of the year, to $ 49,400 million at the end of the first quarter of 1971 and to $ 55,500 million at the end of the first half of that year.[1]

Table 21

Gold and Exchange Reserves of the Federal Republic of Germany and Japan
(million US dollars)

At the end of the period	Federal Republic of Germany		Japan	
	Gold	Foreign exchange	Gold	Foreign exchange
1970, first quarter	4,081	6,286	530	2,423
1970, fourth quarter	3,980	8,455	532	3,188
1971, first quarter	3,977	10,392	539	4,285
" second quarter	4,046	11,199	641	6,238
" September . . .	4,077	11,380	679	11,939
" October	4,077	11,589	679	12,653

S o u r c e: *International Financial Statistics*, December 1971 pp. 21, 23.

The table shows that, although the movement of the foreign exchange reserves of the FRG and Japan differed, the result was the same: excessive accumulation of dollars not dictated by the requirements of current balance settle-

---

[1] *International Financial Statistics*, December, 1971, p. 23.

ments. Japan found herself in a worse position because, relying on the stability of the dollar, she did not accumulate a sufficient gold stock, as was done by financial circles of the FRG and other West European industrial countries, which at the end of the first half of 1971 had at their disposal gold valued at $ 17,800 million, or considerably more than the United States ($ 10,500 million).

At the beginning of May 1971 some European countries were compelled to allow the free floating of the rates of their currencies in relation to the dollar under the influence of supply and demand.

This was one of the measures designed to protect the reserves of central banks from the excessive influx of dollars. But this measure—floating rates—completely upset the usual currency relations regulated by IMF rules (prevention of the upward or downward fluctuation of rates in relation to the dollar by more than one per cent). The Federal Republic of Germany was the first to take this path on May 9, although the free floating of its currency in relation to the dollar ran counter to the Common Market countries line of maintaining minimal fluctuations between the rates of their currencies. The example of the FRG was followed by the Netherlands, and this disorganised currency relations within the Common Market.

The Governments of Austria and Switzerland, countries which do not belong to the EEC, officially revalued their currencies: the Austrian schilling by 5 per cent and the Swiss franc by 7 per cent. Thus, the system of regulating currency rates, with the dollar serving as the standard, practically stopped functioning. The currency rates of most countries of the capitalist world began to climb upwards.

The threat of imminent monetary chaos alarmed international financial and banking circles. The sudden massive shifting of capital from country to country became particularly dangerous. Under these conditions guidance of the monetary system by the IMF, like the maintenance of the fluctuation of currency rates upwards or downwards within the bounds of one per cent in relation to the dollar, became impossible.

US financial circles took no measures whatsoever to maintain the rate of the dollar. They expected that a depressed dollar would help to increase exports and reduce imports, resulting in a more favourable trade balance, which is the backbone of the country's balance of payments. In 1971, for the first time since 1898, the balance of trade became unfavourable to the tune of some $ 2,700 million. Let us recall that in the first half of the 1960s the favourable balance of trade exceeded $ 5,400 million annually on average. The sharp deterioration of the trade balance in 1971 could not but affect US monetary policy. It is largely this factor that explains the exceptional measures in US monetary, financial and trade policy in 1971.

TWO DEVALUATIONS OF THE DOLLAR
AND EXPLORATION OF WAYS FOR REFORMING
THE MONETARY SYSTEM

In his radio speech of August 15, 1971 President Nixon announced measures which sharply altered not only US financial and economic policy but also monetary and financial relations in the capitalist world as a whole. The USA announced its refusal to convert dollars into gold at a time when world circulation and the exchange reserves of other countries were clogged with dollars. It also introduced a 10-per cent import surcharge. This measure was regarded as a big step towards protectionism. The US Administration also introduced a wage freeze, tax privileges on capital invested in expanding production, and so on. All these measures were designed to improve the competitive ability of American goods.

The August 1971 measures of the United States caused consternation among its partners. To eliminate differences, intensive negotiations were started. In the course of the talks the United States demanded a revaluation of the currencies of a number of countries, sought the creation of favourable conditions for American exports, insisted on increasing the share of other countries in NATO military spending, and so on.

The Council of the Six EEC countries which met in Brussels on August 20 was marked by sharp differences. This was reflected even in newspaper headlines: "A Torn Europe; Failure in Brussels" (*L'Aurore*); "French and Germans Clash Sharply" (*Le Figaro*); "Clash of Giscard d'Estaing and Schiller" (*Paris-Jour*).

On August 22, 1971 the news agencies of the world, transmitted the text of a telegram sent by Pierre-Paul Schweitzer, managing director of the IMF, to all member states of the organisation: "Unless prompt action is taken, the prospect before us is one of disorder and discrimination in currency and trade relationships which will seriously disrupt trade and undermine the system which has served the world well and has been the basis for effective collaboration for a quarter of a century."[1]

He was referring to the postwar monetary system of capitalism founded on the US dollar as an international currency. As director of the IMF, Schweitzer called for the earliest convocation of the financiers of the Group of Ten, which usually preceded major IMF measures.

Finance Ministers and managers of the central banks of the Group of Ten met on September 15-16 and discussed a wide range of issues raised by the August measures of the US Administration.

To judge from the official communiqué, the financiers of the ten countries merely examined factors pertaining to the proper rearrangement of exchange rates, "fair" trade agreements and questions of sharing the burden and the necessity of reforming the international monetary system. The latter was an open admission that the mechanism of the postwar monetary system could no longer function normally without radical changes.

After the floating rate of the Japanese yen was introduced on August 28, all the principal capitalist countries refused in fact to support the market rate of the dollar. Its rate in relation to other currencies continued to drop, while the price of gold began to rise not only in dollars, but also in other currencies. The capitalist world once again was made aware of the importance of gold as the cornerstone of the monetary system of the commodity capitalist economy regulated by the objective law of value.

Abolition of the conversion of the dollar into gold placed

---

[1] *Keesing's Contemporary Archives*, December 25, 1971-January I, 1972, p. 25004.

it in the position of a "king without a golden crown": it was no longer recognised as the pivot of the monetary system.

As the year 1972 was drawing near, the ruling circles of the capitalist countries felt impelled at all costs to create, at least temporarily, a semblance of some stability of monetary relations, since the completion of international settlements of old trade contracts and the conclusion of new ones was associated with the advent of the new year. Hence the proposal for summit meetings.

Of particular significance was the meeting of two presidents—Richard Nixon and Georges Pompidou—in the Azores on December 12-14, 1971. Pompidou in fact represented the interests not only of France but also of the other EEC countries. As a result of the talks Nixon agreed to lift the import surcharge, making this conditional on the consent in principle of other countries to revalue their currencies and also on a certain devaluation of the American dollar by raising the price of gold in dollars. President Pompidou stated on this score that a return to firm parities of currencies determined by the relation to gold was in line with the principle advocated by France.

On December 17-18 Finance Ministers and managing directors of central banks of the Group of Ten assembled in Washington. The meeting, presided over by US Secretary of the Treasury John Connally, adopted decisions corresponding to the Nixon-Pompidou understanding reached in principle in the Azores.

The agreements on monetary questions reached in Washington (they were named Smithsonian, after the institute where the financiers met) initiated a restructuring of the international monetary system.

The United States undertook to raise the official price of gold from $ 35 to $ 38 per troy ounce of pure gold, and thereby devalued the dollar by 8.57 per cent. At the same time the question of restoring the actual convertibility of the dollar into gold, abolished in August, remained unsolved because the available US gold stock remained at the level of about $ 10,000 million, while the sum of dollars in the reserves of banks of other countries, estimated earlier at $ 50,000 million, increased still more towards the end of 1971,

Other countries, in turn, officially agreed to revalue their currencies raising them as follows in relation to the dollar: the Japanese yen by 16.88 per cent, the West German mark by 13.57 per cent, the Belgian franc and the Dutch gulden by 11.57 per cent. The gold content of these currencies was raised by 7.6, 4.61 and 2.76 per cent respectively.

The gold content of other national currencies either changed insignificantly or remained unaltered (the French franc and the British pound), but with respect to the dollar they also were raised to the same degree to which the dollar was devalued, i.e., by 8.57 per cent. Simultaneously, a decision was adopted on allowing the upward or downward fluctuation of currencies from parity by 2.25 per cent (in the case of opposite trends of rates this could create a difference of up to 4.5 per cent). The legislative procedure of approving the devaluation of the dollar by the US Congress was completed only in April 1972.

Having achieved the revaluation of a number of currencies of its partners, the United States agreed to lift the 10-per cent import surcharge. The US ruling circles acted on the principle that the revaluation of currencies in relation to the dollar would bring into action the monetary mechanism of stimulating American exports, especially to countries with a revalued currency. But owing to the cluttering of the channels of world circulation with US dollars and widespread world trade settlements in US dollars, the stimulating influence of the new correlation of settlement rates was diminished.

More than 40 countries, including members of the EEC, under US pressure, agreed with the proposal to extend the fluctuation rates from 1 to 2.25 per cent. This complicated mutual settlements among Common Market countries: it was becoming exceedingly difficult to apply the common policy of agricultural prices within the framework of the EEC, and so on.

Let us assume, for example, that the rate of the currency of one EEC country, the FRG, rises by 2.25 per cent as compared with the dollar, while the rate of the currency of another country, Italy, decreases by 2.25 per cent. In that case the divergence between their currency rates may reach 4.5 per cent. What complicated the situation was that in 1972 the question was settled of admitting Britain, Eire, Denmark and Norway to the Common Market (Norway's application was subsequently withdrawn).

Enlargement of the Common Market during a period of monetary troubles could exert a particularly adverse effect on reciprocal trade and settlements between the EEC countries. That is why the question of more effective currency solidarity of the EEC countries, including future members, after the Smithsonian agreements acquired even greater urgency. These countries agreed to cut by half the permissible fluctuation of the rates of their currencies as compared with the level accepted by the Group of Ten at the Washington meeting in December 1971. In March 1972 Britain acceded to this decision. But this solidarity of the principal West European countries proved to be short-lived.

As prior to the devaluation of US currency, the reason for the extreme instability of currency rates was the oversaturation of the exchange reserves of capitalist countries with dollars. In the very first months of 1972 it became clear that the Smithsonian agreements did not lead to an equilibrium in currency relations and that a radical reform of the monetary system was imperative. At the end of June 1972 the British Government, suffering from financial strain and pressed by US capital, decided to let the rate of the pound float. This struck a blow at the currency solidarity of the Common Market countries. The floating sterling demolished the plans for regulating the currency rates of the EEC countries. On the eve of the 27th session of the IMF the EEC was deprived of the possibility of acting in a more organised way on questions of reforming the monetary system. This impelled EEC countries to hold additional talks on currency problems so as to create at least a semblance of solidarity before the IMF session.

On September 11-12, two weeks before the opening of the IMF session, ministers from ten countries (members and prospective members of the EEC, including Norway) agreed to set up a so-called European Fund of Monetary Co-operation. The centrifugal forces which were destroying the Bretton Woods system thus continued to operate.

US financial circles made use of the IMF session which opened in Washington on September 25, 1972 to capture the initiative in the contemplated reform of the monetary system. On September 26, George Shultz, the new US Secretary of the Treasury, outlined the general principles of the reform. He voiced the opinion that the reform would require a transitional period. It became clear that the USA had no intention of accelerating the adoption of a reform. American ruling circles, undoubtedly, acted on the principle that time was on their side. France's representative, Giscard d'Estaing, who reflected the opinion of the EEC countries, made a proposal for three-stage reform. The first stage, the conclusion of agreements on exchange rates and the problems of developing countries, was to be discussed at the IMF session in Nairobi in 1973. The second stage was to be consummated by the restoration of the convertibility of currencies and the third was to establish an initial monetary standard.

An examination of the essence of the US proposals on the monetary reform makes it possible to single out the following two problems.

First, Shultz tried to set international financial circles against gold as the foundation of the monetary system and spoke in favour of an artificial medium of international settlements. "I do believe," he said, "orderly procedures are available to facilitate a diminishing role of gold in international monetary affairs in the future".[1] "We contemplate," Shultz said, "that the SDR would increase in importance and become the formal numeraire of the system."[2] From this it seemed to follow that gold as an objective measure of value, standard of prices (in the form of the gold content of money units) and a universal equivalent could be replaced by an arbitrary "numeraire". How an SDR unit, equal to the dollar or its gold content prior to devaluation, would break its link with gold was not explained, however. "Contemplation" of the future role of SDRs, of course, could not offer a suitable basis for a discussion on this question at a broad international forum.

---

[1] *Vital Speeches of the Day*, October 15, p. 5,
[2] Ibid.

Second, the US Secretary of the Treasury spoke at length about the regulation of the balance of payments. The gist of his proposals was that in future an increase or decrease of foreign currency reserves of the respective countries should be regarded as the "indicator" of the favourable or unfavourable nature of the balance of payments. Measures were necessary for reaching an equilibrium in balance of payments, for eliminating a surplus or deficit. In other words, both countries with a favourable and unfavourable balance of payments had to take measures for removing the deficit or surplus.

The former had to revalue their currencies and take other measures necessary to eliminate the favourable balance. The latter could devalue their currencies and resort to direct restrictive measures for regulating their balance.

Thus, the representative of the United States, a country with an unfavourable balance of payments, prepared the ground for the subsequent measures of the USA, specifically, for the second devaluation of the dollar. Other proposals of the US representative, particularly, wider fluctuation of currency rates and liberalisation of the movement of capital, in fact, reflected former US policy.

The procedure for regulating balances of payments proposed by Shultz has aroused doubts. Its legalisation, within the framework of the IMF, would doom member countries to the constant changes of the exchange rates of their currencies during settlements and extreme instability of monetary and credit relations.

A special agency at the level of finance ministers, known as the Committee of Twenty, was set up within the framework of the IMF at that session to work out the reform of the monetary system. In the interval between meetings of the Finance Ministers various aspects of the reform were to be settled by a working group at the level of their deputies headed by Jeremy Morse (Britain). All questions of the reform of the monetary system were handed over to the Committee of Twenty. Having outlined in detail the basic principles for the reform of the monetary system at the IMF session in September 1972, US financial circles steered in advance the work of the Committee of Twenty into the channel of their monetary and financial policy. The second devaluation of the dollar by 10 per cent, effected on February 12, 1973, was an important step of this policy.

In his statement about the second devaluation of the dollar US Treasury Secretary Shultz in fact repeated the main principles for reshaping the monetary system that he outlined at the 1972 September session of the IMF.

Specifically, he laid emphasis on the necessity for procedures which could reduce the role of gold and enhance that of SDRs, thus overshadowing the question of restoring the dollar's convertibility. At the same time Shultz emphasised that the US Administration assumed no commitment to intervene in the foreign money market to restore the "currency equilibrium", leaving this to other countries. On behalf of the US Government, the Treasury Secretary also insisted on the need for liberalising the movement of capital between countries and mentioned the contemplated annulment of the so-called Interest Equalisation Tax on American capital flowing out abroad. Thus, he expounded a programme for the further expansion of American capital, and not a drive to eliminate the monetary disequilibrium which intensifies inflation.

After this preamble to the second devaluation of the dollar it became clear that the vast Eurodollar market would remain an uncurbed factor promoting speculative shifts of capital and instability in international monetary relations.

Indeed, during the 12 months in the interval between the September 1972 IMF session in Washington and the session held in Nairobi in September 1973, instability of currency and credit relations in the capitalist world was intensified. All attempts to eliminate or, at least, to slow down the inflation process in capitalist countries were of no avail.

The inflationary rise of prices, especially of consumer goods, worsens the material condition of the masses, particularly the workers, and arouses their resistance.

The class struggle assumes the form of open protests, mass action and strikes, which is compelling the ruling circles of the principal capitalist countries to step up the work of preparing the monetary reform,

The fundamental issues of the reform of capitalism's monetary system, however, remain outstanding and will, apparently, for a long time be the subject of discussion by statesmen at different levels.

The main fallacy of the unsuccessful search for ways of reforming the monetary system is undoubtedly rooted in the incorrect premise that under present-day commodity capitalist relations it is possible to disregard the objective regularities based on the law of value. Hence the attempts to eliminate the functions of gold as a measure of value, the standard of prices and universal equivalent in international monetary relations. By putting up against them the utopian ideas of an international medium of circulation— a voluntarist "numeraire"—the would-be "reformers" of the system are, on the contrary, aggravating the situation which is already exceedingly tense.

The exertions of bourgeois economists and statesmen who, disregarding the inflationary derangement of monetary relations, are trying to eliminate the operation of the law of value through reform cannot lead to success.

The monetary reform plan which the USA is seeking to force upon other countries obviously cannot eliminate the intrinsic flaws in the currency and credit relations of the capitalist world. Hence, the acute disagreements between the major capitalist countries. Under such circumstances, the Committee of Twenty has not been able to formulate acceptable proposals for a monetary reform. This came to light during the IMF session, held in Nairobi (Kenya) in September 1973.

Since then the Committee of Twenty and international financiers have arranged several meetings which, however, failed to get the monetary reform moving. As a result, uncertainty in the monetary sphere of the capitalist world has been increasing.

The year 1974 witnessed further chaos in the currency and credit relations of capitalist countries. Two cases in point are the decision of the French Government to let the French franc float and the new rise in the price of gold.

The announcement introducing the floating of franc particularly aggravated currency relations among EEC countries. The monetary solidarity of the Common Market countries was thrown into jeopardy, and the establishment of a monetary union of the Nine was deferred indefinitely. The prospects of agreement on a monetary reform within the framework of the IMF grew dimmer.

The capitalist monetary crisis continues apace, and new upheavals in the field of currency, trade and credit relations may be expected.

REQUEST TO READERS

Progress Publishers would be glad to have your opinion of this book, its translation and design and any suggestions you may have for future publications.

Please send all your comments to 21, Zubovsky Boulevard, Moscow, USSR.

PROGRESS PUBLISHERS PUT OUT RECENTLY

KORBASH E. *The Economic "Theories" of Maoism*. Progress. Theories and Critical Studies Series

The author musters an array of facts from Chinese sources to analyse some of the concepts propounded by China's present-day leaders on various crucial economic problems and the results of their implementation in the Chinese economy over the past 10 to 12 years. In his study of Chinese reality, the author shows the economic "theories" of Maoism to be petty-bourgeois, adventurous and scientifically untenable and harmful to socialist construction.

PROGRESS PUBLISHERS
PUT OUT RECENTLY

OSADCHAYA I. *From Keynes to Neoclassical Synthesis (A Critical Analysis)*. Progress. Theories and Critical Studies Series

The authoress examines the evolution of Keynesian macro-economic theory and describes its place and role in the bourgeois political economy.

She gives a critical analysis of the latest views of bourgeois economists on attaining a dynamic balance in the development of modern bourgeois economy; of the problem of an economic cycle, and Marxist evaluation of anti-crisis measures in the modern bourgeois state. She shows the influence exerted by the latest economic conceptions on economic policy of the ruling circles in capitalist countries.